THE
GREATER & LESSER WORLDS
OF
ROBERT FLUDD

In lumine tuo Videbimus lumen.

Si tu illustres lucernam
meam, Iehova Deus
Splendentes efficies
tenebras meas.
Ps. 18. 29.

Matthæus Merian Bahlsen fecit.

THE
GREATER & LESSER WORLDS
OF
ROBERT FLUDD

Macrocosm, Microcosm & Medicine

JOSCELYN GODWIN

Inner Traditions
Rochester, Vermont

Inner Traditions
One Park Street
Rochester, Vermont 05767
www.InnerTraditions.com

Originally published in 2018 in Spanish under the title *Macrocosmos, Microcosmos y Medicina: Los Mundos de Robert Fludd* by Ediciones Atalanta, S. L., Girona, España
First U.S. edition published in 2019 by Inner Traditions

Cataloging-in-Publication Data for this title is available from the Library of Congress

ISBN 978-1-62055-949-9 (print)
ISBN 978-1-62055-950-5 (ebook)

Printed and bound in India by Replika Press Pvt. Ltd.

10 9 8 7 6 5 4 3 2 1

Text design by Priscilla H. Baker and layout by Virginia Scott Bowman
This book was typeset in Garamond Premier Pro, Goudy Oldstyle, and Avenir with NixRift used as the display typeface

To send correspondence to the author of this book, mail a first-class letter to the author c/o Inner Traditions • Bear & Company, One Park Street, Rochester, VT 05767, and we will forward the communication.

Contents

	Preface and Acknowledgments	vii
One	Fludd's Life and Work	1
Two	How the World Is Made	29
Three	Nature's Ape	81
Four	How Man Is Made	129
Five	Psychology and Divination	153
Six	Kabbalah	167
Seven	Anatomy	183
Eight	Meteorology	201
Nine	Universal Medicine	217

❈ ❈ ❈

Appendices	243
1. Astrology Solves a Crime	244
2. The Wisdom of the Ancients	244
3. Fludd on His Own Times	245
4. Symbolic Ornaments	246

5. Fludd Finds "Star Jelly"   249

6. Three Stories of Prophecy   249

Bibliography   251

Abbreviations   251

Plan of Fludd's *History of the Macrocosm and
the Microcosm*   252

Plan of Fludd's *Medicina Catholica*   253

Fludd's Writings   254

Manuscripts   255

Modern Editions and Translations   255

General Bibliography   255

Index   260

Preface and Acknowledgments

Robert Fludd (1574–1637) was the first encylopedic author to appreciate the power of illustrations and to have the resources to put it into practice. He wrote, of course, in the universal language of Latin, with a prolixity and redundancy that are a translator's nightmare. However, nothing better confirms the adage that a picture is worth a thousand words. Fludd's illustrations, entrusted to some of the best copper engravers in Europe, often bypass the text and make his point directly via the eye. They also include some of the most impressive abstract compositions in the history of engraving. Once understood, they provide a master key to the blend of Neoplatonism, Hermeticism, and Christianized Kabbalah that is at the center of the Western esoteric tradition.

I became interested in Robert Fludd in the early 1970s as part of an exploration of esoteric writings on music. In 1979 the London house of Thames & Hudson published my two short books in its Art and Imagination series: *Robert Fludd, Hermetic Philosopher and Surveyor of Two Worlds* and *Athanasius Kircher: A Renaissance Man and the Quest for Lost Knowledge*. With translations into French, German, Spanish, Greek, and Japanese, they gave many readers access to the marvelous imaginations of these two seventeenth-century polymaths. Thirty years on, with interest in Athanasius Kircher growing exponentially, it was time to do him better justice. The result was a large-format book, *Athanasius Kircher's Theatre of the World*, copublished in 2009 by Thames & Hudson and Inner Traditions, with over four hundred illustrations and a text to match. This too has appeared in French and Italian.

Fludd also deserved a fuller and a fresher presentation, especially as there had been surprisingly little scholarship and almost no new publications about him. Two works by William Huffman stand out, one a historical study and the other an anthology (see the bibliography). The present book aims to fill the gap, taking advantage especially of recent German scholarship. After decades of absence from the field, I returned to the original volumes at Cornell University for a fresh reading and mining of their illustrations. Only the account of Fludd's controversies with his contemporaries has been lifted from my previous book. Having outgrown the somewhat "New Age" approach of the 1970s, I resolved to follow Fludd's own program rather than imposing a thematic one of my own. Hence the greater emphasis placed here on his medical writings, which were the grand project of his later years.

For all the immediacy and ingenuity of Fludd's illustrations, they still need exegesis and the translation of Latin terms. Whenever possible, the captions provide this in Fludd's own words (sometimes paraphrased and distinguished from my text by being set in a different type style), and the appendices add some passages selected for pure pleasure and even humor. While almost everything about the Fluddean philosophy is alien to today's world, its consistency and grandeur can only command admiration.

In the captions to the illustrations, Fludd's works are cited by abbreviations, to be found at the beginning of the bibliography on p. 251. The final citation in a caption is to the relevant book of Fludd's and to the page therein on which the illustration occurs. Any internal parenthetical citations following passages of text or translations refer to the book in question.

I thank Jacobo Siruela for proposing this new book on Robert Fludd and first publishing it in a Spanish edition (see bibliography). For the illustrations, I thank the Deutsche Fotothek, Kroch Library of Cornell University, and the Biblioteca Nacional de España.

JOSCELYN GODWIN
HAMILTON, NEW YORK

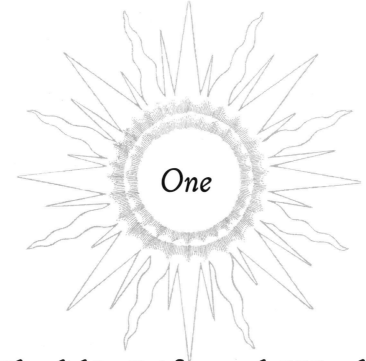

One

Fludd's Life and Work

A MEMORY PALACE

An encounter with the works of Robert Fludd (1574–1637) is like exploring a Renaissance memory palace, perhaps on the scale of the Pitti Palace in Florence or the Escorial in San Lorenzo, and equally labyrinthine and laden with meaning. I imagine two vast symmetrical wings marked with the signs of the Macrocosm and the Microcosm, the latter still unfinished. At the juncture of the two is a library, where grandiose lecterns support the Holy Scriptures and the works of Hermes Trismegistus, with those of Plato within easy reach. The central hall of each wing is hung with heraldic shields celebrating Fludd's ancestry and views of the foreign cities he visited. From it, many corridors radiate, their walls lined with charts, tables, and diagrams, leading to further clusters of rooms, no two alike. One room may hold a collection of cannons; another, a bubbling alchemical furnace or a giant mechanical harp. Here a group of students is spattering paper with ink dots, to be interpreted through geomancy; there, they are reading each other's palms.

At the back of the main building is a third wing, half built and more austere in architecture. Pictures of all the organs and internal details of the human body decorate its walls, as well as portraits of the angels and demons who take an interest in it. No surgery is done here, but corpses are sometimes smuggled in, for concoction of the weapon salve. The official faculties are those of urinomancy and astrology, with a research institute for studying the pulse in the light of the recent discovery of the circulation of the blood. There is a consulting room, and a Protestant chapel in which prayer is offered when medicine fails.

Outside the palace is a yard for military drill, a large herb garden, and some ingenious waterworks, but nothing affording pleasure for its own sake. Statues of Fludd's friends and opponents dot the parterres. The former, more numerous, include King James I, King Charles I, the royal physician Sir William Paddy, and one or two archbishops. The second group incudes Johannes Kepler, Pierre Gassendi, and two twisted, leering figures labeled "Father Mersenne" and "Parson Foster." A small pavilion, its door sealed, is marked with Rosicrucian symbols. Other outbuildings house a meteorological station and, surprisingly, a factory for the forging of steel. The whole complex is surrounded by moats and bastions in the shape of a star. Nowhere in it is a single woman to be seen.

Thus, emulating Fludd's flair for visualization, we may sketch an intellectual world unrivaled in its breadth and ambition; for the era would soon pass in which one man's mind could encompass so much of human knowledge. This very ambition was one cause of the obscurity into which Fludd fell, almost as soon as he was dead. He was not original enough in any of the disciplines that would make history, such as astronomy, mechanics, philosophy, medicine, or the arts. Another reason was his obsession with a few dominant ideas, such as the pyramids of spirit and matter, the monochord, the weatherglass, a theory of winds, geomancy, and an alchemical experiment with wheat. Each of these generated book-length studies in which every circumstance and combination is laboriously explained, with frequent recourse to biblical authority. The reader can usually get the point in a fraction of the time from the illustrations, as Fludd himself admitted when he wrote against Kepler's prolixity: "What he has expressed in many words and long discussion, I have compressed into a few words and explained by means of hieroglyphic and exceedingly significant figures."[1] The number of illustrations in Fludd's works exceeds those in any

1. *Veritatis Proscenium*, p. 5.

encyclopedic literature before Diderot's. It was these that kept Fludd's reputation alive and his books in the libraries of bibliophiles, though more out of curiosity than respect.

Historians, at least until recently, have neglected the current of thought to which Fludd made his most permanent contribution: it was the esoteric tradition, and specifically the blend of Christian Hermetism with the occult sciences. Here his amplitude of mind found its true range, which was not the horizontal one, taking in the multiple fields of man's activities, but the vertical one that starts from the first principles of theology and metaphysics, and descends the chain of being to its limit.

EARLY LIFE AND TRAVELS[2]

Fludd's paternal family originated in the county of Shropshire, their surname being a variant of the common Welsh name of Lloyd. Robert's father, Thomas Fludd, came from a landed and armigerous family, but as a younger son he had to take up a profession. He entered the law, and thereafter worked in the service of the crown. According to his epitaph he was a victualler (supplier of provisions) for the garrisons at Berwick-on-Tweed, near the Scottish border, and at "New-Haven in France" (now Le Havre). From 1568 he was surveyor of crown lands in the county of Kent, and settled at Milgate House, Bearsted. This was situated on the main road from London to the Channel ports of Folkestone and Dover, and close to the northern port of Chatham. Thomas fathered twelve children with his wife, Elizabeth Andrews, of whom we know little more than the date of her death, 1592.

By the end of the 1570s Thomas Fludd was a justice of the peace, and by 1582 collector

of revenues from the three counties of Kent, Surrey, and Sussex. In 1589 Queen Elizabeth knighted him and appointed him paymaster for the army in France. Two years later he supervised the repairs to Dover harbor. He was also Member of Parliament for Maidstone in 1593, 1597, and 1601. In 1597 he was briefly treasurer-at-war, responsible for financing the English forces supporting the Dutch revolt, but court intrigues terminated his post.[3] This slender information adds up to a portrait of an ambitious and largely self-made man, trusted by his government with large sums of money and respected both locally and nationally.

Robert was one of Sir Thomas's younger sons, born in Milgate House shortly before his baptism on January 17, 1574. He was presumably educated by private tutors until 1592, when he entered St. John's College, Oxford. Among his contemporaries there was William Laud (1573–1645), later archbishop of Canterbury and a leader of the anti-Puritan wing of the Church of England. An older member was Sir William Paddy (1554–1634), a lifelong friend of both Laud and Fludd, who later presented his college with copies of some of Fludd's works. Fludd's tutor at St. John's was John Perin (ca. 1558–1615), professor of Greek, who once called on his student's astrological expertise to catch a thief.[4] Fludd may have known John Rainoldes (1549–1607) of Corpus Christi College, expert in Hebrew and rabbinic studies and, like Perin, a member of the 1611 Bible committee.[5] However, Fludd's writings give no evidence of a fluent knowledge of Greek, nor of Hebrew, for which he relied on Latin translations. His warmest tribute to a teacher

2. For a more extensive biography, see Huffman, *Robert Fludd and the End of the Renaissance,* to which the following overview is indebted.

3. *The History of Parliament: The House of Commons, 1588–1603,* ed. P. W. Hasler. Accessed online.

4. Fludd tells the story in *UCH* I, 2, p. 701. For abbreviations of Fludd's titles, see the bibliography.

5. On Rainold(e)s, see Craven, *Doctor Robert Fludd,* p. 13.

is to his master in astrology, Thomas Allen (1542–1632) of Gloucester Hall, a mathematician and collector of medieval manuscripts.[6]

By the time Robert Fludd graduated as bachelor of arts in 1596 he had already compiled treatises on music and astrology, later included in his *History of the Macrocosm*.[7] Almost his only Oxford reminiscences are in this connection (see appendix 1, "Astrology Solves a Crime"). Clearly the young student was unlike the typical sons of the gentry, who attended the university for social reasons and did not complete a degree. Fludd remained at Oxford for two more years, during which he wrote a treatise on cosmography to help his father's observations in France and the Netherlands. In 1598 he took his master of arts degree, then announced his intention of going abroad.

After his six years at Oxford, Fludd spent nearly six more traveling, supported by his father and by occasional tutoring in aristocratic families. He was thus one of the first Englishmen to complete his education with what was later known as the "Grand Tour" of continental Europe. He visited France, Spain, Italy, and Germany, possibly on several separate trips, and writes of this period: "I have traversed and surveyed with my eyes and mind almost all the provinces of Europe: the surging deep seas, the high mountains and slippery valleys, the crudities of villages, the rudeness of towns and the arrogance of cities."[8] Unfortunately these travels and the people he met are only recorded in a few tales and passing references in Fludd's philosophical books.

Fludd's time in France coincided with a relatively open religious climate, following the Edict of Nantes (1598), which allowed freedom of worship to Protestants. Throughout his travels, and also when describing the reception of his books, he remarks on his friendly relations with Catholics, Lutherans, and Calvinists alike. Naturally he was in Paris, where he saw the king's collections in the Louvre[9] and made friends with Antoine de Bourdaloue, counselor and steward to Charles, Duc de Guise. The two of them shared an interest in weird phenomena, such as chemical experiments on blood that produced apparitions.[10] Through Bourdaloue, who remained in touch for years after, Fludd gained an entrée to aristocratic circles in the South of France. But he did not travel first class. His only companion seems to have been his dog, a water spaniel, as we learn from an anecdote in *Mosaicall Philosophy*. On the way to Lyon he left behind the valise containing letters of exchange (his vital financial resource), and his hired post horse stubbornly refused to turn back. In desperation, Fludd sent the dog, which retraced his route, found the valise by scent, and brought it to him half an hour later.[11]

We next find Fludd in Provence, on his way to Italy but delayed by snow in the Saint Bernard Pass. He spent the winter of 1601–2 in Avignon, still a papal enclave and the site of his best-documented contacts. They included both the eldest and the youngest sons of Henri de Lorraine, Duc de Guise (1549–88), the leader of the Catholic League who had been assassinated in the Wars of Religion. The elder was Charles de Lorraine, fourth Duc de Guise (1571–1640), who had almost become king of France and was now governor of Provence and admiral of the Levant. Charles invited Fludd to Marseille, to instruct him in arithmetic and probably with political motives too, considering Fludd's likely insights, through his father, into court and military matters at the close of

6. See *UCH* II, 1, 2, p. 73.

7. See the bibliography for details of this and Fludd's other writings.

8. Huffman, *Robert Fludd: Essential Readings*, p. 56.

9. "Truth's Golden Harrow," quoted in Huffman, *Robert Fludd: Essential Readings*, p. 169.

10. See *AA*, p. 233.

11. *MP*, p. 227.

In lumine tuo Videbimus lumen.

Si tu illustres Lucernam meam, Iehova Deus Splendentes efficies tenebras meas. Ps. 18. 29).

Matthæus Merian Basilien fecit.

1.1. Robert Fludd, 1626

Matthaeus Merian's engraving of Fludd, published in 1626, has served as the model for all subsequent portraits. We do not know the original artist whose drawing was presumably sent from London to Frankfurt to be engraved, but the result is a fine and memorable one. Fludd's right hand is on his heart, his left on a book. He wears a tunic and lace collar somewhat similar to those in the Droeshout portrait of Shakespeare (1623). The quarterings of the heraldic shield show six armigerous ancestors on the male side, five on the female (two of the quarterings being the same). The crest on the helmet is a leopard's head issuing from a marquess's coronet. Further research by heraldic experts would be desirable. The words (*top left*) mean "In thy light shall we see light" (Psalm 36:9); those in the rays (*top right*): "If you light my lamp, Jehovah God, you will make my darkness bright" (Psalm 18:29). *PS*, fol.):(2'. For abbreviations of Fludd's titles, see bibliography, p. 251.

Elizabeth's reign. The younger Guise brother, the posthumously born François-Paris de Lorraine, Chevalier de Guise (1589–1614), was the dedicatee of Fludd's treatises on geometry (i.e., surveying), perspective, and the military art. When Fludd came to publish these treatises, he recalled the thirteen-year-old François as an ardent learner, eager if possible to surpass his tutor, and mourned his early death through the accidental explosion of a cannon.[12]

Another adult pupil, for whom the treatises on music and the art of memory were compiled, was André, Marquis d'Oraison and Vicomte de Cadenet. He too came from a distinguished family favored by Henry III, but little is known of him beyond his marriage in 1597 to Louise de Castellane-Laval.[13] While in Avignon, Fludd enjoyed the open table of a "captain" who was probably Pompée Catilina (d. 1613), a hero of the Turkish wars and now colonel of the papal garrison.[14] This led indirectly to Carlo Conti (or Comti, 1556–1615), who was the papal vice-legate from 1599 to 1604. Conti came from a family that had produced three popes, and was later made a cardinal. His meeting with Fludd followed an effort by some malicious persons to cause trouble by telling him that Fludd was practicing divination through geomancy. The Jesuits, who had just been readmitted to the papal city after their expulsion in 1594, formally condemned this practice. As it turned out, the vice-legate himself was eager to practice the art, and Fludd dedicated his geomancy treatise to him. Conti's entourage included an apothecary called Malceau who regaled Fludd with hair-raising stories of sadistic poisoners.[15] Last among Fludd's pupils, a young

and "very dear friend" named simply Reinaud of Avignon received the dedication of the treatises on motion (i.e., mechanics) and astrology. Reinaud remained unidentified until François Ferté found a likely candidate in François de Renaud, "lord of Alleins, Lamanon, and Auron, gentleman of the King's Chamber, later elected first consul of Aix, procurer of the region in 1623 and royal *viguier* [judge] of Marseille in 1617 and 1632." Ferté's research into Fludd's Avignon sojourn complements that of Frances Yates into the Palatine connections, and reveals Fludd in the midst of an esoteric and cosmopolitan confrerie in which confessional differences were of no account.[16]

Making these contacts in Provence must have eased Fludd's passage in Italy, where he spent a considerable time in Rome. All we know of his activity there is his praise of a Swiss-born "Master Gruter," who was "much esteemed by the Cardinal Saint George" and taught Fludd "the best of his skill" in "the Art of motions and inventions of Machines." Gruter's identity is a mystery. He cannot have been either the Flemish scholar Jan Gruter (1560–1627) or the Strasbourg-born engraver Matthaeus Greuter (1564–1638), though Fludd may have known them both.[17] The cardinal, however, is identifiable as Marco Sittico Altemps (1533–95), nephew of Pope Pius IV, owner of the Palazzo Altemps in Rome and builder of the Villa Mondragone in Frascati. The expertise of Fludd's Gruter evokes the fountains, waterworks, and automata that adorned the Frascati villas, summer residences of the papal aristocracy. There is also a Swiss connection: Cardinal Altemps founded the

12. *UCH* I, 2, p. 3.

13. Nostredame, *L'histoire et chronique de Provence,* p. 629; Brianson, *L'état et le nobiliaire de Provence,* p. 414.

14. On this captain, see Ferté, "Robert Fludd et la philosophie hermétique," p. 285.

15. See *MP*, pp. 236–37.

16. Ferté, "Robert Fludd et la philosophie hermétique," pp. 292–93.

17. See Ferté, "Robert Fludd et la philosophie hermétique," pp. 291–92, for the many connections between Fludd and Matthaeus Greuter.

Collegio Helvetico in Milan for the training of Swiss Catholics. Whoever Gruter was, he also revealed a "magnetic" cure for atrophied limbs that sowed the seeds of Fludd's later enthusiasm for the weapon salve.

Of Fludd's time in Spain we know nothing, and little more of his travels in Germany. Beside Augsburg, they may have included Heidelberg, seat of Frederick, Count Palatine, who was married to King James's daughter Elizabeth; and Cassel, where the Landgrave Moritz von Hesse-Cassel ("Moritz the Learned," 1572–1632) pursued his alchemical and Hermetic interests. One thing is certain: that Fludd returned from his travels committed to a career in medicine and full of the novel doctrines of the Paracelsians.

By early 1605 Fludd was back in Oxford, this time enrolled at Christ Church where he took his medical degrees of MB and MD. His Paracelsianism and contempt for the prevalent Galenic system soon caused difficulties with the medical establishment. He failed his first examination by the College of Physicians and was not allowed to practice. In February 1606 he was examined a second time, and according to the College's records "Although he did not give full satisfaction in the examinations, he was thought not unlearned and therefore allowed to practise medicine." By May he was exhibiting all the zeal of a convert, "prating about himself and his chemical medicines and heaping contempt on the Galenic doctors." His name was removed from the physicians' roll, and he was told to behave himself better.

In July 1606 Fludd returned to France for consultation with some Italian and French physicians whom he already knew.[18] The police at the Channel port of Hythe mistook him momentarily for a suspect whose description he resembled: "small stature, lean visage, auburn hair, etc." The next year he reapplied to the College of Physicians, was thrice examined, and admitted as a candidate in December. In March 1608, he "conducted himself so insolently as to offend everyone," and was once more rejected. Not until September 1609 was he finally admitted, and settled into his career as a fashionable London doctor.

EARLY WRITINGS AND THE ROSICRUCIANS

Fludd's first appearance in print was prompted by the appearance of the Rosicrucian manifestos. These anonymous publications, which aroused strong emotions of sympathy and antipathy, were *Fama Fraternitatis* in 1614 and *Confessio Fraternitatis* in 1615. (Fludd does not mention the third original Rosicrucian work, the *Chemical Wedding of Christian Rosenkreutz* published in 1616.)[19] The *Fama* and *Confessio* purported to come from the Brotherhood of the Rose Cross, a secret society that announced an imminent reformation of the whole world and invited prospective members to make themselves known.

Appearing in the midst of a century of religious wars, the idea of a universal reformation and reconciliation was welcomed by many, but not by Catholics, whose pope the manifestos had grossly insulted. Its esoteric aspects and claims of occult knowledge also met with resistance, even fear. In 1615 and 1616 Andreas Libavius published tracts denigrating the Rosicrucian doctrines as expressed in the *Fama* and *Confessio,* especially those of harmony between macrocosm and microcosm, magic, Kabbalah, and the use of Hermetic texts. This was an attack, by implication, on the very foundations of the *History of the Macrocosm and Microcosm* that Fludd had already completed and was preparing for publication.

---

18. See Huffman, *Robert Fludd and the End of the Renaissance,* p. 28.

19. For the texts of the three original Rosicrucian documents, see Godwin and McIntosh, *Rosicrucian Trilogy.*

He immediately sprang to the defense of the Rosicrucians, writing *Apologia Compendiaria,* a "compendious apology" for them.[20] At the end of this he took the opportunity, as many others had done, to appeal to the mysterious brotherhood to accept him as a member. The next year (1617) he published an expanded version, *Tractatus Apologeticus,*[21] in which he set out the philosophy and intentions of his forthcoming major work. Both were published in the Netherlands. Not content with this, he also produced *Tractatus Theologo-Philosophicus,* a theological discussion of life, death, and resurrection (see ill. 1.3, p. 10–11). This too was dedicated to the Rosicrucians, confident that they would understand and sympathize with Fludd's approach, and that they shared his disgust with the mores of the modern world. (See appendix 3, "Fludd on His Own Times.") The publisher was now Johann Theodor de Bry, of whom more later.

The Rosicrucians' failure to reply to Fludd's defense and appeal put him in a quandary of self-doubt. While being a seemingly perfect candidate—chaste, religious, and devoted to medicine—was he still not good enough for them? He of course knew nothing of the real circumstances surrounding the Rosicrucian manifestos. These have generated an immense amount of literature, but only recently has scholarship made it possible to reconstruct them.[22] The *Fama* and *Confessio* originated in a circle of Lutheran scholars in Tübingen, and were probably intended for private circulation alone. The *Fama* introduces the character of Christian Rosenkreutz (1378–1484), who traveled in the East and learned a wisdom beyond anything known in the West. On his return he founded a brotherhood to put his ideas into practice. After his death at the age of 106 he was laid in a seven-sided vault whose location was lost for 120 years. In 1604 it was discovered by chance and found to contain Rosenkreutz's uncorrupted body, books, and symbolic objects. The Rosicrucians thereupon reconstituted themselves and invited applications for membership. The *Confessio* is a more doctrinal work, explaining the theological, philosophical, and practical principles espoused by the brotherhood in expectation that the end of the world is near. The two manifestos are an erudite fantasy, rich in esoteric symbols and associations, reflecting the Tübingen circle's concern with the state of the world and their conviction that little time remained for its reformation.

The manifestos were already written in 1610, after which Johan Valentin Andreae (1586–1654), who seems to have been the chief author, turned his attention to other things. But the manuscripts escaped, with effects that resonated far beyond the Tübingen circle. The world first learned of them in 1612, when the composer Adam Haslmayr published a booklet in praise of the brotherhood, for which he was arrested and condemned to the galleys. The texts then came into the hands of the court printer of Hesse-Cassel, who published them, surely at the behest of Landgrave Moritz (see above). Most readers took the existence of the Rosicrucians as literal truth. Rumors spread and emotions became heated, both for and against a brotherhood that refused to reveal any more of itself, or to answer applications for membership. Andreae, disconcerted by these overreactions, took steps to discredit the myth that he and his friends had invented. In 1616 he revised and published *The Chemical Wedding,* an alchemical novel that he had written years earlier, making the protagonist none other than Christian Rosenkreutz, yet

---

20. *AC,* translation in Huffman, *Robert Fludd: Essential Readings.*

21. *TA,* partial translation in Fabre, "Robert Fludd et l'alchimie."

22. See especially Gilly, *Cimelia Rhodostaurotica.*

IN EFFIGIEM D. AVTHORIS.

POe on a commendent laudentque Machaona prifci,
    Iactes Phœbigenam tuque Epidaure tuum.
Nos te ROBERTVM noftris celebrabimus annis,
    Nomina qui gelidis FLVCTIBVS orfageris.
Scilicet infando fubnixus robore mentis
    Defcribis quicquid cofmus vterque tenet.
Suauis es ore, grauis, FLVDDI, fimul arte medendi
    Dicendus patriæ verus Apollo tuæ.
Sit licet Argolicà præcinctus Daphnide Pœon,
    Quæ datur à Phœbo Laurea, totà tua eft.

                                        I. E. Chriſtannus.

1.2. Robert Fludd, 1631

This portrait reverses Merian's of 1626. Since it would be inappropriate for Fludd to
have his left hand on his heart, he holds a pair of gloves in it. *Beneath*, a Latin poem
by "I. E. Christannus." Alluding to Fludd's "Apollo's Oracle" at the end of the work,
the poem compares Fludd to the classical healers Paion and Machaon and lauds him
as the "true Apollo of his nation." *MC* I, 2, 1, verso of title page.

יהוה

TRACTATVS

Theologo-Philosophicus,

In Libros tres distributus;

Quorum

I. } { VITA.
II. } de { MORTE.
III. } { RESURRECTIONE.

Cui inferuntur nonnulla Sapientiæ veteris, Ada-
mi infortunio superstitis, fragmenta: ex profun-
diori sacrarum Literarum sensu & lumine, atque
ex limpidiori & liquidiori saniorum Philo-
sophorum fonte hausta atque
collecta,

Fratribusáż, à CRUCE ROSEA *dictis,*
dedicata
à

RUDOLFO OTREB Britanno.
ANNO
CHRISTVS MVNDO VITA.
Oppenheimii typis HIERONYMI GALLERI,
Impensis JOH. THEOD. de BRY.

so different in character, age, and activity from the Rosenkreutz of the *Fama* as to unmask that work as equally fictitious.

It did not work. The Rosicrucian myth answered too well to the hopes and fears of the times. Both Fludd and the alchemist Michael Maier (1569–1622) have gone down in history as enthusiasts for Rosicrucianism, which they were, and as members of the brotherhood, which they were not (whatever is claimed by later orders going under that name). They were also assumed to be bosom friends, but recent research has banished even this happy notion, since neither man acknowledged the other's existence except for a few scathing remarks on Maier's side.[23]

---

23. See Figala and Neumann, "Author cui nomen Hermes Malavici,'" pp. 133–35.

HISTORY OF THE MACROCOSM AND MICROCOSM

While Fludd was busy with the Rosicrucians, his long-prepared work of universal learning was gathering dust, having been partly written during his student days and mostly finished by 1610. From 1617 to 1621 his *History of the Macrocosm and the Microcosm* appeared in annual installments from the presses of Johann Theodor de Bry (1561–1623) in the Palatinate region of Germany. Frances Yates, in *The Rosicrucian Enlightenment,* has pieced together the fascinating story of de Bry's work in Oppenheim and Frankfurt and its connection with the short reign of Frederick and Elizabeth. The huge works of Fludd and the many alchemical books of Maier, all

---

⟨ 1.3. The Fall of Man

Theological-philosophical treatise in three books: 1. On Life; 2. On Death; 3. On Resurrection. In which are included some fragments of ancient wisdom witnessing to Adam's misfortune: derived and compiled in the light of Holy Writ and from the limpid fount of the wiser Philosophers, dedicated to those called the Brothers of the Rose Cross by Rudolfo Otreb, a Briton, in the year "Christ, life to the world." At the Oppenheim press of Hieronymus Gallerus, at the expense of Johann Theodor de Bry.*

The name of "Roberto Floud" is concealed as an anagram, and the date in a chronogram (found by adding the capitalized letters of ChrIstVs MVnDo VIta: CIVMVDVI = 1617). The title page shows God creating Eve from Adam's side, Adam and Eve with the fruit of the Tree of Knowledge, the expulsion from the Garden of Eden, and the Resurrection of the Dead. Further symbols (fruits and skulls) appear in the decorations. The major part of the book reiterates traditional Christian doctrine concerning man's fall and redemption, amplified by many quotations from the Hermetic writings. Fludd offers this, his second work, to the Rosicrucians, joining them in the expectation of an imminent renewal of heaven and earth. *TTP,* title page.

---

*Throughout this book, translations and direct paraphrases of Fludd's Latin texts are distinguished by this contrasting type style.

1.4. Rosicrucian Emblem

"The rose gives the bees honey." This engraving appeared on the title page of *Summum Bonum* (1629), a book by a Scottish friend of Fludd's who went under the name of "Joachim Frizius."* Fludd adopted it for his *Clavis Philosophiae et Alchemiae Fluddanae*. The rose has seven circles of seven petals each, and its stem is cross-shaped. The whole figure resembles the astrological sign for Venus. *On the left* is a grape trellis with two spiderwebs, also with sevenfold divisions, and the wingless insect on the rose may also be intended as a spider. *On the right* are four beehives. Adam McLean identified the source in an emblem book of 1615 illustrated by Merian.[†] Frizius, *Summum Bonum*, title page; *CP,* title page.

---

*On Frizius's possible identity, see Schuchard, *Restoring the Temple of Vision,* pp. 392–94; Heisler, "Robert Fludd."
[†]See McLean, "A Source for Robert Fludd's Sevenfold Rose."

illustrated with symbolic engravings by de Bry's Swiss son-in-law Matthaeus (Matthieu) Merian (1593–1650), take on a new meaning when placed in their political setting.[24] The hopes of all those of a "Rosicrucian" outlook (i.e., anti-Catholic, devoted to the Bible, and open to occult doctrines) were pinned on Frederick: hopes that he could initiate the reform of which the manifestos spoke and heal the rifts that were soon to split central Europe apart in the Thirty Years' War.

It was probably Fludd's friend Justus Helt who took the manuscript of his *History of the Macrocosm* to show to publishers at the 1616 Frankfurt Book Fair. In April 1617 Helt wrote to Fludd to announce his success in securing publication by Johann Theodor de Bry, one of the foremost publishers in Europe.[25] De Bry had the first tractate of 214 pages ready for the autumn fair, and the much larger second tractate, *De Naturae Simia,* by Easter 1618, when Kepler saw it.[26] The speed with which the hundreds of illustrations were engraved is astonishing. The German firm's efficiency and experience came as a godsend to Fludd, for he says in his answer to Foster that "our home-borne Printers demanded of me five hundred pounds to print the first volume, and to find the cuts in copper; but, beyond the seas, it was printed at no cost of mine, and that as I would wish. And I had sixteen copies sent me over, with forty pounds in gold, as an unexpected gratuity for it."[27]

These "cuts in copper" were the engraved illustrations that play such a prominent part in Fludd's work. Several factors had prepared for this approach. First there was the popularity of emblem books, in which pictorial symbols were combined with mottoes and poems to make an ethical or philosophical point, or just for the sake of a conceit. Innumerable emblem books followed on the prototype, Alciati's *Emblemata* of 1531, and the genre flourished well into the seventeenth century. The idea that a picture could show what words could not tell also lay behind the beautifully illustrated alchemical texts, which appeared in great numbers in the fifty years around 1600. When copper engravings succeeded woodcuts as the favorite means of printing such pictures, the quality of illustration improved markedly. The de Bry firm was largely responsible for the change, through their massive illustrated books describing America and other recent discoveries. The extraordinary cosmological plates of Fludd's *History of the Macrocosm* have been attributed to Theodor de Bry himself, but Lucas Wütrich, the authority on Merian, holds that the younger man, still in his twenties, was responsible for them all.[28] After inheriting the press on his father-in-law's death, Merian concentrated on engraving topographical and biblical scenes, in a style already visible in his Fluddean illustrations.

Fludd's go-between, whether Helt or someone else, wanted the work to be dedicated to the "Landgrave of Hesse," a title held by several nobles beside the learned Moritz. De Bry, on the other hand, wanted it dedicated to the Elector Palatine.[29] Fludd had higher ambitions and a more patriotic plan. On the first page he dedicated the work to "God, best and greatest, my incomprehensible creator," and on the second page to "The most serene and potent prince,

24. They were also placed on the Catholic "Index of Prohibited Books." See Van Groesen, *Representation of the Overseas World,* pp. 283–84.

25. Helt's letter is in "A Philosophical Key," Trinity College, Cambridge, Western Ms.

26. On these transactions, see Hauge, "Robert Fludd (1574–1637): A Musical Charlatan?" pp. 21–22.

27. *DFA,* p. 21.

28. Wütrich, *Das druckgraphische Werk von Matthaeus Merian,* 2:81.

29. See "Declaratio Brevis" in Huffman, *Robert Fludd: Essential Readings,* pp. 87–88. On the various possible Landgraves of Hesse, see Figala and Neumann, "'Author cui nomen Hermes Malavici,'" pp. 133–35.

HONORI, PIETATI, MEMORIÆ,
OPTIMI, INTEGERRIMI, DEQVE PVBLI-
CO BONO LITTERARIO OPTIME MERITI VIRI, SVMMIQVE AR-
tificis noſtrorum temporum IOHANNIS THEODORI de Bry, ciuis
Franeofortenſis, qui die 8. Menſis Auguſti, Anni
M. DC. XXIII. ad beatorum ſedes
translatus eſt.

Æri ſuam ipſius effigiem incidenti

Corporis effigies ſculptores fingere multi   Iane refert Theodore tuam tamē iſta tabella
Sat bene ſæpe ſolent; aſt animi nequeunt.   Arte tuâ, effigiem corporis atque animi.
                    Amicitiæ ergò poſuit I. C. D

V Erſibus accuſent alij crudelia fata   Heu probitas! Heu priſca fides! Heu candida mentis
    Neſcia præclaris parcere fata viris,   Fibra iacet nulla ſat lacrymanda die.
Perq̗ leues Elegos deducant flebile carmen,   Vix ego, Sancte Senex, lectus tibi numine dextro
    Orba parente ſuo tot monimenta gemant: Sum Gener & nondum filia facta parens:
Lugebunt alij jacturam & publica damna   Occidis, & grata rumpis conſortia menſæ,
    Ingenium flebunt artificemq̗ manum.   O Socer & plusquam mî venerande pater!
O Theodore tuam Socer exoptate Bryæ,   Sic olim pueros Solis vix lumen adeptos
    Quem triſtis rapuit morbus & atra dies.   Principio vitæ Mors inimica rapit.
Cauſa mihi lacrymas vicinior exprimit vdas   Ergo cape has lacrymas, & teſtes ſortis acerbæ
    Et mea triſtitia pectora mole grauat,   Verſiculos, tremula lemmata poſta manu:
Nam tua me pietas, amor, indulgentia, virtus, Atq̗ vale, & Chriſtus (nec erit mora longa) ſepulcro
    Deſerit, & luctu proximiore premit.   Ereptum ætherei collocet arce Poli.

Iohannes Ammonius Ambergenſis Socero
meritiſſimo cum lacrymis poſuit.

James, thrice-greatest, minister and first ruler in the kingdoms of Great Britain, France and Ireland of the emperor of heavens and earths and of his incomprehensible creator."

It is usual to ask permission before dedicating a book, especially to a king. Word of this indiscretion soon reached King James's ears, and with it the insinuation that Fludd and the Rosicrucians had sinister and heretical intentions. Fludd was summoned to explain matters to the king in person: a potentially dangerous interview that he carried off with great aplomb. James, who was unusually learned for a monarch and deeply interested in religious controversy, while being known as a difficult and prickly person, approved of Fludd's views and remained his patron for life.

Another complaint that was settled through royal influence could not have been more different: it concerned a steelmaking workshop that Fludd had started by 1618. He had brought over a French metallurgist to make steel that was better and more economical than anything currently manufactured in England. Two holders of the royal monopoly on steelmaking filed a complaint that came before the Royal Council in 1620. It was dismissed, and Fludd was granted a patent and congratulated for contributing to the national welfare. This episode, which was first described by William Huffman, gives insight into Fludd's practical talents.[30]

Returning to the *History of the Macrocosm and the Microcosm,* volume I and the first part of volume II were published from 1617 to 1621 at the rate of one large tome a year. De Bry died in 1623, and the following year his heirs published a second edition of the most popular part, *De Naturae Simia* (Nature's Ape). This is a bibliographical curiosity, as in one issue the existing plates were used, while in another the hundreds of illustrations were re-engraved, almost indistinguishably from the originals, by someone who found it worth the trouble and expense.[31] Meanwhile Fludd continued with his great project, which exceeded

---

30. See Huffman, *Robert Fludd and the End of the Renaissance,* pp. 23–24.
31. See Hauge, "Robert Fludd (1574–1637): A Musical Charlatan?" pp. 22–24.

꧁ 1.5. Johann Theodor de Bry

On the verso of the title page of *Anatomiae Amphitheatrum* is a memorial to Fludd's chief publisher, Johann Theodor de Bry (1561–1623), who had died on August 8. In this self-portrait, dated 1615, he holds a plate engraved with Hendrik Goltzius's design of a putto perched on a skull and blowing bubbles, with the motto *Quis evadet,* i.e., "Who will evade [death]?" The answer beneath comes from Saint John's Gospel: "Truly, truly, I say to you, he who hears my word and believes him who sent me, has eternal life" (John 5:24). The scroll on the table quotes from Psalm 139:21–22: "Do I not hate them that hate thee, O Lord, and do I not loathe them that rise up against thee? I hate them with a perfect hatred; I count them my enemies." It is not hard to guess who the Calvinist printer had in mind, having been driven from his native Netherlands by the invaders from Catholic Spain. Piled up on the right are unbound sheets of the illustrated travel narratives for which the de Bry firm was best known. *AA,* verso of title page.

all reasonable proportions as he divided and subdivided it (see the breakdown on p. 252). Later parts carried different titles, probably to promote sales: *Anatomiae Amphitheatrum* (Theatre of Anatomy) and *Philosophia Sacra et Vere Christiana* (Sacred and Truly Christian Philosophy). By the time the latter appeared in 1626, being portion IV of section I of tractate II of volume II, the master plan was beyond repair, and Fludd abandoned it, only to start another one.

MEDICAL PRACTICE AND PRINCIPLES

Once Fludd's troubles with the College of Physicians were over, his standing improved, and he served several times as censor (examiner). He set up his medical practice in London, living first in Fenchurch Street and later in Coleman Street. We learn from his will that his house there cost him four hundred pounds, plus a hundred pounds in building and repairing.[32] He employed his own apothecary—a necessity for a physician whose herbal and chemical remedies were not compounded by every pharmacist. Early biographers mention his ability to talk his patients into believing in his cures, and cynically attribute his success to this alone. Among his patients was John Selden, the eminent lawyer and antiquary, and among his close friends William Harvey, who discovered the circulation of the blood.

The expressed intention behind Fludd's medical writings was to replace the heathen authorities, Aristotle, Galen, and Hippocrates, with a properly Christian medicine. Although the disputes with the College of Physicians make much of his Paracelsian convictions, these play little part in his writings. Instead we have the ponderous and neglected *Medicina Catholica* (Universal Medicine), a second encyclopedic project that overlapped with the *History of the Macrocosm and Microcosm,* one of whose treatises had been devoted to anatomy.[33] The first volume of *Medicina Catholica* was published in four installments from 1629 to 1631. It appeared in Frankfurt, which, despite the Thirty Years' War and occupation by the Swedes, was still a thriving center of the book trade.[34] Fludd's publisher was now William Fitzer (1600–1671), an English bookseller who was one of Theodor de Bry's sons-in-law.[35] Communications were more difficult now: Fitzer apologizes in the first volume that he has not been able to submit the proofs to the author, but has done his best to illustrate them according to the author's intentions. Presumably on Fludd's instructions, he reused a number of copper plates from the earlier project. Whereas they had originally served to illustrate cosmological principles, now they were applied to medical conditions, fully in accord with the macro/microcosmic philosophy.

Fludd's medical encyclopedia undertook a complete theoretical reconstruction of the causes of disease. In his view, they did not come from below—for example, from the imbalance of the four humors, as taught in the official Galenic system of medicine—but from above. The first part of *Medicina Catholica* sets out these principles. They begin with the leading idea of Fludd's entire philosophy: that God has a dual power, one self-contained and inactive, the other outwardly oriented and creative. From the human point of view, these two powers manifest respectively as the qualities of darkness and light, contraction and expansion,

---

32. Fludd's will: see Huffman, *Robert Fludd and the End of the Renaissance,* p. 224.

33. See bibliography for details.

34. Weidhaas, *History of the Frankfurt Book Fair,* p. 65.

35. Van Groesen, *Representation of the Overseas World,* p. 100.

destruction and preservation, death and life, evil and good, demons and angels, disease and health. As regards the latter, God sends sickness to mankind as a punishment for sin. Whether the sin is always on the individual's part, or whether due to the original sin that weighs, in Christian doctrine, on the entire human race, is a question Fludd prefers to avoid. But in effect, if we get ill we have none to blame but ourselves, and like Job must suffer patiently and prayerfully. (The book of Job is one of Fludd's most-used sources for his medical philosophy.) Whether we recover depends less on the doctor's skill than on the ineluctable course of the disease, and ultimately on what God intends for us. Perhaps this was inevitable when official medicine had no cure for the ever-present dangers of infections, malaria, smallpox, or bubonic plague, and falling ill was as likely as not to result in death. Such was Fludd's own condition in November 1629. At the very moment when he decided to write a treatise on the role of "crisis" in disease, he was struck by a fever and in a short time was completely helpless.[36] The crisis came on the fourth day, after which, by God's grace, he began to recover.

In all fairness, we should add that *Medicina Catholica* is an unfinished work. We have only the first volume, which treats the causes of disease, and not the second, which was to treat their cures.[37] The latter was planned on a threefold division similar to that of Cornelius Agrippa's *Three Books of Occult Philosophy,* with reference to the supercelestial, celestial, and elementary worlds. Each of these apparently has its own medicaments. There was also to be a section on external applications, and one on magnetic cures and the "mystical pronunciation of words." Lacking this volume, we can only gather a few hints about Fludd's actual

medical practice. For all his independence from established medicine, he took for granted its standard remedies of bleeding and "purging" (inducing vomiting and diarrhea), only with careful attention to timing, weather, and planetary positions.

Medicina Catholica starts, as one would expect, with metaphysical principles. It then descends step-by-step to the theological roots of disease, the angels and demons that are agents of God's dual nature, the qualities of the zodiacal signs and the planets, the four elements, and the four humors: choleric, sanguine, phlegmatic, and melancholic. These form the necessary background to the physician's study of the individual patient. Whereas in the *History of the Macrocosm and Microcosm* it was the monochord that supplied a symbolic and numerical representation of creation, here it is the weatherglass, a primitive barometer to which Fludd attached great importance. In the second part of the work it becomes the centerpiece of a grand universal theory of angelic and planetary influences, meteorology, and especially the winds and their connections with disease. More is explained in the captions to the relevant illustrations (see ills. 9.3–9.11, pp. 220–29). A large section is devoted to a review of the experiments from Fludd's earlier work. It recycles over forty of the engravings from the *History of the Macrocosm* that depict cauldrons, siphons, fountains, musical pipes, furnaces, altars, and other devices, as well as the woodcuts illustrating Fludd's experiment with wheat and some pictures of the human brain from *Anatomiae Amphitheatrum.* Each is now reinterpreted as illustrating the workings of the human body and the causes of disease.

The third published part of *Medicina Catholica* likewise looks back to some of the microcosmic arts that Fludd had treated in his *History of the Microcosm:* mathematics, geomancy, physiognomy, chiromancy, and astrology.

---

36. *MC* I, 2, 2, p. 10.
37. See the plan on p. 253.

He now applies them to medicine as so many methods of divination. The doctor uses them to calculate and predict the course of a disease, discovering which are the good and bad days, when the disease will reach a crisis, and whether recovery will follow. Physiognomy and chiromancy require actual contact with the patient, whose facial features and hands contain answers to these questions. In geomancy and astrology, the doctor consults higher sources of knowledge. Geomancy, the most occult of Fludd's arts, extracts answers from the patterns of pebbles randomly thrown on the ground, or from random dots made on paper. Astrology finds answers in the current state of the heavens and the planetary influences at work on the patient.

In Fludd's time, as in ours, uroscopy or diagnosis through a patient's urine was a well-established method. We learn the typical procedure from Fludd's exhaustive treatise on the subject. When people fell ill and were unable to leave their house, a messenger (relative, servant, or friend) would take a sample of their urine and bring it in a bottle to the doctor's office. The doctor would examine it carefully for color, consistency, smell, and even taste, then pronounce his verdict on the disease. Fludd grounded uroscopy, as he did all his methods, in his cosmological principles (see ill. 9.10, "The Colors of Urine," p. 228). But he seems to have preferred urinomancy, divination, rather than diagnosis. In this he followed a medieval theory revived in the Elizabethan period by Simon Forman (1552–1611), the astrologer whose work Fludd acknowledges as his primary influence. The theory assumes the scenario sketched above, of a patient's urine being brought to the doctor, but now the actual sample was of minimal interest. What was important was the actual moment at which the messenger arrived, and the circumstances under which he or she had obtained the sample. The physician asked only the name (which indicated the sex) and age of the patient, then drew a horary chart for that moment, showing the positions of the seven planets and the moon's nodes relative to the signs of the zodiac. The other element in horoscopy, the assignment of planets and signs to the twelve "houses," depended on the relationship of the messenger to the patient, and whether or not the latter was aware and willing that a urine sample was being taken to the doctor. Through complex calculations, the doctor then identified the nature of the ailment and its likely crisis and outcome.

The last completed part of *Medicina Catholica* deals with diagnosis through the pulse. To his credit, Fludd was among the very first to accept William Harvey's recent discovery that blood circulates around the body, and that the motive force behind pulsation is not the veins but the heart. His own system characteristically calls on other arts and sciences: arithmetic for calculating the pulse beats, music for timing their rhythm, and geometry for calculating the width, depth, and length of the veins. He tabulates every astrological combination, every effect of demonic and angelic influence on wind and weather, every variation of pulsation, in order to diagnose a patient's disease and to divine its progress. The whole process, for all its prayerfulness and piety, is extremely mechanical and impersonal, and quite at variance with the few contemporary reports of Fludd's relation to his patients. It seems unlikely that the work was as successful as the *History of the Macrocosm and Microcosm,* and perhaps for that reason the promised second volume never appeared. Fludd planned it so meticulously that the mere outline fills a large folding plate at the end of *Pulsus,* titled "Apollo's Oracle." In a half playful use of classical figures, the physician is imagined as Aesculapius, receiving oracles from his father Apollo.[38] Fludd explains:

---

38. Compare the use of Apollo and Dionysus in ill. 9.1.

By Aesculapius we understand the spirit of any gifted physician who appears inebriated by Apollo's gifts, influences, and properties (thought to be given by the sun god). Thus his spirit is inspired by the healing influences of the sun; indeed, his whole attention is given to the medical art and the cure of illness. He accepts this gift or property from Apollo, or from eternal wisdom, the son of Jehovah. Thus the whole mystery of the following volume takes the form of a dialogue between Apollo, the son of eternal light (whose nature is all in curing, salvation, and the expulsion of sin, which is the root of sickness and death), and the human spirit, regenerated, instructed, moderated, and as it were led by the hand to obtain this gift.[39]

One exception to Fludd's reticence over cures, though a bizarre one, is the weapon salve. This was an ointment with which one anoints not the wound but the thing that caused it, being careful not to wipe off any blood. The salve works on the blood and, by occult sympathy, transmits its curative power to the wound. After Fludd published the recipe for the salve, which included human blood, flesh, fat, and the moss that grows on a dead man's skull, the Reverend William Foster attacked it with suitable scorn in his *Sponge to Wipe Away the Weapon-Salve*. Fludd responded with *The Squeesing of Parson Foster's Sponge*. As in all his controversies, he gave as good as he got.

Fludd compares the weapon salve to the acoustic phenomenon of a lute or viol lying on a table that resounds when another instrument is played nearby. This demonstrated the possibility of action at a distance, provoked by sympathy between similarly tuned strings. Another practical demonstration was the magnet or lodestone, with its power to attract without contact.

Fludd was aware of William Gilbert's magnetic researches, and of their cosmic dimension, for the magnet is not only attracted by iron nearby, but by the distant North Pole. Magnetism seemed to be a universal phenomenon, not limited to metals but present in other substances, as the Scottish doctor William Maxwell reported after a meeting with Fludd:

When I was visiting Dr Robert Fludd last year with my friend Stafford, and we came to discuss these things, Dr Fludd spoke, as was his wont, very sagaciously but also secretively about this art. Among other things he was able to tell me of the wonders of a magnet which I had heard of but never myself tried: it had such power of attraction that when he applied it to his heart it drew him with such force that he could not have held out for long. The Fluddian magnet is nothing other than dessicated human flesh, which certainly possesses the greatest attractive power; it should be taken, if possible, from a body still warm, and from a man who has died a violent death.[40]

After completing the first volume of *Medicina Catholica,* Fludd published no more major works. In 1638, the year after his death, a publisher in Gouda produced *Philosophia Moysaica,* supposedly a summation of his philosophy, and in 1659 an English translation as *Mosaicall Philosophy* made this the most familiar of Fludd's works. However, Johann Rösche questions its authorship, regarding it as a "foreign body" in the Fluddean corpus.[41] He analyzes significant differences from Fludd's other writings, and finds an emphasis on sympathetic medical cures, especially ones from German sources of 1629–30, that is at variance with the

---

39. *MC* I, 2, 3, p. 94.

40. Peuckert, *Gabalia*, p. 271.
41. See Rösche, *Der Versuch einer hermetischen Alternative*, pp. 325–72.

FLUDD'S LIFE
AND WORK

19

1631 plan of the second volume of *Medicina Catholica*. In general there is a greater presence of German materials than is usual in Fludd's work. Rösche concludes: "Might a German follower have taken Fludd's fragments, perhaps out of the planned therapeutical part of *Medicina Catholica,* and incorporated them in a textbook on sympathetic medicine, trying to anchor it in Fludd's system?"[42] Certainly *Philosophica Moysaica* is anticlimactic, coming after the two great projects and the densely argued controversial writings, while the quality of illustrations is pitiful.

CONTROVERSIAL WORKS

Wilhelm Schmidt-Biggemann classes Fludd's controversies with his hunt for the Rosicrucians as "fruitless activities" that hindered the completion of his great encyclopedic works.[43] Fruitless they were, yet an inevitable part of his character. As Allen Debus says, "Acutely self-righteous, outspoken at all times, Fludd could not easily accept criticism."[44] His early Rosicrucian works were already defensive, as were the two treatises written after his interview with King James. Among his critics, Johannes Kepler (1571–1630), and to a lesser extent Pierre Gassendi (1592–1655), expressed their differences firmly but courteously, as one scholar arguing with another. Marin Mersenne (1588–1648) and William Foster (1591–1643), on the other hand, wrote intending to damage Fludd's reputation and even endanger him by association with black magic and witchcraft.

The following summaries highlight some of the many ideas exchanged in these debates,

concentrating on the ones most revealing of Fludd's attitudes. More thorough treatments, with reference to the original documents on both sides, are to be found in the given sources.

1619 Johannes Kepler, in *Harmonices Mundi,* criticizes Fludd's theory of world harmony.[45] Kepler was a Platonist and a Pythagorean, whose search for the planetary motions was part of a quest for God's secret plan. Like Fludd's scheme, Kepler's had a basis in musical harmony, as well as in the geometry of Plato's *Timaeus.* But his method was diametrically opposed to Fludd's. He sought harmony in the mathematics of actual planetary motions, whereas Fludd looked for it in the relation of light to darkness, and in his artificial system of pyramids. Kepler finds Fludd's work too extravagant and symbolic, having little to do with the actualities of the solar system.

1621 Fludd answers Kepler's criticisms at ten times their length in *Veritatis Proscenium.* He points out that Kepler's dependence on the Platonic solids for the explanation of planetary distances is no less artificial than his own pyramids. He criticizes Kepler for believing that the influence of the stars comes from light rays, whereas it is from the *spiritus vitae;* also for situating the world soul in the earth rather than in the sun. While Kepler relies on logical argument alone, for Fludd this is only one method of knowing among others. By ignoring those other methods, Kepler stays on the surface. He does not understand the differences between the three worlds, nor the pyramidal doctrine, which is not about planetary distances, but about the various densities of form and matter.

1621/1622 Kepler replies with *Prodromus Dissertationum Cosmographicum,* saying that Fludd does not understand his (Kepler's) planetary harmonies. He (Fludd) confuses string

42. Rösche, *Der Versuch einer hermetischen Alternative,* p. 372.

43. Schmidt-Biggemann, *Geschichte der christlichen Kabbala,* 2:63.

44. Debus, "The Synthesis of Robert Fludd," 1:208.

45. On the controversy with Kepler, see Rösche, *Der Versuch einer hermetischen Alternative,* pp. 463–95; also Pauli, "The Influence of Archetypal Ideas."

lengths, which only apply to human music, with planetary motions. While Fludd only relies on ancient teachings, Kepler is offering something entirely new and is doing it in a straightforward way, free from Hermetic mystification. He can tolerate Hermetism and alchemy as having a place somewhere between poetry and mysticism, but they should not interfere in the mathematical description of nature. As for the heliocentric system, which Fludd says is contradicted by Scripture, the Bible makes no distinction between stars and planets. Fludd's arguments from everyday experience (of the sun going round the earth) do not outweigh Kepler's mathematical demonstrations.

1623 Fludd answers Kepler again in *Monochordum Mundi,* issued as part of *Anatomiae Amphitheatrum.* This largely repeats Fludd's former arguments. He can admire Kepler's mathematical discoveries and wish him well, yet Kepler does not value Fludd's. The mathematical approach cannot solve basic metaphysical questions. Kepler wants to banish Hermetic natural philosophy from natural science, relegating it to poetry or rhetoric, but wrongly, for it is deep and real knowledge. In six questions, Fludd undermines the basis of Kepler's geometrically based theory of harmony. He closes with the evidence of his own experiment with wheat, which showed that there is a higher knowledge, based not on riddles and symbols but proven through experiment and the Bible. All the practical sciences are merely images of the inner and hidden knowledge. There are, in short, two ways of knowing, each of which should give place to the other.

1623 Marin Mersenne, a Franciscan friar, attacks Fludd and the Hermetic philosophy in *Quaestiones Celeberrimae in Genesim.*[46]

Fludd only discovered this in 1628, and was outraged. Mersenne calls him an atheist, on the grounds that Fludd denies the immortality of the soul, and an evil magician. Mersenne exclaims: "O how blind is a man who in Europe, among Christians, goes unpunished for not only practising such foul and horrendous magic, but boldly dares to publish it!" In the Europe of witch hunts, this was no light accusation. Mersenne, who is a mechanist, wants a clear division between body and spirit. This entails the complete immateriality of the soul, and the complete elimination of psychic ideas from matter. All ideas of a World Soul and of *spiritus* are anathema to him, as are all methods of divination, all occult sciences, and the Hermetic doctrines that support them. He takes the Bible as literal truth and rejects any Platonic, Hermetic, or Kabbalistic readings and commentaries. He presents Fludd, both by name and with unattributed quotations from his work, as a prime example of the opposition, but allows that if Fludd should convert to Catholicism, there might be hope for him.

1623 Patrick Scot (active 1603–25), who was probably a civil servant and/or royal tutor, attacks Fludd in *The Tillage of Light.*[47] His particular bugbear is alchemy, which he takes only in the material sense, saying that making gold would be fatal to the economy. He deplores the curiosity of those who search the Scriptures for evidence of occult sciences, and urges simple faith and orthodoxy as the pillars of society.

1624? Fludd answers Scot in a manuscript titled "Truth's Golden Harrow." Fludd emphasizes the symbolic and theological interpretation of alchemy, but insists that there is also a physical Philosophers' Stone.

1629 Fludd answers Mersenne in *Sophiae cum Moria Certamen.* He asks how Mersenne

---

46. On the controversy with Mersenne, see Schmidt-Biggemann, *Geschichte der christlichen Kabbala,* 2:147–84; Rösche, *Der Versuch einer hermetischen Alternative,* pp. 495–509.

---

47. On the controversy with Scot, see Janacek, *Alchemical Belief,* pp. 48–54.

can accept the soul in man yet deny it in God's creation. Fludd's experiment with wheat proves that there is a universal soul in plants and animals. He attacks the Catholic dogma of transubstantiation: in the Church of England, the bread and wine are reminders of Jesus's death and resurrection. The presence of Christ in special substances is superfluous in a world picture where Christ is the universal spirit or world soul. Fludd defends himself against the accusation of magic. There is a licit magic, as found in the Wisdom of Solomon, and an illicit. Man has three natures, light, dark, and the will in the middle; hence is subject to three guardian angels. Mersenne was evidently writing under the influence of his dark nature. He misunderstands Platonism, rejects authors like Giorgi and Ficino, and knows nothing about Kabbalah, rooting about like a pig in a dunghill and missing the buried gems. Fludd is his fellow Christian, yet Mersenne is intent on sowing discord between the sects.

1629 Fludd's friend Joachim Frizius answers Mersenne in *Summum Bonum*. In *Clavis Philosophiae* (see below), Fludd insists that it was not written by him, but by a friend, and that the publisher, against Fludd's wishes, printed it in uniform format with his works. Thus Frizius's defense of the Rosicrucians added fuel to the belief that Fludd himself was one of the brotherhood, something he explicitly denies.[48]

1630 Pierre Gassendi, in *Epistolica Exercitatio*, supports Mersenne in principle, though he thinks his criticisms too aggressive.[49] He calls Fludd one of the most learned men of his time, but dislikes his dogmatism. Fludd is

not an evil magician, as Mersenne says, though his ideas are very far from Catholic doctrine. His idea of three guardian angels is ludicrous. Gassendi rejects all forms of divination and Kabbalah; he finds the scriptures self-evident without the need for complex interpretation. Appended to his letter is a *Judicium de Roberto Fluddo* by Lanovius (François de La Noue, 1595–1670), vicar-general and historian of Mersenne's order. He too considers the alchemical interpretation of Scripture to be blasphemous, and Fludd to be even more impious than Calvin.

1631 William Foster, the vicar of Hedgerley in Buckinghamshire, attacks Fludd and the weapon salve in *Hoplocrisma-spongus*, pinning a copy of the pamphlet to Fludd's doorway.[50] Foster is revolted by the grisly ingredients of the salve. He believes that healing can only come from contact, and that healing at a distance is unnatural, hence forbidden. If it occurs, it can only be through demonic agency. He maliciously repeats Mersenne's exclamation about King James allowing such a man as Fludd to live in his kingdom.

1631 Fludd answers Foster in *Doctor Fludd's Answer unto M. Foster*.[51] He points out that the recipe was already published by Paracelsus, and reproves Foster for relying on Catholics like Mersenne, Gassendi, and Lanovius to attack a fellow Anglican. He defends the doctrine of the universal spirit and its special presence in blood. It is the necessary link between the two extremes of form and matter. Since all healing, as well as all sickness, comes from God, to attribute any kind to the Devil is blasphemous. This is Fludd's only

48. See Huffman, *Robert Fludd and the End of the Renaissance*, p. 157.

49. On the controversy with Gassendi and Lanovius, see Rösche, *Der Versuch einer hermetischen Alternative*, pp. 509–30; also Cafiero, "Robert Fludd e la polemica con Gassendi." Fludd summarizes it in *DFA*.

50. Kassell, "Magic, Alchemy and the Medieval Economy," p. 91.

51. On the weapon salve controversy, see Rösche, *Der Versuch einer hermetischen Alternative*, pp. 530–39; also Debus, "Robert Fludd and the Use of Gilbert's *De Magnete*"; Sugg, *Mummies, Cannibals and Vampires*.

publication in English, and it includes many anecdotes and unique biographical facts.

1633 Fludd answers Mersenne, Gassendi, and Lanovius in *Clavis Philosophiae et Alchymiae Fluddanae,* pointedly addressing it to Gassendi alone. While Mersenne had pointed out Isaac Casaubon's redating of the Hermetic writings to the early Christian era, rather than to the time of Moses, Fludd does not consider this significant. Its truth is not dependent on dating. As for angels, Fludd has the support of Trithemius and Reuchlin, who are approved by the church, as well as the evidence of everyday experience. He thanks Gassendi for the courtesy of his answer. But Gassendi is wrong in taking Fludd's "world monochord" literally. It is the closest symbol of the cosmic nature. Likewise Fludd's pyramids are not real objects, but describe the refinements of matter. There is a long discussion (as in all the Mersenne controversy) of blood, the heart, and the role of *spiritus.* Fludd also reproves Gassendi for his ignorance of Kabbalah: it is not wordplay, but a source of deep truth. Likewise the Bible contains secret knowledge, to seek which is not impiety. It teaches that God is not directly knowable, but revealed in his creation. Thus through observing nature, we rise to supernatural things, as Fludd found in his experiment with wheat. In response to the Catholic suprematism of his opponents, Fludd asserts that all Christian sects, plus Jews, Muslims, Arians, Brunians, and Anabaptists, are striving for inner truth.

DEATH AND REPUTATION

Fludd became a wealthy man. Not only had he inherited property, manufactured steel, and enjoyed a successful medical practice, but King James's succesor, Charles I, continued as his patron. At various times, and for reasons unknown, the king gave Fludd income-generating properties and also the income from a will whose beneficiary, being a foreigner, was denied inheritance.[52]

Fludd died at his home in Coleman Street on September 8, 1637, aged sixty-three. His will directed that his body be carried, preferably at night, to Bearsted, accompanied by the mourners whom he provided with money for appropriate garments, and buried in the church. As he was unmarried, his chief heir was his nephew Thomas Fludd, and he made many smaller bequests to relatives, friends, and the College of Physicians. Another nephew, Lewin Fludd, MD, received all his books. Fludd had designed his own monument, and Thomas had it sculpted and placed prominently in the chancel of the church (it was moved to the vestry in the nineteenth century). The monument has a marble bust of Fludd with an open book, resting on a plinth with an inscription that Craven (see below) translates as follows:

Sacred to the Memory

Of that most brilliant and most learned man, Robert Fludd, alias De Fluctibus, doctor of both medicines, who, after several years' travelling, which he had happily undertaken into regions beyond the sea for gaining the culture of genius, at length was restored to his country, and was, not undeservedly, elected to the society of the most distinguished College of Physicians of London. He calmly exchanged life for death on the 8th day of the month of September, An. Dom. 1637, in the 63rd year of his age.

No costly perfumes from this urn ascend,
In gorgeous tomb thine ashes do not lie,
Thy mortal part alone to earth we give,
The records of thy mind can never die,
For he who writes like thee—tho' dead—
Erects a tomb that lasts for aye.

---

52. See Fludd's will in Huffman, *Robert Fludd and the End of the Renaissance*, pp. 222–29.

This monument, Thomas Fludd, of Gore Court, in Otham, in Kent, Esquire, erected to the most happy memory of his very dear uncle, on the 10th day of the month of August 1638.

The name of Robert Fludd soon passed as a catchword for arcane and incomprehensible philosophy, and indeed, his books are not easy to read. The first serious effort to understand rather than just wonder at them was made by the Reverend James Brown Craven (1850–1924), rector of Saint Olaf's Church in Kirkwall, Orkney. Although working on an island in the most remote corner of the British Isles, Craven had access to virtually all of Fludd's publications, and also to those of Michael Maier, on whom he wrote the first book-length study.[53] Craven was familiar with the researches of the Societas Rosicruciana in Anglia, a society founded in 1867 and open only to master masons. He also read some Theosophical literature (citing H. P. Blavatsky's *Isis Unveiled,* in which Fludd is several times mentioned), A. E. Waite's books on the Rosicrucians, and Hargrave Jennings's chaotic book *The Rosicrucians: Their Rites and Mysteries* (1870).

After improvements in printing made it feasible to reproduce the engravings from Fludd's work, they appeared frequently in esoteric literature of the earlier twentieth century. Manly Palmer Hall's *The Secret Teachings of All Ages* (1928) gives Fludd due consideration[54] but is symptomatic of the split in approaches to esoteric philosophies and occult sciences: either they were taken uncritically by believers such as Hall and the various orders calling themselves Rosicrucians, or else were dismissed as part of an irrational and superstitious past.

In the post-World War II period the Warburg Institute in London created a climate in which Frances A. Yates could reconsider Fludd, Giordano Bruno, Ramon Llull, and other esoteric philosophers on their own terms, not those of modernism or sectarianism, and place them in a historical context. At the same time, Allen Debus at the University of Chicago made a close study of Fludd from the point of view of the history of science. My own early book has been mentioned in the introduction. In 1988 William Huffman published what has become the standard study, *Robert Fludd and the End of the Renaissance,* bringing forth much archival material such as Fludd's last will and his genealogy, and drawing attention to his status as a late representative of Renaissance thought. Huffman followed this in 2001 with a selection from Fludd's writings.

The growth of scholarly interest in esoteric traditions during the 1980s and 1990s created an intellectual space between the extremes mentioned in which those traditions could be recognized as a veritable "third force" in Western civilization, alongside religion and science. But Fluddean studies were sparse, especially compared to the international industry that grew up around his near-contemporary Athanasius Kircher (1602–80). Only in recent years, and largely thanks to German scholars, has Fludd begun to receive the attention that he deserves.[55] And thanks to the libraries that have allowed their copies to be scanned and placed online, nearly all of Fludd's works are freely accessible to anyone with the ability and the patience to read them.

FLUDD'S PHILOSOPHICAL SYSTEM

At the summit of Fludd's cosmos is one Absolute God, whom he usually represents

53. See bibliography.
54. See Hall, *Secret Teachings,* pp. opposite cix, cxxii, cxlii.

55. See especially the works of Hauge, Rösche, and Schmidt-Biggemann.

by the Hebrew Tetragrammaton יהוה or its transcription as "Jehovah." This supreme, impersonal principle is beyond the distinctions of good and evil. But although it is a perfect unity, it has a dual power: it can either remain in itself, contained in a state of potentiality, or it can act. The Kabbalists call both of these powers by *Aleph* (א), the first letter of the Hebrew alphabet, distinguishing them as the "light Aleph" and the "dark Aleph." Fludd says that God's dark side seems like an abyss of chaos, the parent of all the evils and discord in the world. It is the source of Satan and the demons who trouble the world and fight perpetually against the angels of light. But since God's unity includes it, we must accept it as an aspect of him and hence ultimately good. God's active state, on the other hand, is obviously good, for it gives the whole universe being and sustains it with all its creatures. Fludd calls this dichotomy a "Sphyngian riddle" that will not be solved until the end of the world, when (as described in the book of Revelation) the seventh seal will be opened. Then the mystery will reveal itself, and the two opposites will return to one harmonious unity.

The process of creation, on every level, fascinated Fludd, and he was anxious to find the common ground of the creation myths in the two books he most respected: the Bible and the writings ascribed to Hermes Trismegistus (*Corpus Hermeticum*). He explains the creation of the universe as the result of a ray of God's active light, sent out into the void and diminishing gradually as it went farther from him. The light was pure spirit, and around it the darkness coalesced in the form of matter. The stronger the ray, the less matter could exist in its presence. But in the outer reaches of God's illumination, the darkness gradually prevailed over light, exceeding and finally extinguishing it. The various compounds of spirit and matter became worlds and regions

of worlds, of which there are three main divisions. First is the empyrean world, or heaven, where light exceeds darkness, the latter taking the form of very rarefied matter. Second is the ethereal world, in which light and darkness are equal and make a substance we call ether (the "quintessence" of Aristotle's system). Third is the elemental world, where darkness predominates over light, producing the four elements of fire, air, water, and earth. The earth itself is the darkest and most material place in the universe, of which, following the geocentric system, it is the center.

There is a curious ambiguity in this image of creation. First we are led to imagine God as the center, presumably of a sphere, and the states of light and darkness surrounding him, getting darker and more material as they are farther away. But then the system is turned inside out, with the earth at the center and God at the circumference. The entire cosmic system is then enclosed as a miniscule bubble within his infinity. This is more like the Kabbalistic idea that God made the cosmos by withdrawing from a part of himself, creating by absence the only space that is *not* God. When we examine Fludd's illustrations we discover that the limitations of graphic design not only force him to represent this "bubble" as a two-dimensional circle, but to show only a slice of this circle from its center to its circumference. The result is a one-dimensional scale with God at one end, the earth at the other. Out of this come his three major symbols, which are all linear: the monochord, the intersecting pyramids, and the weatherglass.

Far from being lifeless spaces, Fludd's worlds are thronged with beings: the empyrean with angels; the ethereal with stars, planets, and demons; the elemental with men, animals, plants, and minerals. All these creatures partake of God's light in measure according to their place on the hierarchy. But there is one level in particular that, though not the top of the scale (or the circumference of the sphere), is especially favored by God. This is the sun, which is placed at the crucial midpoint of the ladder of being, where spirit and matter are in perfect equality and balance. As the psalmist says, God has set a tabernacle in the sun,[56] and from this secondary residence his active power radiates anew to all the lower realms. God's powers, says Fludd, are transmitted to the three worlds by his ministers. The angels are the servants of his light aspect, the demons of his darkness: two parallel hierarchies that strive perpetually one against the other. They are not exactly equal, however, for the demons were beaten down from the empyrean heaven by the archangel Michael and his host before the lower worlds were even created, and Michael then took up his abode in the sun.

Fludd's theogony and angelology are complicated and intertwined in such a way that some very remarkable conclusions emerge. His most important concepts are those of nature, the anima mundi (world soul), the Kabbalists' Metatron, the archangel Michael, the Messiah, and God the Son. Nature is the feminine, maternal principle, whom Fludd describes in glowing terms as God's first creation and also as his spouse. As such, we see her dominating the great frontispiece of the *History of the Macrocosm* (see ill. 2.1, pp. 30–31). In later works Fludd speaks less of nature and more of the world soul. This is the same thing, though less personified: the creative forces of light, will, intellect, and so on, which sustain the cosmos. He describes its origin as follows: the Logos gives off an emanation of light, which is the "eternal spirit of wisdom." This creative principle infuses the humid chaos, turning it from a potential state to an active one, so that it becomes the substratum for the world. From

the world's viewpoint, this divine light is its very soul. In the words of *Mosaicall Philosophy*, "the soul of the world, or *mens divina in mundo* [the divine mind in the world], simply taken, is that divine mental emanation absolutely in itself, being distinguished from the created spirit" (149).

In the same chapter Fludd draws a parallel with the individual soul, which gives life to the body and spirit (the latter meaning the subtle substance between body and soul). Analogously, the world soul provides the essential life of the world's body and spirit. Fludd recognized the same principle in Metatron, which he translates as "the gift of God." Again, in the words of *Mosaicall Philosophy,* he calls it "that universal Spirit of Wisdom which God sent out of his own mouth, as the greatest gift and token of his benignity . . . which reduceth the universal Nothing into a universal Something" (151–52).

Fludd's answer to Kepler implies that he considered this principle to be none other than the second person of the Trinity. Here he actually says that the Light Aleph is the Son, or Wisdom, or Light, or the Word, adding "And the Platonists accept this 'Wisdom' of the Hebrews, and 'Messiah' of the Christians, and 'Mittatron' of the Cabbalists, and 'Word' of the Prophets and Apostles as the true Soul of the World, whom they say filled harmonically all the intervals of the world in threes, squared and cubed" (302–3). The reference here is to the description of the world's creation in Plato's *Timaeus* where, following Pythagorean number theory, the universe is organized mathematically and harmonically.

This kind of syncretizing had its roots in the Florentine Platonists of the fifteenth century, especially Marsilio Ficino and Pico della Mirandola, who sought to reconcile the pagan philosophers with the Jewish and Christian revelations. (See appendix 2, "The Wisdom of

---

56. Psalm 19:4.

the Ancients.") By Fludd's time the Counter-Reformation had made such compromises suspect, and Marin Mersenne objected in virulent terms. Nothing could be more impious, said the friar, than Fludd's equating this world soul that permeates all beings—angels, demons, men, and beasts—with the angel Michael, Metatron, the Messiah, and ultimately with Christ.

Fludd's reply explained that he was not equating these to one another, but that they are manifestations of a single principle in different worlds. In the archetypal world (above even the angels), it is Adonai, the Lord, whose light is Ensoph, the infinite. In the angelic (empyrean) world the principle is the soul of the Messiah, whose light is Elchai, the living God. In the celestial (ethereal) world it is the anima mundi or Metatron, whose light is Sadai, the all-powerful. And in the human microcosm it is the soul, illuminated by mind. This dispute highlights the most essential principle of Fludd's philosophy: the correspondence between worlds or levels of being. That the whole of magic rests on this presupposition may explain why Mersenne, the enemy of all things occult, found it so repellent.

The same principle underlies Fludd's demonstration of the harmony between microcosm and macrocosm. According to this, man is a miniature universe, and the universe is structured like a great man. Therefore if one understands the little world, one will have a key to understanding the greater one. Fludd interprets in this spirit the words that God speaks in Genesis: "Let us make man in our own image," and also the Hermetic axiom "That which is above is like that which is below."

Harmony implies relationships, and nowhere are quantitative relationships so keenly felt as when they manifest as musical proportions. Here quantity becomes quality and numbers are experienced as feeling. The ratio of 1:2 gives the octave, 2:3 the perfect fifth, and so on with other intervals. The chords and intervals that he posits between different levels of being may not be scientifically demonstrable or even accurate, but they testify to Fludd's faith in an orderly world, in which nothing is related by chance and all is imbued with a harmony that we will one day understand and hear for ourselves.

These areas of Fludd's thought illustrate his independence from sectarian Christian theology, his readiness to recognize wisdom wherever he found it, and his conviction that reality consists of multiple states of being. All three set him apart from the dominant philosophical and theological concerns of his own day and of the centuries that followed. Seen from one viewpoint, he did represent, in William Huffman's phrase, "the end of the Renaissance." But the Renaissance, with its respect for antiquity, its curiosity about the origins of religion, its practice of concordance between different systems and faiths, and its vision of the dignity, even the divinity, of man, did not end with the Scientific Revolution. Seen from another viewpoint, Fludd takes his place in the tradition of Christian esotericism that includes figures as disparate as Hildegard of Bingen, Roger Bacon, Albertus Magnus, Nicolas of Cusa, Marsilio Ficino, Cornelius Agrippa, Paracelsus, Michael Maier, Jacob Boehme, Thomas Vaughan, Jane Leade, Emanuel Swedenborg, Louis Claude de Saint-Martin, Franz von Baader, Eliphas Levi, Rudolf Steiner, and Valentin Tomberg.

Two

How the World Is Made

2.1. Macrocosm and Microcosm

The title page of Fludd's 1617 volume announces his program in words and image. It is to treat, first, the metaphysics and physics of the universe, and second, the creations of man in the external world. The image is a slice through the geocentric cosmos, which should be imagined as a series of nested spheres. *Counting inward,* they are the primum mobile, which "gives movement and life to all the inferior spheres" (see ill. 8.4, p. 210); the fixed stars, including those of the twelve zodiacal constellations; the seven planets Saturn, Jupiter, Mars, Sun, Venus, Mercury, and Moon; and four unmarked spheres representing the elements fire, air, water, and earth.

Inside the macrocosmic circles is a second and parallel scheme of stars, planets, and elements. This is the microcosm of man, in whom the heavenly bodies manifest as his psychic faculties, and the elements as the four humors of Galenic medicine (choleric, sanguine, phlegmatic, and melancholic). His genitals are at the center of the earth, which in Fludd's system is the limit of materiality and darkness. The symbolic figure touches the outer circle at five points, outlining a pentagon and the golden section derived from that figure, which is a model for generation and growth in the natural world.

Outside the circles, in a rare example of Fluddean humor, is Time. In the sixteenth century his image changed from an old man hobbling on crutches to a muscular figure, often with diabolic attributes like these goat's legs.* Striding on the supercosmic clouds, he tugs a rope that turns the cosmic machine. He shows us his backside (because Time is always getting away from us), his wings (because *tempus fugit*), and the forelock by which one should try to seize the opportune moment (*carpe diem*). On his head is an hourglass, topped by the escapement of a clock. *UCH* I, 1, title page.

---

*See Cohen, *Transformations of Time,* p. 166.

2.2. The Sun

All spiritual and invisible splendor derives from God, and all things are inwardly illuminated by him, just as all externally visible light comes from the Sun. Just as in the material world the Sun is the Emperor, so in the spiritual world God holds the fiery scepter. According to the Wisdom of Sirach, three essences are to be seen in the Sun: the Sun itself, its light or clarity, and its life-giving heat. The Sun itself refers to God the Father, the light to the Son, and the heat to the Holy Spirit. The splendor arises and derives directly from the one solar body; the effects and benevolent virtue of heat descend from both. *UCH* I, 1, p. 9.

2.3. The Trinity Enclosing the World ↝

God may be compared to an incomprehensible triangle that comprehends all things in itself and by its virtue extends itself everywhere. Inspired by the Kabbalistic system of the four worlds or heavens, this shows the infinite heaven of the Trinity enclosing the three created heavens (empyrean, ethereal, and elementary) and the earth. *UCH* I, 1, p. 20.

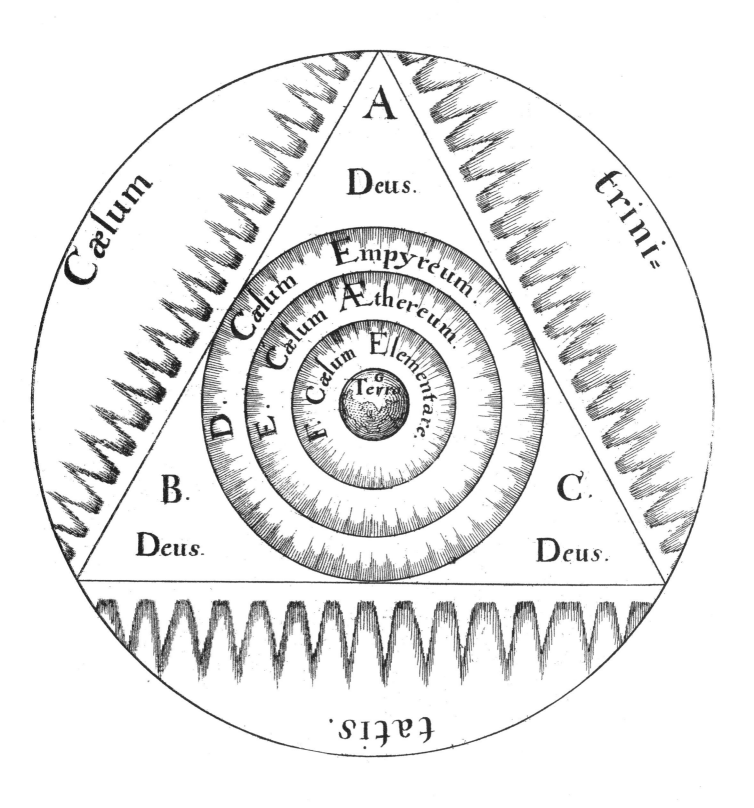

2.4. The Great Darkness ⤿

And thus, to infinity.

From all the writings of ancient and modern philosophers we conclude that this first matter (materia prima) is the primordial Being, infinite, formless, of any potential and of none; of no quantity or dimension, so that it cannot be called large or small; of no subtle, gross, or perceptible quality; without property or inclination; neither moving nor quiescent; without any color or elementary quality. . . . Hence it is called the mother of the world, containing as in a maternal womb the ethereal orbs decorated with glowing fire and the four elements suspended around the center (p. 25). This image captured the imagination of early modernist painters, among whom Kazimir Malevich with his "suprematist compositions" came closest to Fludd's metaphysical vision. *UCH* I, 1, p. 26.

Et sic in infinitum

2.5. The Appearance of Light

The all-wise architect of the world, who said "I am the light of the world, the true fire, the father of lights," first freely communicated his light to the empyrean heaven, and secondly to the ethereal heaven, to the sun and its other spheres. Thus by their virtue, as by an instrument, the ethereal heaven might be ornamented, and lower creatures given form and life (p. 27). *UCH* I, 1, p. 29.

2.6. The Division of the Waters

The prime matter, fecundated by the divine light, divides into two. The part furthest from the light [the dark cloud in the middle of the picture] remains passive, while in the surrounding part dwells the active fire of love. These are the lower and upper waters. The light cloud in between is a mysterious state, neither spiritual nor corporeal. It is called the Earth Spirit, the Spirit of Mercury, the Ether, or the Quintessence. It can penetrate and alter bodies, and thus acts as the vehicle of the soul's descent into matter (pp. 56–57). *UCH* I, 1, p. 37.

2.7. The Chaos of the Elements

The lower waters have now been stirred into a confused and undigested mass, in which the four elements fight against each other, hot against cold, dry against wet. Manly P. Hall points out the resemblance of this figure to the human intestines.* Elsewhere, Fludd has the elemental realm correspond to the bowels of the microcosmic man (see ill. 4.8, p. 138). *UCH* I, 1, p. 41.

───────────

*Hall, *Man, the Grand Symbol*, pp. 48–49.

2.8. The Central Sun

Resolving the chaos of the previous plate, the elements arrange themselves into concentric circles of fire, air, water, and earth. Part of the light is trapped in the center, later to be released and placed in the heavens as the sun. This idea came from an alchemical experiment that Fludd witnessed performed by a friend, in which a precious solar substance was extracted from the heavy, black, and fetid matter. *UCH* I, 1, pp. 43, 141.

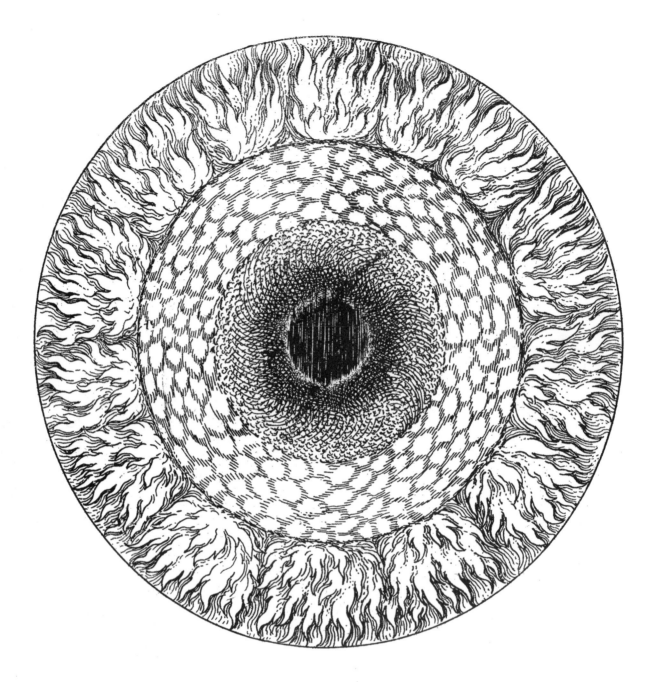

2.9. The Three Worlds

The world substance now divides into three spheres, differentiated by their purity or impurity. The highest is that space which contained the igneous spirit and the primal substance of light, extending from the sphere of the Trinity to the convex surface of the starry sphere. The middle part is adorned by the fixed and wandering stars, containing the whole space between the moon's sphere and the concavity of the primum mobile. The lowest part is embraced by the concave surface of the moon's sphere. So the whole universe is divided into two principal parts: one incorporeal, spiritual, pure, and subtle, hence superior; the other corporeal. But the latter too is divided into two parts, one subtle, tenuous, and incorruptible, which is the middle zone; the other impure, gross, and subject to corruption (p. 45). *UCH* I, 1, p. 46.

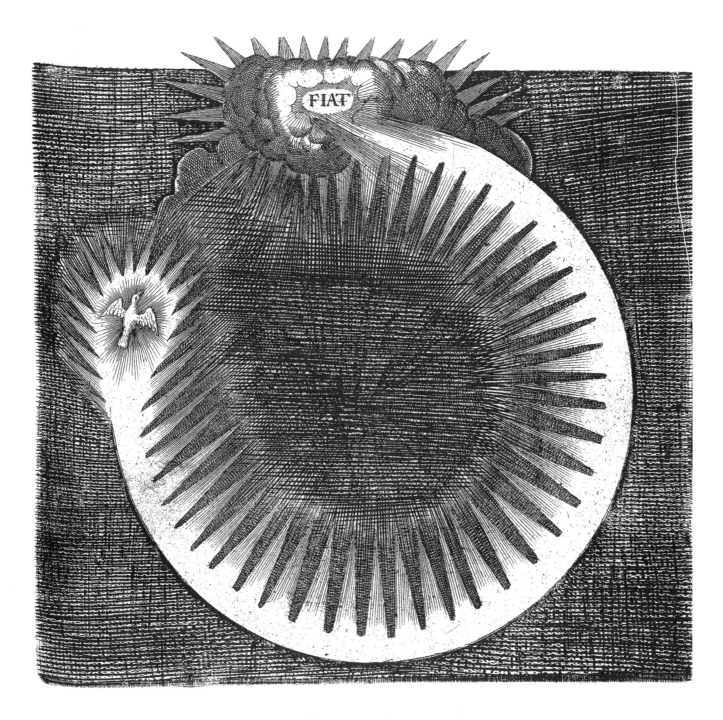

2.10. Let There Be Light

In book 2 Fludd recapitulates the creation of the three spheres, identifying them with the first three days of creation as told in Genesis. Each day is defined by a circuit of the Spirit of God, shown here as a dove, with the command *Fiat! UCH* I, 1, p. 49; *PS,* p. 157.

2.11. Creation of the Empyrean Sphere

Here we begin our history of created things, depicting for our imagination the operation of the uncreated rays through the convex surface of the first region down to its base. . . . The uncreated light of the Spirit is reflected in the empyrean sphere as in a mirror, and these reflections are in turn the first manifestation of created light. Without this light every world or creature would perish. . . . This region is now filled with created light, whose lucid virtue thrusts down the darkness that filled its tenuous substance (pp. 54–55). *UCH* I, 1, p. 55.

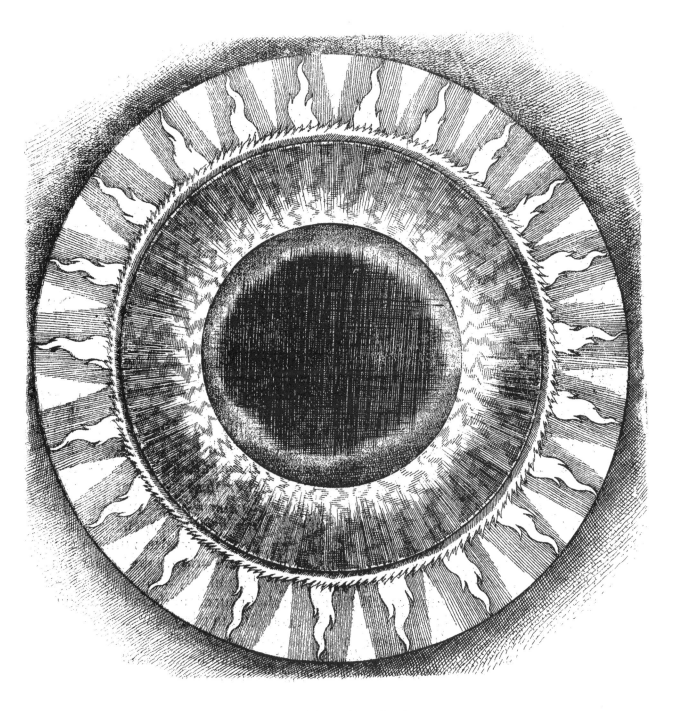

2.12. Creation of the Ethereal Sphere

The second day witnessed the creation of the ethereal sphere, which contains the fixed stars and wandering planets. It is constituted of ether, also known as quintessence and *spiritus,* a substance free from the corruption that affects the four lower elements. Above, in the empyrean, form predominates and matter is totally absent. Below, in the elemental sphere, matter is supreme. The ethereal sphere between them is the region of equality, in which the formal and material qualities are held in balance. *UCH* I, 1, p. 58.

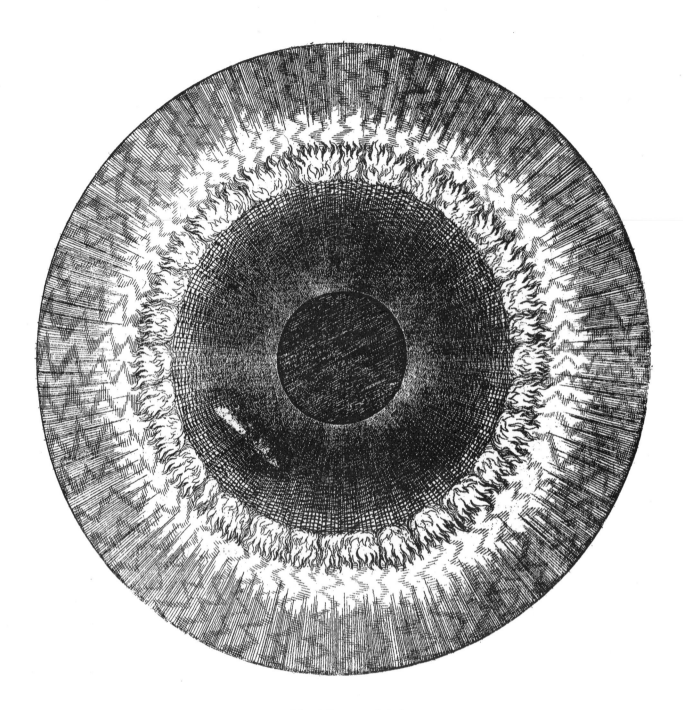

2.13. The Elemental Sphere: Fire

The finest and most volatile of the four material elements is fire, and it naturally rises to the outermost region of the elemental sphere. It is not the essence of the pure light, but as it were the last effect of its action, coming directly from the motion of matter. Thus it does nothing for the functioning of life, except as concerning the constitution of the body, which is the seat of life. Nor is it that invisible fire of the Philosophers from which all things are said to be born. It is simply that fire by whose dominion over natural heat all things are brought to putrefaction. *UCH* I, 1, p. 63.

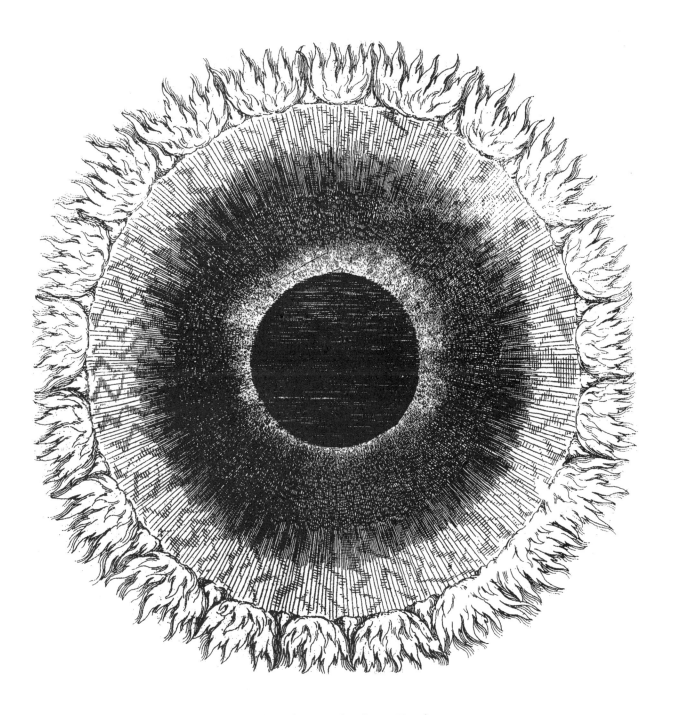

2.14. The Elemental Sphere: Earth

The qualities of earth are cold and dry, and as the darkest and heaviest element it condenses to the very center of the universe. This plate shows it as a dark ball inside the sphere of fire. No wonder, says Fludd, that Earth is such a vale of misery, since it is formed from the very dregs of creation and houses the Devil himself, enemy to God and man. But you, O celestial creatures, inhabitants of the sweetest Paradise, thrice blessed and more beyond human telling, are freed by the ineffable power of light from the miseries and chains that shackle us (p. 65). *UCH* I, 1, p. 66.

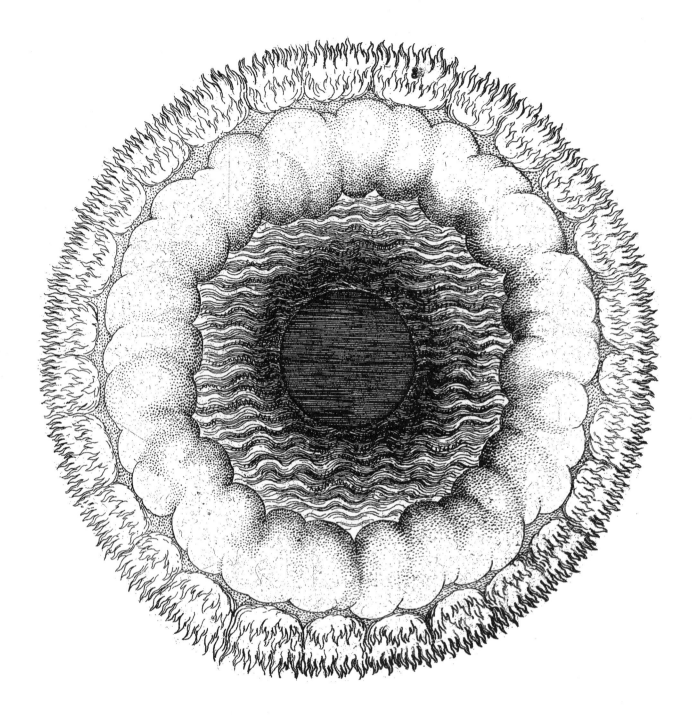

2.15. The Elemental Sphere: Air and Water

In between the fire and earth spheres is a humid zone, compounded of earth's coldness with fire's heat **like the coitus of male with female** (p. 66). Three parts of igneous heat and one of terrestrial cold make the element of air; the reverse proportions give water. These seek their stations adjacent, respectively, to the sphere of fire and to the earth, completing the fourfold world of the elements. *UCH* I, 1, p. 69.

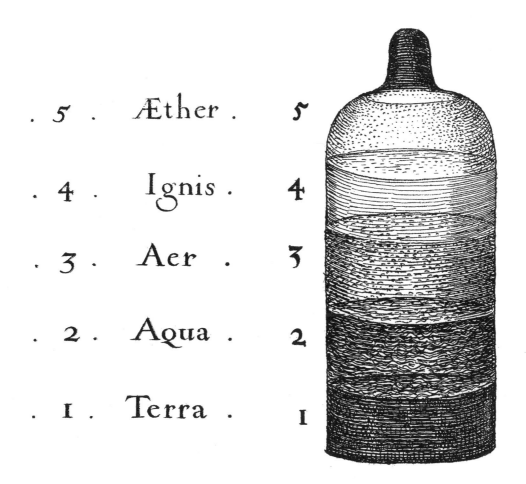

.5. Æther. 5

.4. Ignis. 4

.3. Aer. 3

.2. Aqua. 2

.1. Terra. 1

2.16. An Experiment with Wine

For all the imaginative genius of Fludd's cosmology, he often comes down to earth to describe some experiment that corroborates the cosmic processes. Here he refers to his own experience:

We can make an excellent experiment with wine, displaying the substances of the elements and even its quintessence in tangible and trustworthy form. After extracting the spirits of wine by a well-known operation, I extracted the oil floating on the spirits. Then I extracted the oil of wine from the dregs, and brought it to the height of purification by a different rectification. After that I repeatedly rectified the phlegm distilled after the extraction of the spirits. Lastly, with many washings I cleansed the muddy residue from the dregs. Then I poured it all by equal proportions into a round bottle, hermetically sealed it, and left it for a whole night. In the morning I found five layers: the lowest one black and veiled in darkness, above which the phlegmatic portion rested; then, covering it, the oil extracted from the dregs. In fourth place were the spirits of wine, and in fifth place, the oil extracted from them. *UCH* I, 1, p. 72.

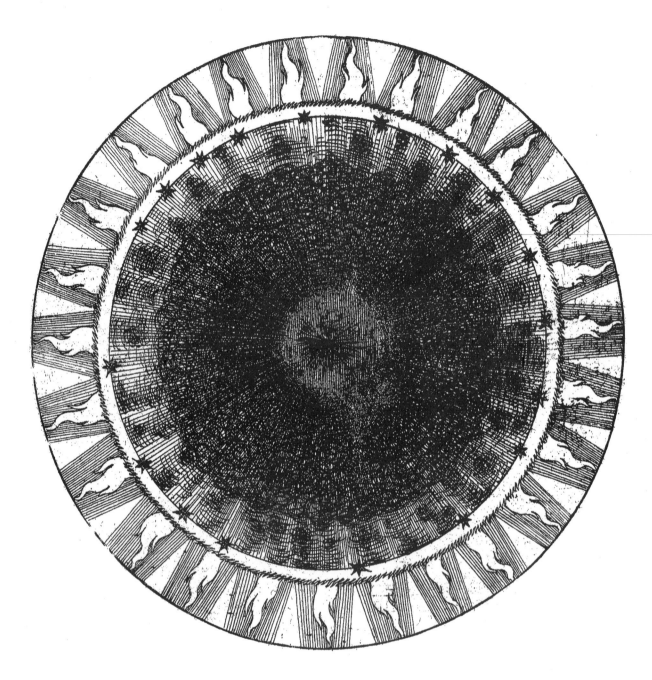

2.17. Creation of the Stars

Continuing the events of the second day, the fixed stars appear on the outside of the celestial sphere. They do not reflect the sun's light but assimilate it and give it off later like phosphorescent fish or rotting wood (pp. 125, 128). Here Fludd gives us another glimpse of his alchemical work: I myself once extracted the spiritual humor from a most noble body and observed its wondrous transmutation into Sol [gold?]. I remember seeing that spirit ascend by its own natural heat, acquired from the sun, without any propulsion from elementary fire. With its newly acquired tincture it rose to the top of the alembic, shining like the brightest ruby (p. 126). *UCH* I, 1, p. 131.

2.18. The Sun in the Empyrean

The light trapped within the earth now emerges and makes its way to its proper place. Spiritual matter ascends from earth to heaven like a tree whose mass diminishes from the roots upward, its lower trunk and branches being thicker than in the upper parts and its leaves and blossoms being the most tenuous part of all. The tree of the heavens is constituted spiritually in the same way. Earth is the grossest of all, followed by water, then air, and fire is like the twigs and leaves. In fact, the planets correspond to flowers surrounding the sun, which collects the seeds of this tree by means of which all things flourish and multiply (p. 137). *UCH* I, 1, p. 136.

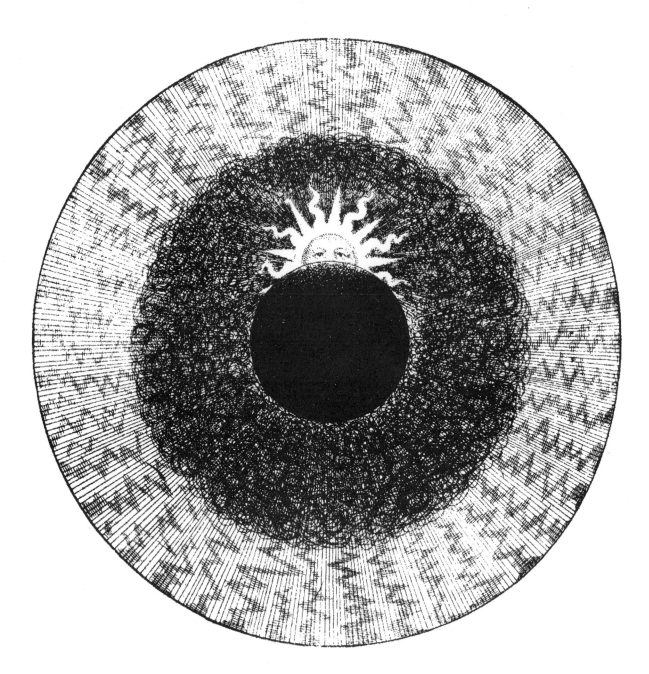

2.19. The Sun Leaves the Earth

In the timeline of creation, this superb illustration precedes the previous one, but Fludd uses it to close the chapter with a meditation on the sorry state of the earth. Now the whole earthly mass is as though soulless and dead, being separated from its moving soul. It lies like a corpse, its limbs frozen, nor does any part of it have a soul like that of living beings. It receives a very little heat from heaven and the stars, like a corpse where worms are generated through putrefaction, flies grow in the bones, and many other things are produced. Is it not thus that animals are born from the earth's surface, as we read in Ovid about the Python's birth, and also vegetation and similar things which cannot multiply without corruption? *UCH* I, 1, p. 138.

2.20. The Production of the Planets

The planets all arose from the action of the Sun's rays, streaming in both directions. The descending solar rays met ascending vaporous material, and at the point where they were equal a battle ensued. And just as the meeting of two opposite winds produces a cloud, so the globe of Mercury condensed at this midpoint, imbued with the opposing tendencies that manifest as its direct and retrograde motions. Venus was similarly formed at the midpoint between Mercury and the Sun; the Moon at the midpoint between Mercury and the lower boundary of the ethereal sphere. The outer planets were formed analogically, Jupiter forming at the midpoint between the Sun and the fixed stars, and Mars and Saturn filling the gaps (pp. 143–45). . . . Since the Sun is the source of heat for the entire ethereal realm, planets will be colder as they are further away from it. Saturn and the Moon are therefore the coldest planets, but they differ in that Saturn shares the dry coldness of the crystalline heavens, while the Moon has the wet coldness of the lowest ethereal vapors. These qualities are consistent with the effects of the planets in astrology (pp. 146–47). *UCH* I, 1, 145.

2.21. A Refutation of Copernicus

Here Fludd invites the reader to imagine what would happen if we lived in the heliocentric universe in which Copernicus believed, and after him William Gilbert, Galileo, and Kepler.

If Earth were not the center of the universe, but a revolving body circling the Sun, as some ancient and modern philosophers maintain, there would be no possibility of life upon it. Violent winds would sweep everything to the ground. Besides, it would be remarkable if Earth alone were to move steadily on its axis, while all the other planets varied in latitude. Finally, as Earth is the largest and densest of all bodies, it stands to reason that it would be at the center of the more rarefied ones, and less apt to move than any of the others. The source of all power and movement is at the periphery of the universe, not in the center—for as our picture shows, a wheel is much more easily turned from its circumference than from its hub (pp. 153–55). *UCH* I a, p. 155.

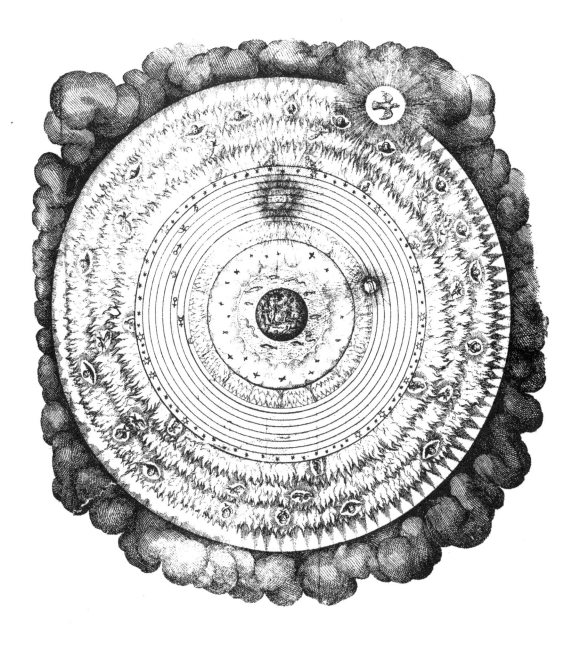

2.22. The Three Worlds

The six days of creation are completed, and the Spirit of God returns whence it came.
The empyrean sphere swarms with angels of various orders. The ethereal (or celestial)
sphere has its fixed stars and seven planets, of which the sun and moon radiate down
through the elemental sphere. Beneath the sphere of fire, those of the other three
elements teem with life: the air with birds, the waters with fish, while earth harbors
the Garden of Eden. In exquisite detail (*center*), the engraver has shown the serpent
wound round the Tree of Knowledge, and Eve reaching up to pick the forbidden
fruit. *UCH* I, 1, p. 9.

← 2.23. An Old Experiment

Fludd says in *Integrum Morbum Mysterium* (*MC* I, 2, 1, p. 9) that he saw this apparatus illustrated in a manuscript at least seven hundred years old—an estimate which he later modified to five hundred. The manuscript is still extant, if, as Sherwood Taylor suggests,* it is the twelfth- or thirteenth-century copy of Philo of Byzantium's treatise *De ingeniis spiritualibus* (Bodleian Library, MS. Digby 40). It belonged to Thomas Allen, Fludd's mentor at Oxford, and later passed to the alchemical physician Sir Kenelm Digby. The relevant page shows an open and a closed vessel joined by an inverted U-shaped tube, with the closed vessel exposed to the sun. Fludd was so impressed by this experiment and its implications that he used the illustration several times. In his version, the globe is filled with air, the ewer with water. When the sun shines on the globe, air bubbles up into the water. When the sun is obscured, water is sucked up through the tube and into the globe.

We can understand this easily because we know that air expands on heating and contracts on cooling. For Fludd, though, the sun's influence purifies the air in the globe, expelling the "dense and dark air," which is absorbed by the water. When the sunlight ceases, **since air in its natural state is not to be found in the vessel filled with water, it attracts the water itself, which is now denser, and forces a quantity into the globe proportionate to what the solar rays expelled during the subtilization and purification** (p. 30). This illustrates Fludd's principle that all purification in this world takes place through the action of light. When the light is withdrawn, matter reverts to its original state. The experiment confirms his belief that on the fourth day of creation all light was concentrated in the sun, and in consequence, the matter at the center of the universe (i.e., in the earth) reverted to its original formless state. *UCH* I, 1, pp. 31, 204; *PS,* pp. 283, 299; *MC* I, 2, 1, pp. 459, 498.

---

*See Taylor, "The Origin of the Thermometer."

DE MVSICA MVNDANA.

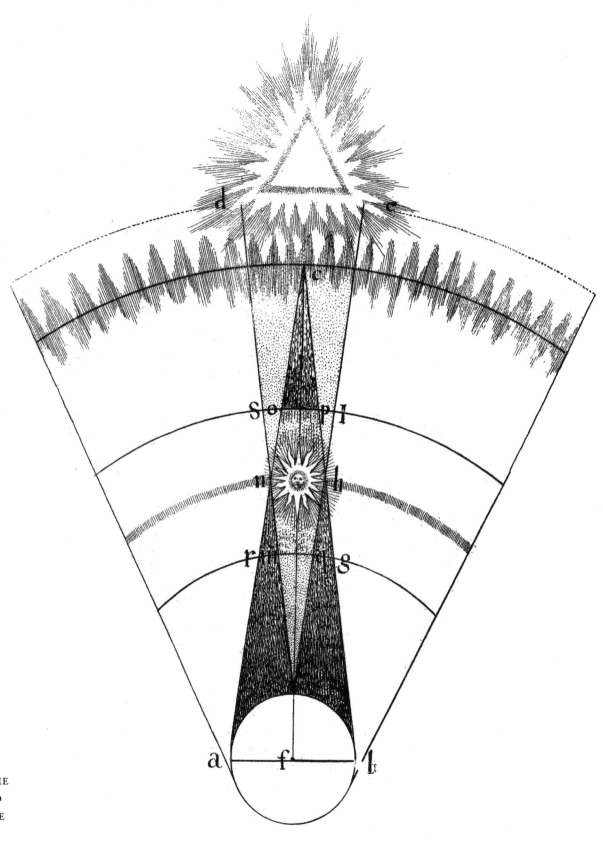

2.24. Pyramids of Form and Matter

This plate introduces Fludd's "science of pyramids," which is a visualization of the twin principles of form and matter, or light and darkness. ABC is the diameter of the material pyramid, whose origin is the Ocean of darkness, namely earth, where it has its base. The lower part of this pyramid (ABRG) gives the lower region of the world its substance and body, with which the formal pyramid pointing downward mixes progressively less. The part of the material pyramid OPGR is the material part of the middle region, which is informed by the equal portion ISMQ of the descending light pyramid. Lastly, the portion OCP of the material pyramid gives what bodily substance there is in the upper region, which is informed by a greater proportion of the radiant pyramid DESI (pp. 81–82). *UCH* I, 1, p. 81.

2.25. Proportions of the Pyramids ⌐⟶

The formal and material pyramids are here separated and placed on the complete circle of the universe, in order to show their internal proportions. The earth contains four parts of matter, none of form; the rest of the elemental world three of matter, one of form. The ethereal world has two parts of each; the empyrean world, three parts of form, one of matter. The arcs to the right of the pyramids contain the Latin names for the harmonic proportions 1:2, 2:3, 3:4, 1:4. These lead directly to Fludd's theory of the harmony of the spheres. *UCH* I, 1, p. 84.

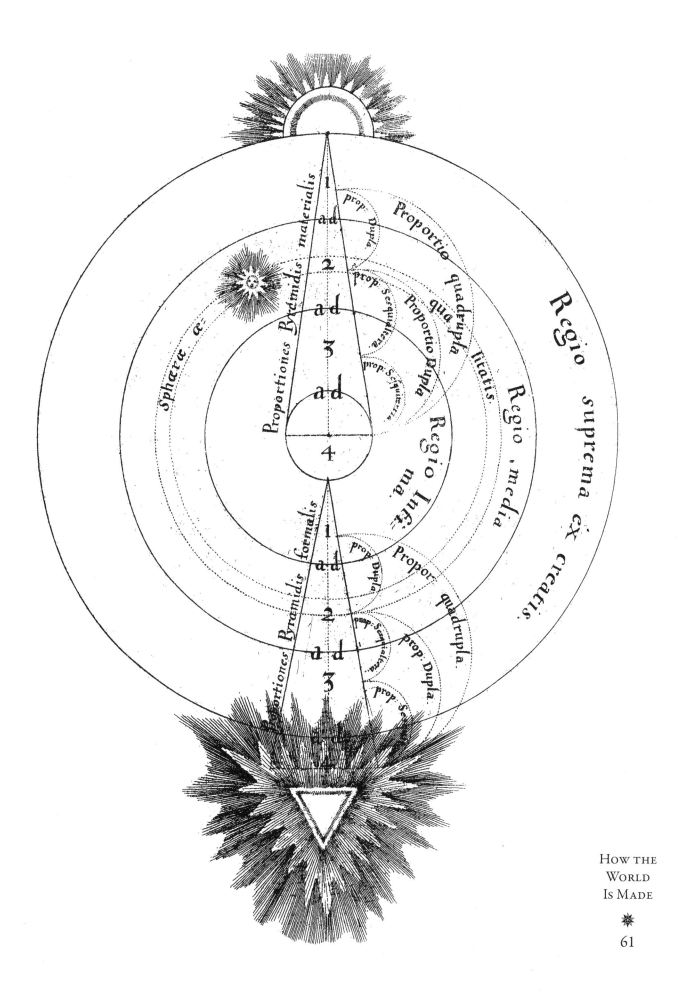

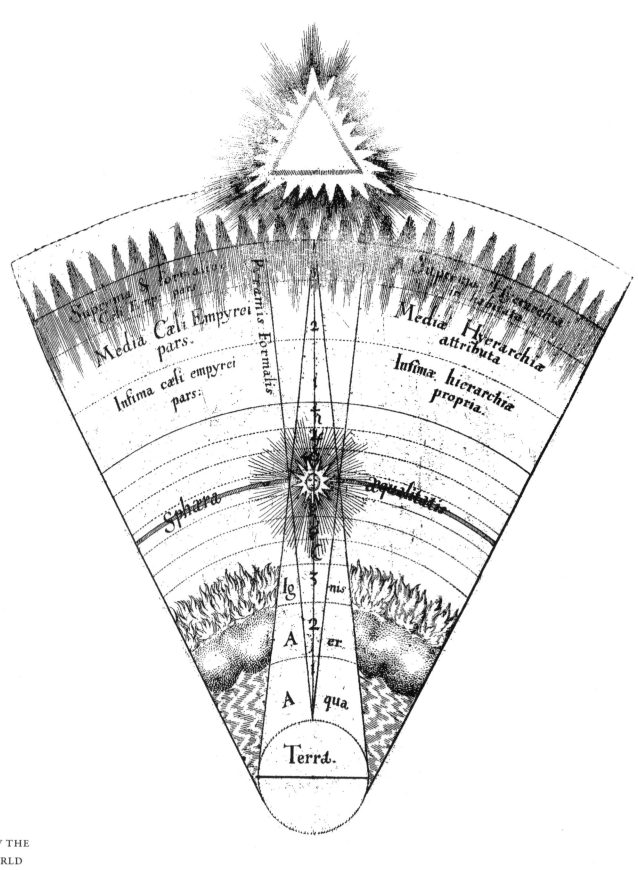

2.26. Proportions in the Three Worlds

The two pyramids of the preceding plate are reunited, and the divisions of each world specified in more detail. The empyrean has three circles, inhabited by the upper, middle, and lower members of the angelic hierarchy. The ethereal world is divided into the circles of the seven planets; the elemental world into four. *UCH* I, 1, p. 89.

2.27. The Divine Monochord ↣

In this famous plate, the three worlds with their divisions are set out along the single string of a monochord, whose tuning peg is turned by the hand of God. The entire cosmos thus sounds the two-octave gamut of Greek and medieval music theory. To the immediate left of the string are the names and symbols of the divisions of each world. (The angelic orders have the Greek names *epiphaniae* = apparitions, *epiphonomiae* = voices, *ephiomae* = acclamations.) Each division is assigned a note of the scale, from low G (the Greek letter *gamma*) for the earth, up through two octaves to the *gg* for the highest division of the empyrean. The arcs on the left indicate the mathematical proportions between the divisions; those on the right, the musical terms: *diapason* = octave, *diapente* = perfect fifth, *diatessaron* = perfect fourth. There is an error in the *diapente materialis*: it should join the sun's G to the C of fire, as should the corresponding *proportio sesquialtera*. And in order for the tones and semitones to be correct, the Fs should be sharpened. *UCH* I, 1, p. 90.

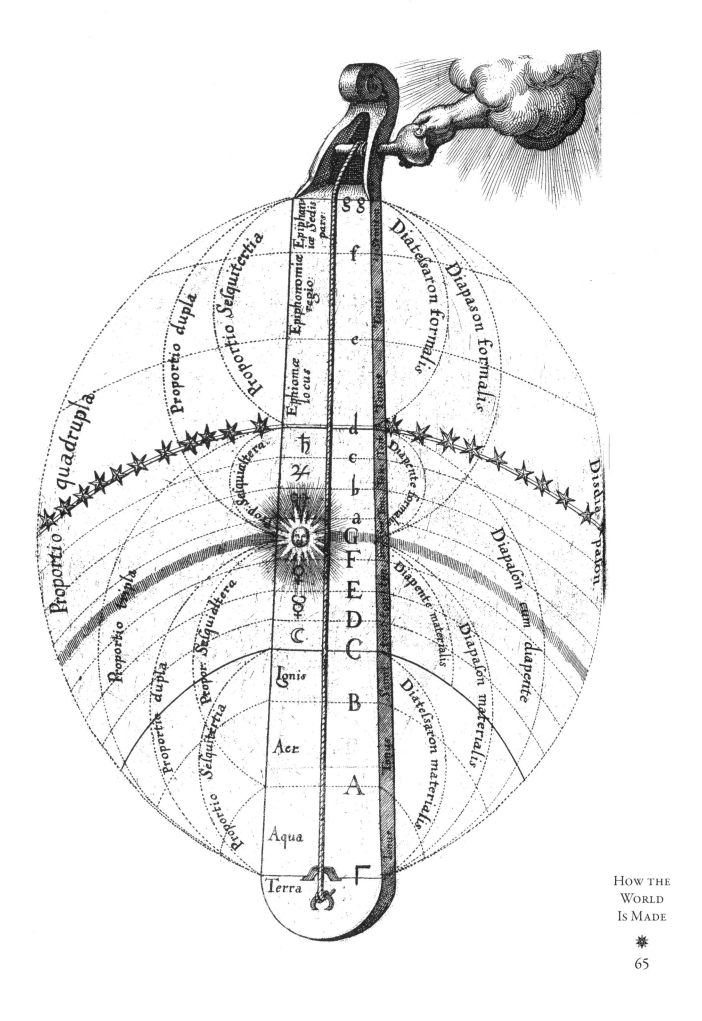

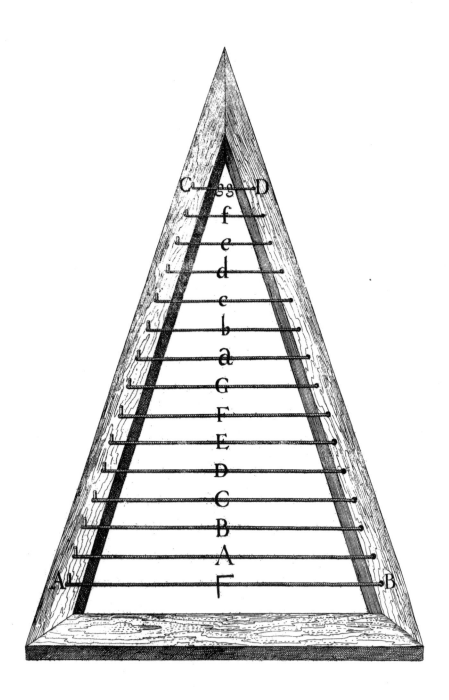

2.28. A Pyramidal Instrument

In order to study the implications of the previous scheme, Fludd suggests making a pyramidal instrument with fifteen strings, tuned to the degrees of the two-octave scale. He incorporated it later into his "great instrument" (see ills. 3.38–3.39, pp. 122–23). *UCH* I, 1, 92.

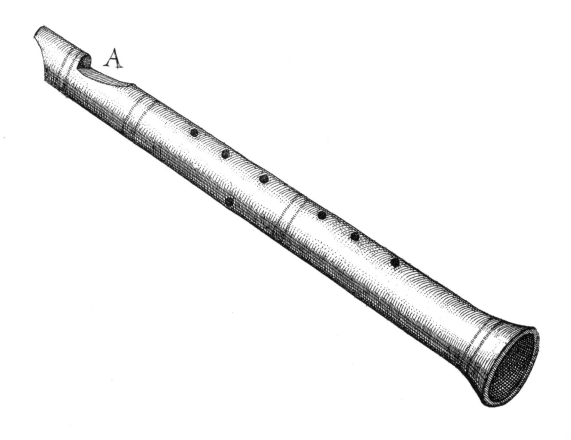

2.29. Symbolism of the Recorder

Behold a remarkable demonstration of how vast secrets often lie hidden in common objects! This musical instrument, called a recorder, truly contains the proportions of the whole world. It is divided into three regions: two lower ones with three holes each denoting their respective beginnings, middles, and ends, and an upper one with only one large hole, showing the nature of the supercelestial heaven whose every part is saturated with the divine unity.... God, the highest mind, at the apex of the device, causes the seams of the world to give forth music, evoking deep tones from the lower parts, and higher and more brilliant ones the closer they approach to the summit. Even so the musician blows life and motion into the top of the recorder from beyond its confines. And the greater the distance of the holes from this inspiring virtue, the lower are the sounds which issue from them.... Oh what great and heavenly contemplation is in this trifling thing, if considered deeply and diligently by the understanding mind! (pp. 94–95). *UCH* I, 1, 94.

2.30. The Harmonies of the Elemental World ⟿

The elemental world is a microcosm of the whole. Its dual principles are fire and earth, which are related analogously to the formal and material pyramids. There is no fire present in earth, no earth in fire, while water and air are produced from mixtures in various proportions. Between water and air is a humid zone, a "sphere of equality" corresponding to the sun in the macrocosm. The arcs show the harmonic proportions between the elements. *UCH* I, 1, 97.

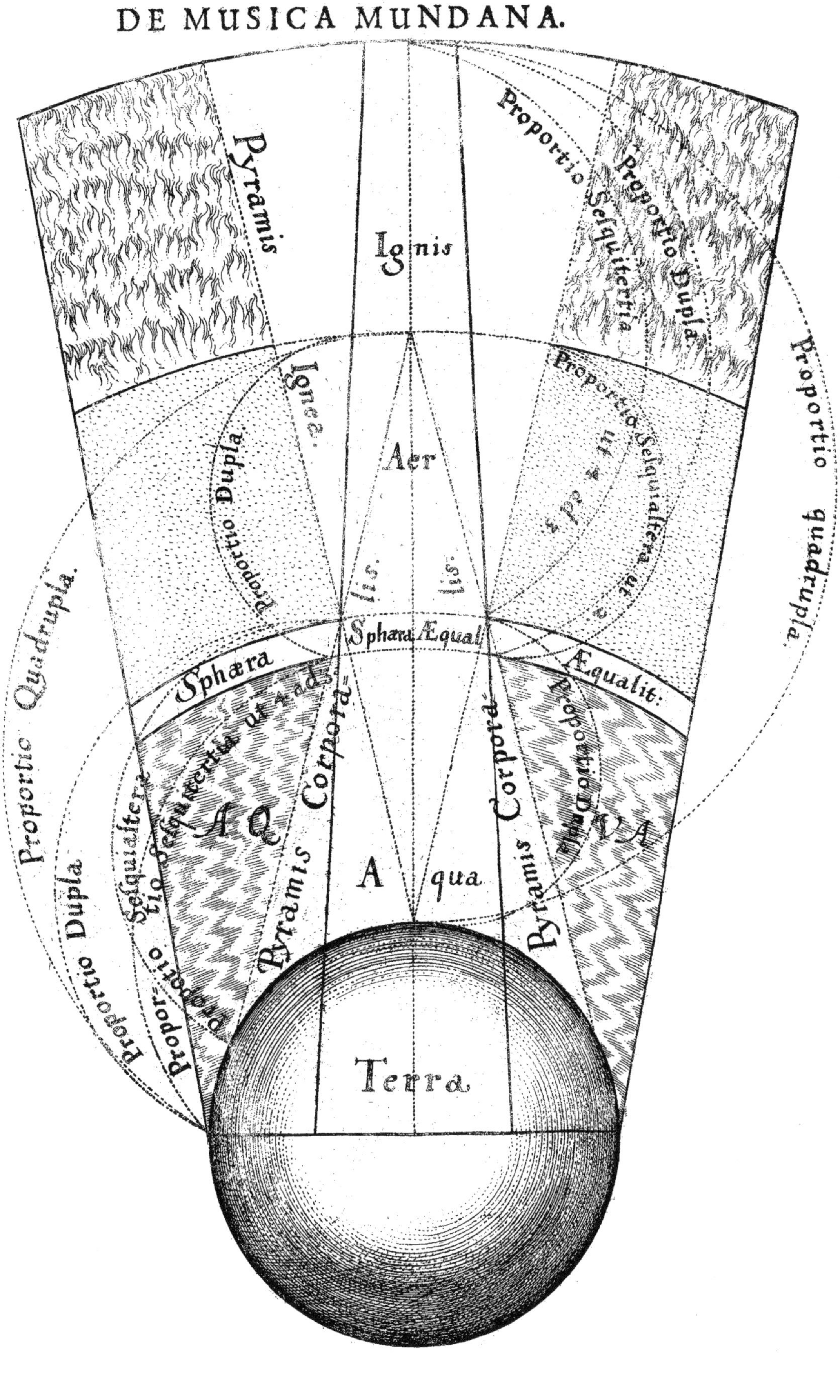

DE MUSICA MUNDANA.

Pyramis

Ignis

Ignea.

Aer

Proportio Dupla

Sphæra

Sphæra Æqual.

lis.

Proportio Sesquialtera ut 4 ad 3

Aqua

Pyramis Corpora=

A qua

Pyramis Corpora=

Æqualit:

Proportio Dupla

Terra

Proportio Dupla

Proportio Sesquialtera

Proportio Quadrupla.

Proportio Sesquialtera ut 4 ad 3

Proportio Dupla

Proportio Sesquialtera ut 4 ad 3

Proportio quadrupla.

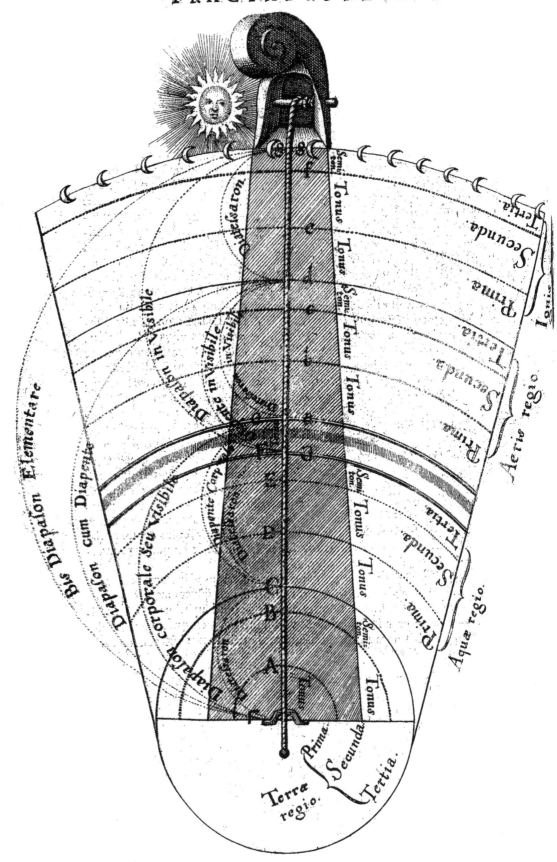

2.31. The Elemental Monochord

Pursuing the analogy of the elemental world with the whole cosmos, Fludd assigns it the full two-octave gamut. Each element is subdivided into three regions, the highest of each being assigned a semitone on account of its closeness in quality to the next element. (Again, some accidentals are missing.) The proportions show the sympathies and antipathies of the elements. In the place of God's hand on the peg of the monochord, here it is the sun, which as Fludd has explained is the source of all life and light in the world. *UCH* I, 1, p. 100.

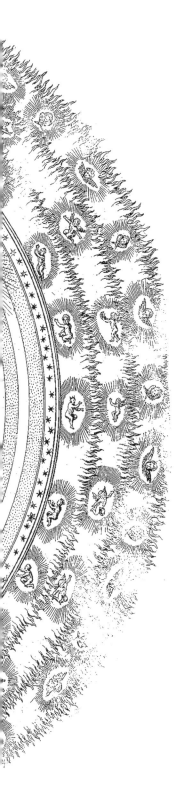

que imago.

↩ 2.32. *The Mirror of Nature and the Image of Art*

This magnificent engraving fills a folding plate at the beginning of Fludd's volume on the macrocosm. It announces the double theme of that volume: first, the cosmology with which our present chapter is concerned, and second, the works of man, who can only ape or imitate nature (see chapter 3). Hence the ape at the center, measuring a globe with a pair of dividers. He is chained to Nature, who in turn is chained to the hand of God. *Reading outward,* we find four circles of arts and sciences:

Art correcting Nature in the mineral realm (alchemical distillation)

Art assisting Nature in the vegetable realm (tree grafting, cultivation of the soil)

Art supplanting Nature in the animal realm (beekeeping, silkworms, egg hatching, medicine)

The Liberal Arts (motion, timekeeping, cosmography, astronomy, geomancy, arithmetic, music, geometry, perspective, painting, fortification)

Next come the three realms:

Mineral (talc, antimony, lead, gold, silver, copper, orpiment, sal ammoniac, each ruled by the appropriate planet)

Vegetable (trees, grapes, wheat, flowers and roots)

Animal (dolphin, snake, lion, man, woman, eagle, snail, fish)

All this belongs to the spheres of earth and water, which are pictured as a landscape. *Continuing outward,* we see the familiar spheres of Aristotelian and Ptolemaic cosmology: the upward-tending elements of air and fire, the spheres of the seven planets

(ill. 2.32 continued from page 73)

(Moon, Mercury, Venus, Sun, Mars, Jupiter, Saturn), and the starry heaven. This concludes Nature's realm. In Fludd's words:

She is not a goddess, but the proximate minister of God, at whose behest she governs the subcelestial worlds. In the picture she is joined to God by a chain. She is the Soul of the World, or the Invisible Fire of Heraclitus and Zoroaster. It is she who turns the sphere of the stars and distributes the planetary influences to the elemental realms, nourishing all creatures from her bosom.

On her breast is the true Sun, on her belly the Moon. Her heart gives light to the stars and planets, whose influence, infused in her womb by the mercurial spirit (called by the philosophers the Spirit of the Moon), is sent down to the very center of the Earth. Her right foot stands on earth, her left in water, signifying the conjunction of sulfur and mercury without which nothing can be created (pp. 7–8).

Beyond Nature are three fiery circles filled with angels. The first circle shows wingless children, whom the engraver has drawn with charming invention, no two alike. They represent the orders of Angels, Archangels, and Virtues. In the second circle the children are winged and some carry crowns, even a trumpet. They are the Powers, Principalities, and Dominions. The outermost circle has only heads, alternately with folded and spread wings. They are the Thrones, Cherubim, and Seraphim. Finally God is symbolized by the Hebrew name IHVH (יהוה) within a small cloud, though he should be imagined as filling infinite space beyond the spheres of his creation.

Wilhelm Schmidt-Biggemann, whose history of Christian Kabbalah includes a deep investigation of Fludd's philosophy, titles this illustration "Sophia Metatron." He explains that Fludd has blended the Sophia of Jewish Talmudic tradition with Metatron, the angel associated with the *sephira* of Malkuth, who joins heaven and earth. She therefore manifests the outward and creative side of God.* Moreover, her stance with one foot on earth, the other in the sea evokes the angel of the Apocalypse who gave Saint John a book (Revelation 10:2). Implicit in this is the doctrine of the Logos, the divine Word that created the universe, incarnated in Jesus (John 1:1), and reveals itself in the twin books of Scripture and Nature. *UCH* I, 1, pp. 4–5.

---

*Schmidt-Biggemann, *Geschichte der christlichen Kabbala*, pp. 69–70.

FURTHER EXPERIMENTAL PROOFS

The Hermetic philosophy ("as above, so below") convinced Fludd that great cosmic events are reflected in small-scale phenomena, hence provable by experiment. Two of them illustrate how comets and meteors are supported in the upper air by cold air rising from the earth and by the attraction of the fiery sphere:

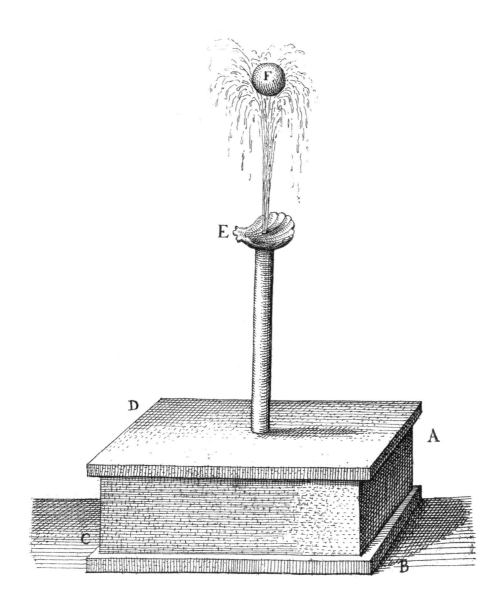

2.33. In this fountain, a wooden ball dances on the rising column of water. *UCH* I, 1, p. 185.

HOW THE
WORLD
IS MADE

✺

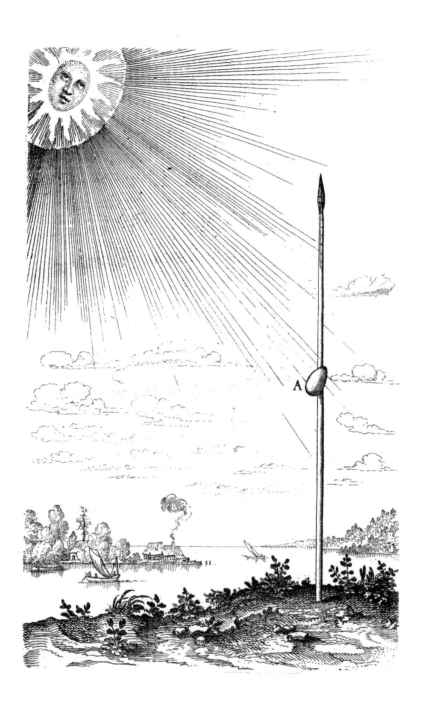

2.34. An eggshell filled with the dew collected from plants (*ros majalis*) and sealed with wax rises up the spear as the solar rays attract the subtle matter enclosed in it. How it is attached to the spear is not explained. *UCH* I, 1, p. 186.

Four experiments demonstrate the origin of winds:

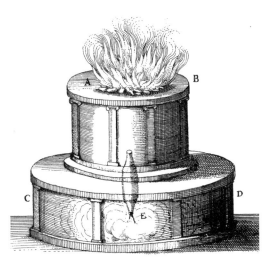

2.35. The fire burning on top of an altar heats the air inside, which escapes through the vent *E*. It shows how the air in subterranean chambers is heated by the earth's central fire and exits through caves and clefts. *UCH* I, 1, p. 189; *MC* I, 2, 1, p. 454.

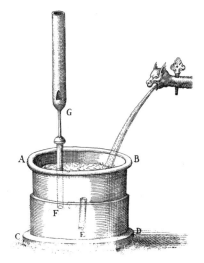

2.36. As the tub *AB* fills with water, it compresses the air in the lower chamber *CD*, which exits through the tube *F*, causing the organ pipe *G* to sound. This illustrates how water falling into the subterranean chambers causes fierce winds. *UCH* I, 1, p. 190; *MC* I, 2, 1, pp. 434, 437.

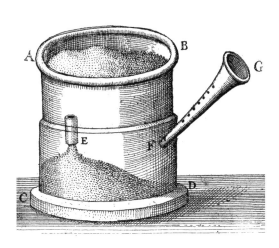

2.37. This device obtains a similar effect through falling sand. It illustrates how hurricanes and earthquakes occur when rockfalls in great caverns suddenly drive the air out. *UCH* I, 1, p. 191 (*upper plate*); *MC* I, 2, 1, p. 435.

2.38. This experiment boils the water in the cauldron, expelling steam through the recorder, just as the waters within the earth may be heated by the internal fires and vaporized. *UCH* I, 1, p. 191 (*lower plate*); *MC* I, 2, 1, pp. 436, 451.

Four experiments replicate on a small scale the causes of thunder and lightning:

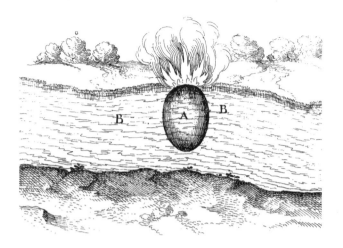

2.39. Mixing the ingredients of gunpowder in a vessel causes an explosion, analogous to the thunder and lightning caused in nature by the mixture of natural saltpeter with sulfur. *UCH* I, 1, p. 193.

2.40. An eggshell filled with a mixture of saltpeter, sulfur, and quicklime burns even when in water. (This is plausible, for these may have been the ingredients of the "Greek fire" used in ancient warfare.) *UCH* I, 1, p. 194.

2.41. This foolhardy gentleman is spitting on an eggshell filled with the same ingredients, thus setting it aflame. *UCH* I, 1, p. 195 (*upper plate*); *MC* I, 2, 1, p. 456.

2.42. Thunder can also be caused by the meeting of subterranean fires and waters. Heating this tightly sealed vessel of water eventually leads to blowing its cork, with a noise like a cannon or thunder. *UCH* I, 1, p. 195 (*lower plate*); *MC* I, 2, 1, p. 452.

2.43. Air and water heated by the earth's internal fires can also rise as vapor, which on meeting the cold upper air is turned to rain. Fludd reused this plate thrice in *Medicina Catholica* to explain the causes of catarrh and other diseases. *UCH* I, 1, p. 201; *MC* I, 2, 1, pp. 424, 432, 446.

Fludd also borrowed some experiments from Hero of Alexandria's treatises.

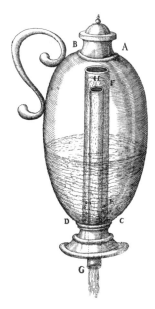

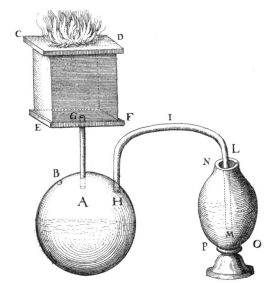

2.44. The vase ABCD is filled with water. When the water rises above the hole H in the tube GH, it leaves the vase by that tube, nor will it cease to rise up the larger tube EF until the whole vase is emptied through the tube HG. This demonstrates the possibility of perpetually flowing springs in the earth. *UCH* I, 1, p. 202.

2.45. Hero describes a version of the experiment in which heat drives air from the sphere into the vase, then when it cools, sucks water back again. This uses fire rather than the sun's heat as agent. *UCH* I, 1, p. 203.

Three

Nature's Ape

3.1. Arts and Sciences ↪

The title page of the second treatise of the *History of the Macrocosm* pictures eleven areas in which man imitates and continues nature's work. An ape squats in the center, pointing like a schoolmaster to an arithmetic book, because all these arts and sciences are founded on number. *Proceeding clockwise* are geometry (applied in surveying), perspective, painting, military science, the "science of motion," timekeeping, cosmography, astrology, geomancy, and music. With the exception of music, which follows arithmetic, this is the order in which the arts are expounded in the treatise.

The image of the ape had many different connotations before Fludd used it.* In Egyptian symbolism it represented the god Thoth, the inventor of writing and other useful arts, whom Renaissance mythography identified with Mercury and Hermes Trismegistus. As an assiduous student of Hermeticism, Fludd may have had this in mind, and with it the idea that by imitating nature in all her operations, man aligns himself with the cosmic design. *UCH* I, 2, title page.

------

*See Janson, *Apes and Ape Lore,* p. 305.

TRACTATUS SECUNDUS,
DE NATVRÆ SIMIA
seu Technica macrocofmi hiftoria,
in partes undecim divifa.
AUTHORE
ROBERTO FLVDD ALIAS DE
Fluctibus, armigero & in Medicina
Doctore Oxonienfi.
Editio fecunda.
FRANCOFVRTI,
Sumptibus hæredum JOHANNIS THEODORI
de BRY; Typis CASPARI RÖTELII.
ANNO M. DC. XXIV.

3.2. Mirror of Proportions ↪

Fludd's didactic writings contain many circular charts intended for ready reference, like this *proportionum speculum* (mirror of proportions). Proportions, whether between the parts of the body or of the cosmos, were important to Greek, medieval, and Renaissance philosophers alike. The most developed application was in music theory, beginning with Pythagoras's discovery that musical intervals can be expressed as the ratios between string lengths. This chart has several errors, e.g., the 5 at the bottom should be 25, so is a poor substitute for the simple mental arithmetic involved. *UCH* I, 2, p. 13.

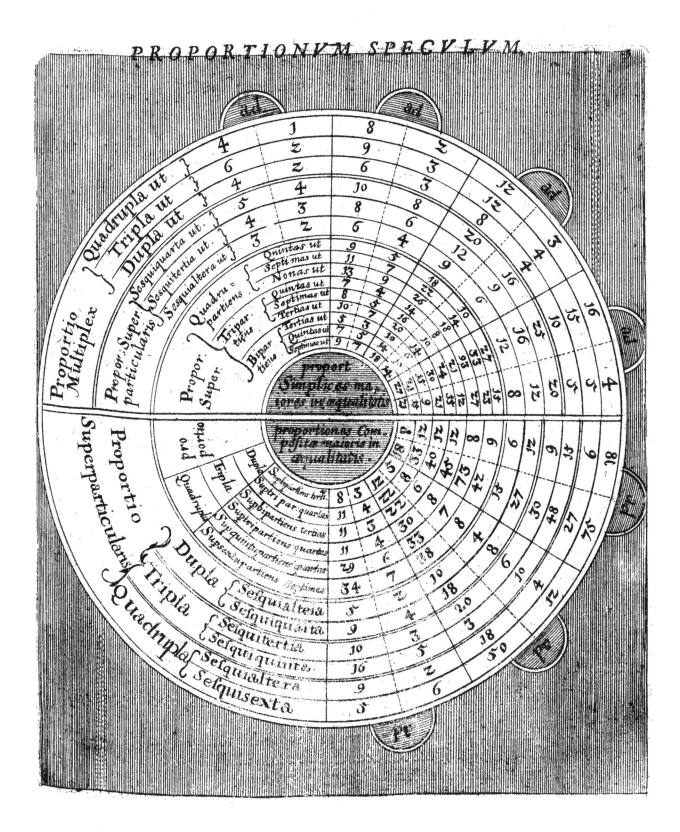

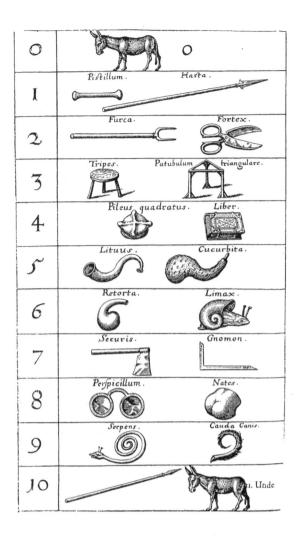

3.3. Mnemonics for Numbers

In the art of memory, everything is given an image, and the more ridiculous the image is, the more easily it is remembered. This set of images is to help one remember numbers by imagining absurd combinations: 0 = donkey; 1 = pestle or lance; 2 = fork or scissors; 3 = stool or tripod; 4 = square cap or book; 5 = horn or squash; 6 = retort or snail; 7 = axe or square; 8 = spectacles or buttocks; 9 = snake or dog's tail. *UCH* I, 2, p. 40.

3.4. Plato's Wheel ↬

This ancient divinatory tool (which has nothing to do with Plato) works thus: Add the numbers corresponding to the name of the person or thing about which you want information. Add the day of the week of the relevant event and the day since the new moon, and divide the total by 30. Look up the remainder on the vertical panel. If it is in the upper half, the answer is Life, victory, success, etc. If in the lower half, the answer is Death, defeat, failure, etc. *UCH* I, 2, p. 151.

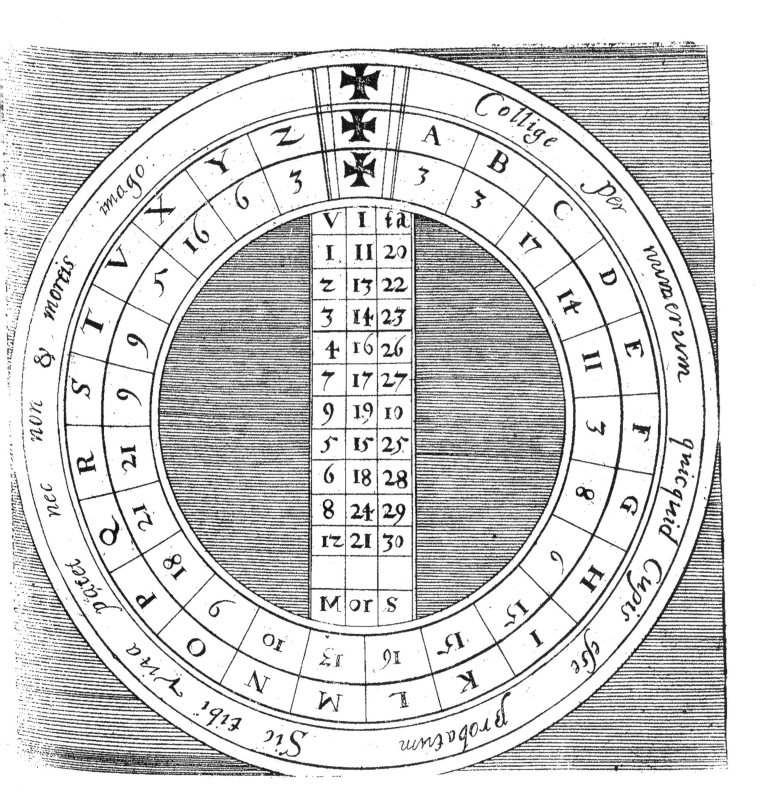

3.5. Apollo and the Muses

Pictorial title pages head the early treatises of *De Naturae Simia,* then disappear as the general quality of illustrations declines, probably for reasons of economy. Here the god Apollo sits under a laurel tree on Mount Parnassus with his head enveloped in a solar nimbus. In his hand is a seven-stringed lyre, indicating that as sun god he is leader of the choir of planets. A cornett and a music book lie at his feet, and around him are the nine Muses, some holding instruments (lyre, cornett, bass viol, lute, trumpet). The Muses traditionally preside over the arts, dispensing inspiration to mortals, while Apollo's direction ensures that the results are true to the cosmic law of harmony and proportion. *UCH* I, 2, p. 159.

3.6. The Temple of Music (overleaf)

This extraordinary structure serves as a mnemonic device as well as a reference chart for music theory.* Starting at *bottom left* we find a lute, an instrument that Fludd held in great regard (see below, ill. 3.8). Next is the legendary scene of Pythagoras entering the forge, where he noticed that the four hammers made consonant pitches. On examining them, he found their weights in the proportion 12:9:8:6, which gave the intervals of octave, fifth, fourth, and whole tone. This was the first insight into the numerical basis of music and the foundation of musical science.

The rusticated foundation obscuring the rest of the arcade illustrates the twin principles of musical notation: pitch and rhythm. The spaces between the stones serve as the staff, with a bass clef. The lowest note is G, the bottom of the gamut. As the scale rises through nine steps, the note values diminish from *maxima* to *semifusa*.

In the second story we find first a column-monochord marked with the complete two-octave gamut, two further octaves being indicated as *gg* and *ggg,* implying that the scale continues *ad infinitum.* Between the first two Tuscan columns is an extended gamut from F to a, the limit of most vocal music of Fludd's day. The next three intercolumnar spaces explain the three species of hexachords, the six-note scale of medieval music whose lowest note, called *ut,* could fall on an F, C, or G. These were called respectively the soft, natural, and hard hexachords. In Fludd's temple the soft hexachord is surmounted by a round tower and a set of seven round organ pipes, the hard hexachord by square ones. These reflect the different versions of the note B as it falls in the respective hexachords. In the soft hexachord it sounds B-flat and is written with a round *b* that became the familiar sign for flat. In the hard hexachord it sounds B-natural, written with a square *b* that became our natural sign. These two accidentals may be seen in the arches of the ground floor. The natural hexachord runs for six notes up from C, hence it omits B altogether. Since it is the highest of the three, Fludd likens it to the highest element, fire, and gives it the highest tower, pointed like a flame, and organ pipes of the same shape.

---

*For a detailed analysis of the temple and investigation of Fludd's musical sources, see Hauge, "*The Temple of Music,*" pp. 7–13.

(ill. 3.6 continued from page 89)

We next consider the clock above the sculpture of Apollo and beneath that of Father Time. The little dial in the gable shows twelve hours, the larger and lower dial the different note values and their corresponding rests. The inner ring contains time signatures.

The area above Pythagoras is divided diagonally. On the left is the scheme described in Plato's *Timaeus,* setting out in the form of a Greek *lambda* the numbers by which the Demiurge constructed the universe. There are two errors, rectified in the text (p. 204): 16 should be 12, and 24 should be 27. Its purpose here is to show the proportions of note values to each other. In medieval and Renaissance notation a breve could contain 4, 6, or 9 minims, depending on the time signature. The possibilities for longer notes were correspondingly greater.

The "chess board" to the right of the *lambda* is an aid to composition, constructed rather like the charts that show the mileage between cities. It shows the distances between the notes of the scale, but includes only consonances. Suppose one has written a low A and wants to write a middle C against it. The chart shows that all is well: the interval is a tenth. Try a B, however, and one meets a blank: the interval is a discord.

The "clerestory" between the three towers is a similar device, enabling one to check the notes respectively an octave, sixth, third, and fifth from any given note. The windows for sixths and thirds are smaller, these being only imperfect consonances as opposed to the perfect consonances of octave and fifth.

Finally, in the alcove beneath the twin portals representing ears, a Muse stands pointing at a phrase in three parts. Neither this nor his three-part dances do any credit to Fludd as a composer.* *UCH* I, 1, between pp. 160 and 161.

---

*See Barton, "Robert Fludd's *De Templo Musicae*," pp. 202–10.

3.7. The Round Tower

This plate shows the uppermost part of the Temple of Music, elaborated with mythological details. Fludd defines sound as made by the striking of air, causing vibrations to propagate in spirals and circles (p. 168). These are fancifully drawn above the two doors that represent the ears. The resemblance of the spiral to the cochlea of the inner ear is probably coincidental, since Fludd's treatise on anatomy (see chapter 7) barely mentions the apparatus of hearing.

The doors are flanked by panels containing (*left*) harp, organ, cornett, (*right*) viol, cittern, lute. On the left is Apollo with a lute, on the right the satyr Marsyas with panpipes. The legend of their musical competition, which ended with the flaying of the loser, was interpreted in Neoplatonism as the painful liberation from one's earthly body (the satyr's skin) in order to hear Apollo's lyre (i.e., experience the celestial worlds).* As Shakespeare writes in *The Merchant of Venice,* "But while this muddy vesture of decay / Doth grossly close it in, we cannot hear it." He continues to speak of the "harmony in immortal souls" and the "young-eyed cherubins." We know from Fludd's diagrams such as the Great Monochord (ill. 7.24) that his concept of universal harmony extended to the empyrean world with its angelic orders. This may be the meaning of the elaborately decorated circles, the first of which contains winged angel heads. *UCH* I, 2, p. 168.

---

*Wind, *Pagan Mysteries in the Renaissance,* pp. 171–76.

3.8. Lute

Since the lute is, as it were, the prince of all musical instruments, we deem it fitting to give it first place in this book; for no other invention, ancient or modern, is more seemly for consorts nor more desirable for symphonies, nor more admirable to the ears of listeners. Time destroys not the sweetness of its sounds, neither do fickle inventions seduce men's affections from it, however rare, unusual, and more easily learnt these may be. *UCH* I, 2, p. 226.

3.9. Orpharion

The orpharion was an English invention of the late sixteenth century, its name fusing those of the mythical musicians Orpheus and Arion. Lutenists could play it, for it was strung like a lute, only with brass wire rather than gut. Fludd states that it was mostly used in consorts. He also mentions its larger relative the pandora (or bandora), which was a member of a characteristic six-piece ensemble of the Elizabethan and Jacobean theatre: treble viol or violin, bass viol, flute or recorder, lute, cittern, and pandora. *UCH* I, 2, p. 233.

3.10. Viola da Gamba

Fludd mentions consorts of viols, a favorite medium for amateur music making, and also the mixed "English consort" (*consortio Anglico*), probably meaning the ensemble defined in the previous caption. He disdains the novel tunings and "fantastic inventions" of the virtuoso school of "Lyra viol" composers. While a competent artist has drawn the other stringed instruments, this illustration comes from an amateurish drawing or woodcut, for several details and all its proportions are wrong. *UCH* I, 2, p. 237.

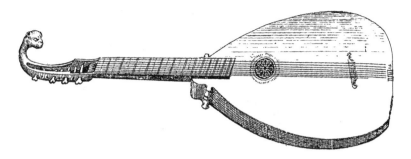

Differt igitur huius instrumenti natura a cæteris prædictis, tum chordarum positione, tum carum numero, ac proinde varium est eius systema et a cæterorum scala differens Huius enim systema hoc modo depinximus.

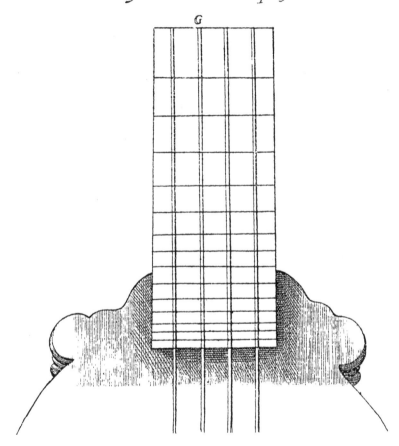

3.11. Cittern

Fludd, like every writer on the cittern, mentions that it hung in barbers' shops for the use of customers. The tuning of its wire strings resembles that of the banjo and ukelele, and like them it served as an easy chordal instrument to accompany singing, as well as having its own solo repertory and a place in the "English consort." *UCH* I, 2, p. 240.

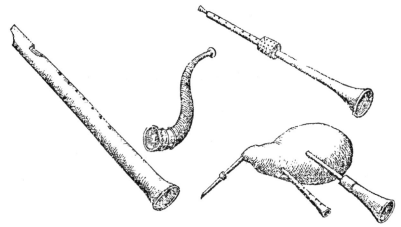

*Aut in diuersis fistulis unico instrumento inservientibus
cuiusmodj sunt Regalia seu Organa et huiusmodj alia.*

*Vel intensiorj aut remissiorj flatus mensura, sine mutatione digi=
torum de aliquo foramine ad aliud diuersæ voces eduntur que=
madmodum in Tubæ clangore, cornuq̃ sonitu euidenter explicatur.*

3.12. Wind Instruments

Fludd's comparative expertise with plucked stringed instruments fails him when he comes to describe wind instruments. He has nothing to say about their mechanism, technique, and tuning. With this single plate he classifies them (*top to bottom*) as those with finger holes (recorder, cornett, shawm, and bagpipe), a keyboard (organetto), and a simple tube (trumpet and posthorn). *UCH* I, 2, p. 242.

3.13. Xylophone

Fludd believed that this was invented by some followers of Pythagoras's teachings, who were inspired to place together dry sticks cut to the proportions of the scale. *UCH* I, 2, p. 243.

3.14. Surveying

This plate heads the section on applied geometry. The two men are measuring the distance and height of a building separated from them by water. The man on higher ground, standing level with the top of the tower, uses an inclinometer to determine its distance (see next plate for explanation). The man lower down, knowing its distance, is measuring its height. *UCH* I, 2, p. 261.

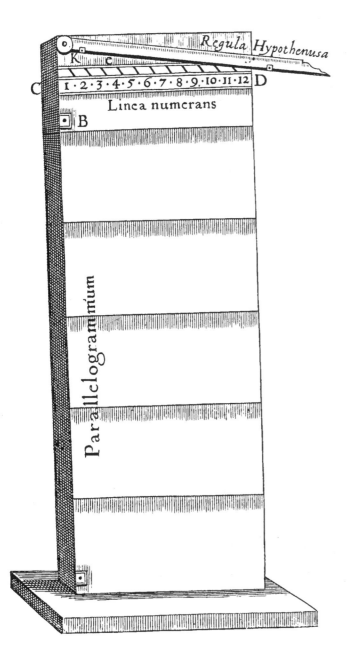

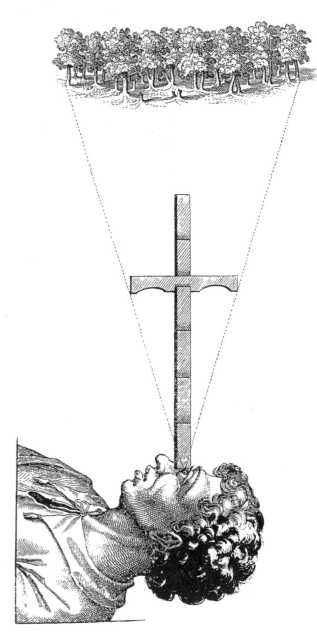

3.15. Inclinometer

An inclinometer measures angles relative to the horizontal. This is an improved model, of Fludd's own design. It measures the distance of an object through similar triangles: one of known dimensions, contained between the cursor (*regula hypothenusa*) and the horizontal bar (*linea numerans*); the other between the entire height of the device and the horizontal distance to be discovered. To the right, a more primitive surveying device, the "Jacob's Staff." *UCH* I, 2, page inserted between pp. 276 and 277.

3.16. Measuring an Obelisk

Once Fludd's inclinometer has measured the horizontal distance of an object, the device is turned on its side to measure its height, through similar triangles or trigonometry. The object here is an obelisk in the mannerist style, which the engraver has decorated with emblems of unknown meaning. *UCH* I, 2, p. 281.

3.17. Principle of Optics

Vision is the sensitive power situated in the optic nerve for apprehending the form of that which enters the crystalline humor from the likenesses of colored bodies, passing through bodies that are diaphanous and radiant in their effect to the surface of the eye (p. 294). The title page of this section shows the visible rays from an object passing through the transparent medium of air to converge on the eye. *UCH* I, 2, p. 293.

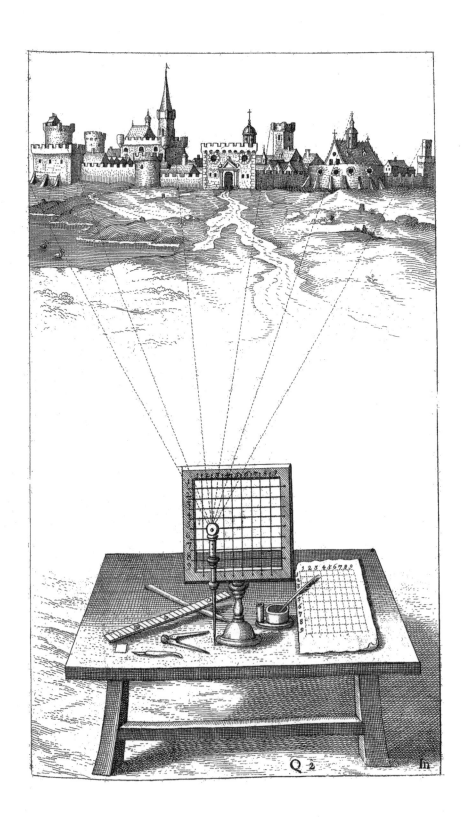

3.18. Perspective Frame

Leon Battista Alberti described this device in the early fifteenth century, when painters began to study scientific perspective. It consists of a frame strung like a tennis racquet and fixed to a table, with an eyepiece through which one views the scene, copying it piecemeal onto paper prepared with corresponding squares. *UCH* I, 2, p. 307.

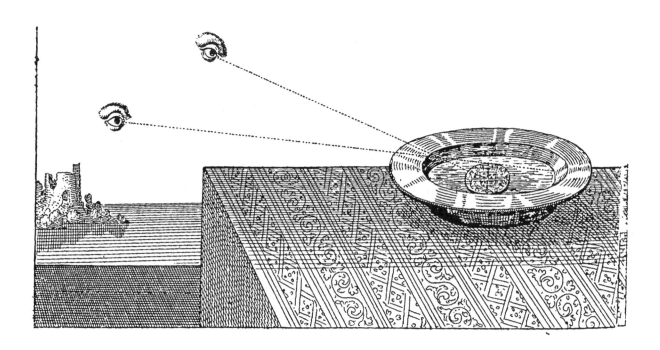

3.19. Experiment in Refraction

Fludd describes a demonstration by an "empiricist" (i.e., an experimental scientist) whom he met in Genoa. He put a gold coin at the bottom of a medium-sized earthenware vessel placed on the ground, and told me to walk backward from it, always watching the coin, until the side of the vessel hid it from me. Then, telling me not to move from there and to keep my eyes on it, he filled the vessel with pure water, and the coin (whose direct rays could not reach the eyes through the opacity) now became visible through the refraction of rays. *UCH* I, 2, p. 310.

3.20. Art Student at Work

Fludd's treatise on the "pictorial art," headed by this illustration, does not discuss painting, only drawing. He lists among the requirements for an artist, first, a heaven-sent gift, then the desire for fame, moral uprightness, erudition in ancient history and mythology (his presumed subject matter, at least in the Protestant world), the ability to imagine all expressions of emotion, and a thorough knowledge of geometry and perspective. Most of the treatise concerns the latter. *UCH* I, 2, 317.

Cuius compositionis gradus (non aliter quàm corporis quantitatiuj quod ex punctis lineis et superficiebus constat) hisce delinetionibus modo sequenti explia.

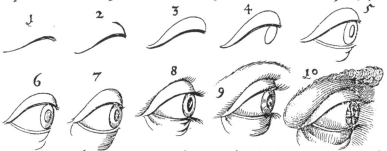

Hoc autem modo cum supercilijs depingitur huiusmodj oculj species, ad dextram quam ad sinistram quam ad sinistram directe ante se prospiciens.

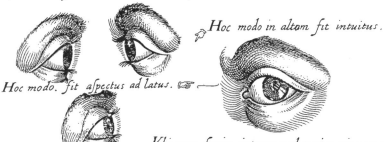

Hoc modo in altam fit intuitus.

Hoc modo. fit aspectus ad latus.

Vbj vero facies integra vel maior eius pars videtur, ibj oculus hoc modo depingendus est, directe ante se prospiciens.

Oculus ad somnum paratus sic depingitur.

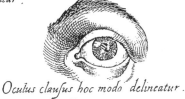

Oculus clausus hoc modo delineatur.

Oculus eleuatus et sursum aspiciens sic sit.

Quæ omnes oculi compositiones semel cognitæ facilime Artistam ad omnem alium aspectum dirigent.

Macrocosmi Tractatus Secundus.   Tt 2   CAP.

3.21. How to Draw Eyes

Below the ten-part instruction are models for left and right eyes, eyes looking up and to the side, a sleepy eye, and one looking straight ahead, another eye looking up, and a closed eye. *UCH* I, 2, p. 331.

3.22. Advice to the Aspiring Artist

After explaining the geometrical bases of the human form, which help one to depict it accurately, Fludd faces the problem of how to draw irregular objects such as animals that do not lend themselves to treatment with the perspective grid. Here is his advice: Sketch it in black or red pencil or charcoal, and lay it aside until the next day. Then, each day, see what parts of it need improvement and amend them bit by bit. In this way one can work on as many as forty drawings simultaneously, and gradually increase one's skill. Imagination and memory are the two nurses and midwives of this art. The engraver here inserted the gratuitous but charming picture of a deer grazing in a rural setting. Comparison with Matthaeus Merian's imaginary landscapes (e.g., in his *Icones Biblicae,* 1625–30) leaves little doubt that this is his work. *UCH* I, 2, p. 338.

3.23. How to Draw in Perspective

There are artists who, when they want to depict something in perspective, draw lines equally distant from a given center at erratic and arbitrary intervals. Then they draw objects according to the direction and extension of the lines relative to the center, which we perceive to be drawn and ordered in perspective. *UCH* I, 2, p. 341.

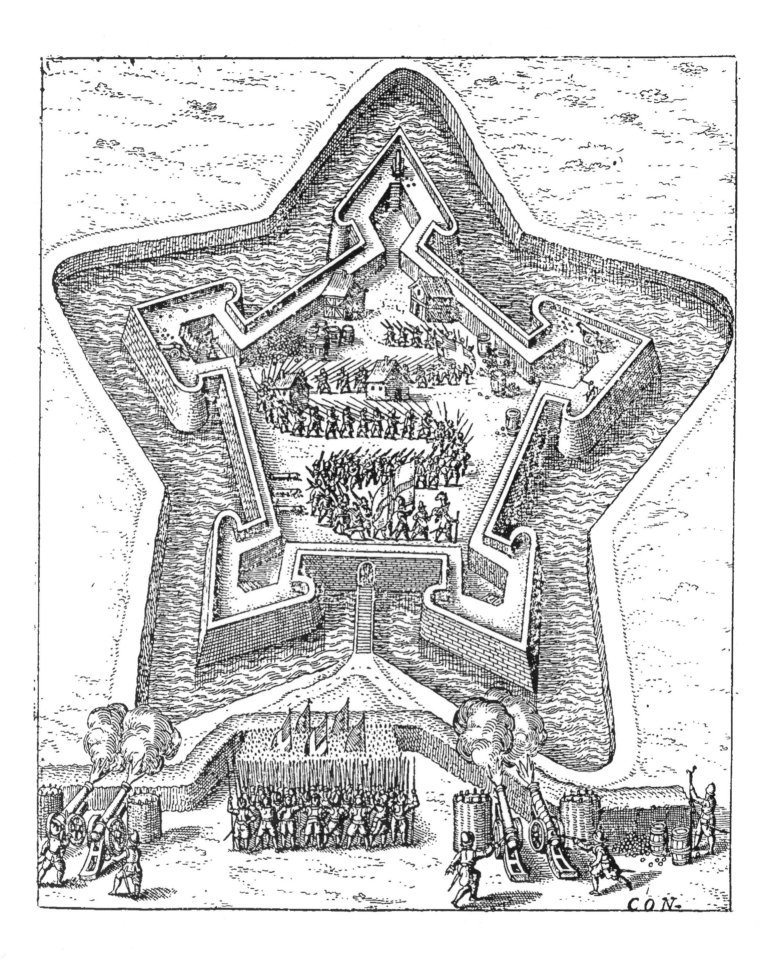

3.24. The Military Art

After his cursory treatment of the pictorial art, Fludd turned with gusto to an art that **does not deal with colors, shadows and fictions, but with rocks, ramparts, and iron, and with real and terrible deeds** (p. 341). The military treatise is his third longest (after arithmetic and music) and the most fully illustrated, with fifty-seven engraved plates, many of them with two scenes, and about twenty woodcuts to which we cannot do justice here. The title page shows a fortress of ideally geometric shape under siege, prefacing a detailed analysis of what makes for victory on both sides. *UCH* I, 2, p. 343.

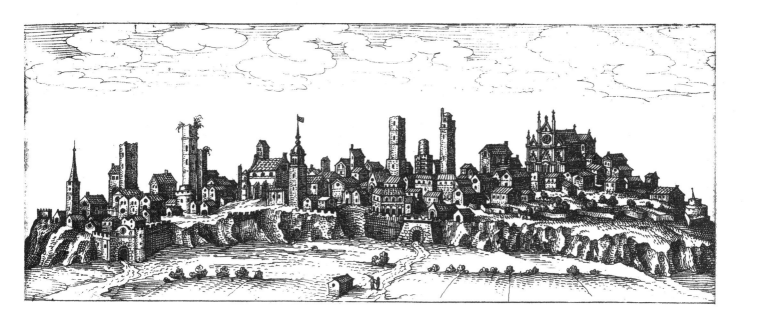

3.25. Orvieto

The Tuscan city is cited as an example of natural fortification, thanks to the steep rocks on which it is built. This and many other views in the present section remind us that Merian was to become one of the great recorders of European townscapes and topography. *UCH* I, 2, p. 345.

3.26. The Perfect Fortress

Hexagonal symmetry, like that of a snowflake or a zodiacal chart, characterizes the perfect fortress. Fludd credits a German with the design, which he finds superior even to the fortress of Livorno, built by Cosimo I of Tuscany and reputed to be impregnable. He does not mention the new city of Palmanova, in the Veneto, planned from the beginning (1593) as a fortress with ninefold symmetry. In its final fortification, under Napoleon, it received an exterior shell of bastions on the exact principle of Fludd's model, lacking only the moats. *UCH* I, 2, p. 390.

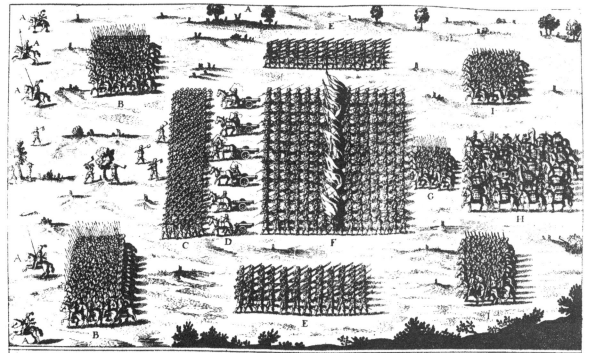

A. Præcursores seu speculatores:
B. Equitum leuium cohortes in duo quadra-
ta dextrum nempe & sinistrum diuisi:
C. Vastatorum banda:
D. Bombardorum campestrium locus.
E. Duæ phalangis alæ seu manicæ:

F. Phalanx seu acies exercitus.
G. Cohores ad Tuldi custodiam constitutus.
H. Tuldum seu impedimenta exercitus.
I. Squadro equitum hargenburas gerentiuᶜ

Italorum exercitus iter faciens.

3.27. The Italian Army on the March

Fludd's military treatise contains three folding plates, showing the order in which the Italian, Imperial, and Spanish armies march. A, scouts. B, troops of light cavalry divided into squares on left and right. C, corps of engineers [clearing obstacles]. D, artillery. E, two wings of the phalanx. F, phalanx or main part of the army. G, guards of the baggage. H, baggage train. I, squadron of mounted arquebusiers.

Fludd also analyzes the military pros and cons of the various nations. He evaluates the Spaniards as follows: The virtues of the Spaniards in war: They are loyal to kings and rarely treacherous. They are seen to obey their leaders and officers. They are good foot soldiers and neat in their arms. They do not desert their companions in trouble. They are peaceful among themselves. They live soberly and without drunkenness. They observe good order on the march. They are vigilant and careful, and wherever they come, they fortify themselves. They know what is to be done before leaving their stations. They keep themselves very safe in reconnoitering. They do not dash into unknown places. They do not act thoughtlessly, even in great danger. They reward and honor those who have done well in war. They are better in action than the Germans, but not so firm against invasions. Their vices: They are proud and haughty. They despise and deride other nations. They think they have more military expertise than impetuosity and courage. They are very often cruel toward the defeated, and devoid of mercy. *UCH* I, 2, p. 410.

3.28. Detecting Enemy Movements

Those under siege who suspect their enemies of tunneling under the walls should place drums above the most suspect points, with needles on their heads or bells hung around them. The slightest vibration underground will cause them to sound. Some also hang bells on posts or in trees for this purpose. The giant harness bells, far larger than a man's head (if we trust the perspective) and with their resemblance to eyes, seem to anticipate the surrealist paintings of Magritte (p. 417). *UCH* I, 2, p. 418.

3.29. Diver

Fludd writes that when the ancients needed to cross a river to retrieve a boat, etc., and had no other means, they sent an experienced man using this method. He wore a watertight leather garment connected to a leather tube that opened above a cork float. To help his progress on the muddy riverbed he carried a staff and wore wide, rounded boots. *UCH* I, 2, p. 419.

3.30. Military Tank

This fearsome machine is the height of a man on horseback, and clad in steel. The horses, vigorously spurred on, drive it rapidly toward the enemy phalanx. It will easily thrust through the spears because of its acute angle and the power of the horses, which must be the strongest and most spirited. The foot soldiers will be so confused that they let through the cavalry who are following the machine. With the phalanx broken and the whole battle array upset, victory will be easily achieved. *UCH* I, 2, p. 421.

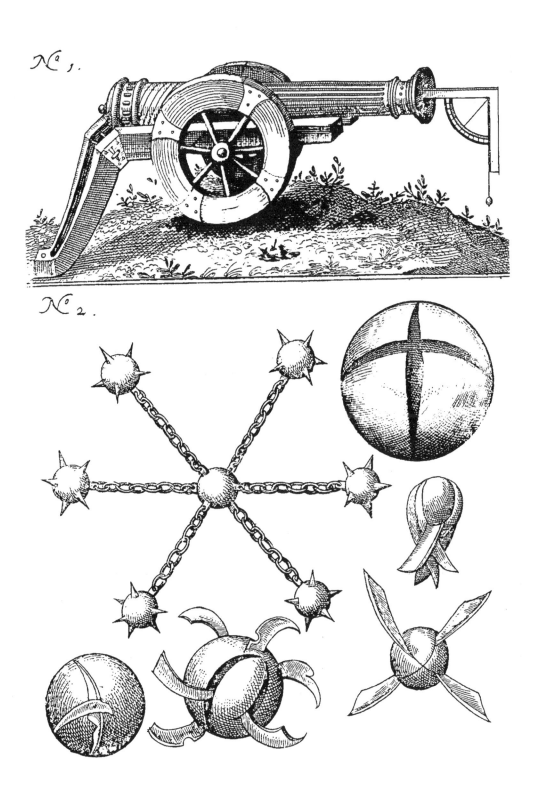

3.31. Cannons and Projectiles

The treatise closes with a catalogue of cannons, each one given with its weight, that of its powder and ball, the number of beasts needed to transport it, and its range. The cannon pictured here is set for "point-blank" range of up to 500 meters, i.e., without compensating for the gravitational fall of the ball that increases with distance. The lower illustration shows some antipersonnel variants on the plain cannonball. *UCH* I, 2, p. 427.

3.32. Perpetual Motion Machine

Fludd shows this ingenious Swiss invention only to reveal the fallacy of perpetual motion. The idea was that as each weight reaches the bottom of the large wheel it is whipped up by the comblike pistons, then somehow rehung on the top of the wheel. The inventor thought that the weights remaining on the wheel could easily raise a single weight in this way and that motion would therefore be perpetual. Fludd points out that a single weight cannot be lifted so far by the much shorter motion of its fellows. *UCH* I, 2, p. 457.

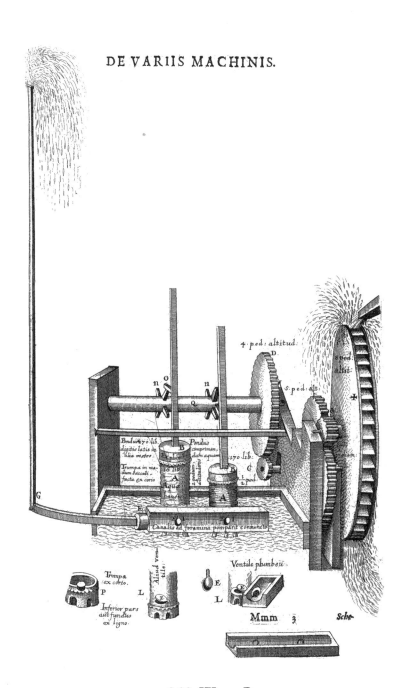

3.33. Water Pump

When I was in Rome, one Gruterus, a Swiss by birth and my master in this art, made this machine for Cardinal Sextus Giorgio whom he served as engineer. It caused the water from a tiny spring, bubbling up at the foot of a mound in his garden, to ascend to the top. I cannot praise enough his artifice and ingenuity, which from so mean a spring raised water to a height with such ease (p. 460).

Unlike some of the machines Fludd illustrates, this one is obviously taken from life and described accurately and convincingly. The British Library owns a sketch of it: the one known example of how Fludd's illustrations may have reached the publisher.* *UCH* I, 2, p. 461.

---

*British Library MS. Sloane 870. See Godwin, *Robert Fludd, Hermetic Philosopher,* p. 87.

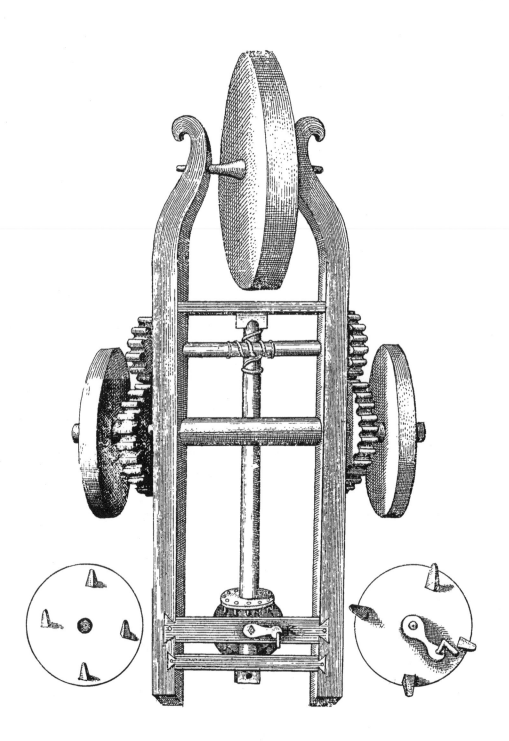

3.34. Hand-Driven Car

While Fludd was in Montpellier, the Lord of Beaulieu showed him a handle-driven car of which he was inordinately proud because it would go both forward and backward: a marvel in the age of horse power. Although Beaulieu refused to disclose its mechanism, Fludd had no difficulty in figuring it out. He went straight to his room, took pen and paper, and drew it to the complete satisfaction of the inventor. The laborious combination of turning handle, crown gear, worm gear, and cogwheels must have absorbed most of the operator's energy before it reached the driving wheels. *UCH* I, 2, p. 465.

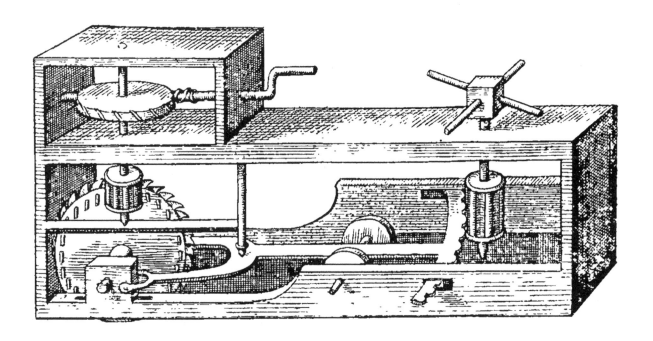

3.35. Steerable Car

While he was in Rome, Fludd had his engineer friend Gruterus make an improved version of Beaulieu's car that could also be steered. The handle again provides the motive power, transmitted to the driving wheels (omitted in the diagram), and the windlass points them to left or right. Presumably there are free back wheels, too. Such machines were used in festivals and processions, with the driver concealed under decorative and allegorical trimmings so that they appeared to be self-moving. *UCH* I, 2, p. 466.

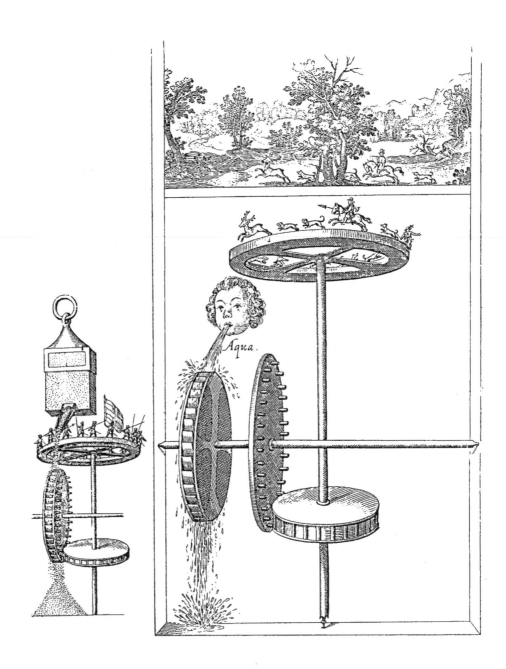

3.36. Revolving Automata

Of the two machines in this plate, one is powered by falling sand and turns a group of model soldiers; the other is powered by water and presents a hunting scene. Above the latter is what the viewer sees, presumably in some grotto or miniature theatre. To enhance the effect, Fludd suggests coupling it with an automatic musical machine, such as he pictures in the same treatise (see ills. 3.38–3.44, pp. 122–27). Salomon de Caus's treatise on motion, published in 1615, shows a similar mechanism coupled to a marine scene.* Both inventors probably drew on machines they had studied in the gardens and grottoes of Europe.† *UCH* I, 2, p. 480.

---

*Caus, *Les raisons des forces mouvantes,* 1:xxvii.
†On Fludd's automata, see Hauge, "Robert Fludd (1574–1637): A Musical Charlatan?" pp. 13–14.

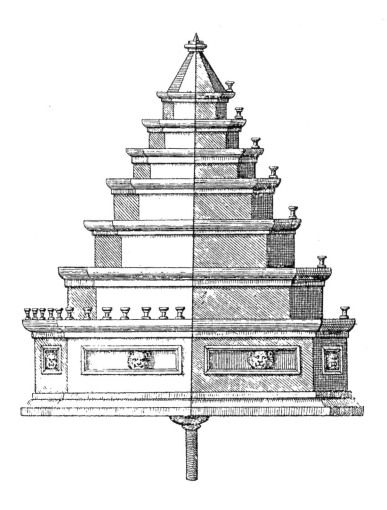

3.37. Fludd's Great Spiritual Machine

This plate gives only the merest hint of the invention with which Fludd closes his treatise on motion. It has seven sides, each of seven steps about one meter in height. The whole apparatus revolves so as to show successive sides to the viewer, each dedicated to one of the seven planets. On the steps are automata depicting the relevant myths, using the devices that Fludd has just described in the book on motion, including mechanical musical instruments concealed within the structure. For example, the side dedicated to Mars depicts, from the top downward, Mars brandishing a sword and spear; then a miniature castle approached by ships in full sail and exchanging cannon fire with them. Lower down, two armies meet with lances and swords; Hercules overcomes the Hydra and Lion; Mars makes love to Venus, watched by Vulcan, who throws an iron net over them. At the lowest level thunder is heard and lightning seen. Fludd assures us that it would not cost too much to build this machine, whose purpose is to demonstrate the visible and invisible powers of the elements. *UCH* I, 2, p. 49.

MECHANICAL MUSICAL INSTRUMENTS

Fludd was fascinated by instruments that play by themselves without human agency, such as were part of the "natural magic" in formal and symbolic garden art. Some of these closely resemble the inventions of Salomon de Caus, who had made such devices for the Jacobean court. Others come from Fludd's fertile and not always practical imagination.

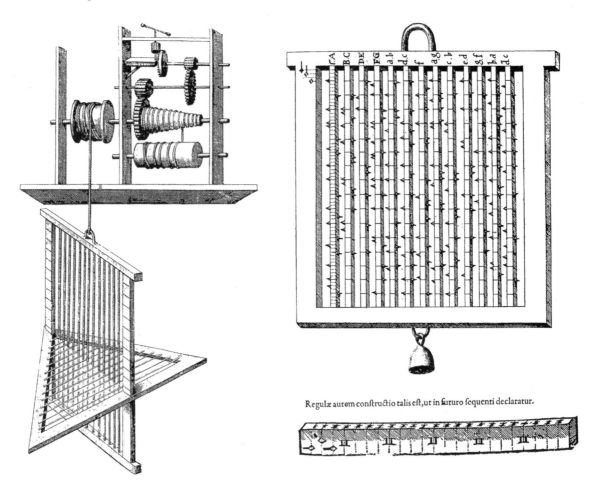

Regulæ autem conſtructio talis eſt, ut in futuro ſequenti declaratur.

3.38, 3.39. Fludd's Great Instrument

This invention of his own forms the culmination of Fludd's book on musical instruments. It is a massive triangular harp or psaltery activated by a rectangular framework fitted with quills and dampers (*plectra tacurnitatis* of felt, not visible here). He makes many claims for its superiority. It needs no player and is a good entertainment at feasts. The same mechanism can be adapted to play wind instruments or bells; and it can play all the parts usually assigned to lutes, pandoras, viols, and so forth. It is all the more effective if hidden from the audience's sight. But any music adapted to it cannot exceed the forty bars that the frame allows: sufficient, Fludd says, for a pavane. Before repeating a piece one has to raise the frame to

3.40. Mechanical Bagpipe

In the section on motion caused by the elements, Fludd returns to the idea of sounding a bagpipe by heated air (compare ills. 2.36–38), to which he adds a pinned wheel that works a three-keyed chanter. This again is a fantasy instrument, ignoring the practicalities of construction and operation. Salomon de Caus has versions of it in which the sun's heat is increased by magnifying lenses. *UCH* I, 2, p. 481.

(ill. 3.38, 3.39 continued from page 122) its high position, whereupon "one will hear something strange and entirely new" (i.e., the same piece played backward). The additional plate shows the plectra in sufficient detail for one to decipher the piece, which consists of many-voiced chords ascending the scale. I do not believe that it was ever constructed as described. For one thing, the absence of any sounding board or resonance chamber coupled to the string frame would make the sound extremely feeble. Athanasius Kircher did Fludd the honor of depicting this instrument in his *Musurgia Universalis,* though doubting its efficacy. *UCH* I, 2, pp. 253, 249.

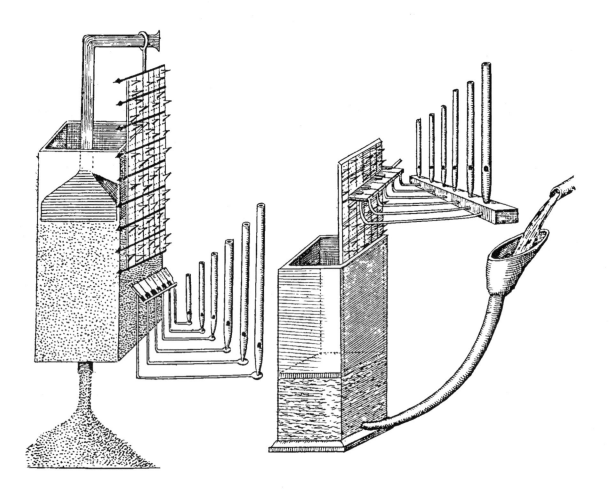

3.41. Mechanical Organ

This works on a similar principle to the Great Instrument, with a pinned framework either descending (as the sand runs out) or ascending (as the water flows in). As it rises or falls, its plectra strike keys that admit air to organ pipes. This too resembles an instrument in Salomon de Caus's 1615 publication, *Les raisons des forces mouvantes avec diverses machines tant utiles que plaisantes. UCH* I, 2, p. 484.

3.42. Mechanical Harp

This works similarly to the Great Instrument, the vertical frame plucking the strings of an Irish harp as the reservoir empties of water. *UCH* I, 2, p. 485.

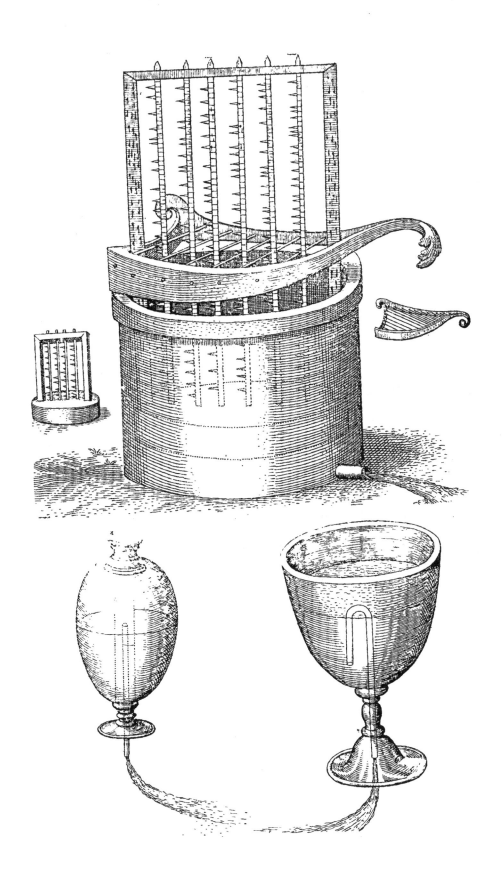

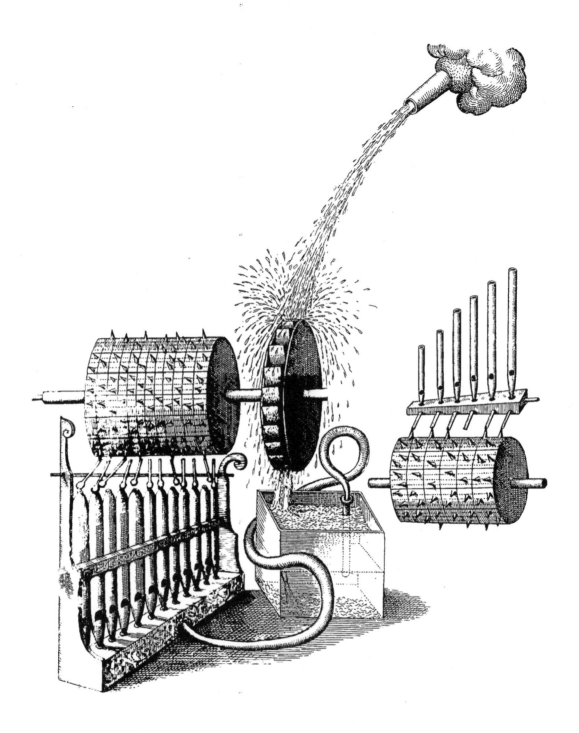

3.43. Water Organ

Water power provides both the compressed air and the playing mechanism for this organ, making it fully automatic, at least in principle. The water in the upper half of the square reservoir is contained in a sliding box that acts like a piston, compressing the air in the lower half. But there is no source for replenishing the air when it is exhausted. The music to be played is encoded on the pinned barrel, as normal. Fludd imagines that organ pipes can be controlled by opening or shutting their upper ends, which is a fallacy. Stopping an organ pipe does not silence it, but causes it to sound an octave lower. *UCH* I, 2, p. 483.

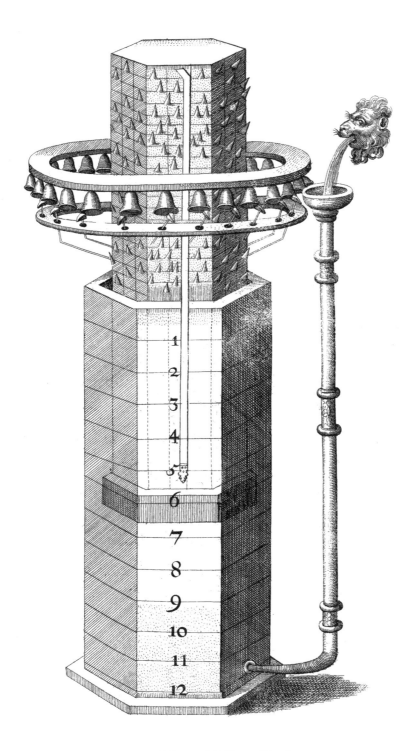

3.44. Musical Water Clock

One of Fludd's own inventions, this is the culmination of his book on time and its measurement. The hexagonal barrel is filled with water that runs out from a tap (not shown) in the course of twelve hours. Floating in the water is a wooden column fitted with a pointer that indicates the hours as it descends. This column also carries spikes that set off a carillon to strike each hour. At noon the barrel is refilled, the float rises to the top again, and the process repeats. *UCH* I, 2, p. 525.

Four

How Man Is Made

4.1. Microcosmic Man ↪

The title page of the *History of the Macrocosm* (ill. 2.1) showed the cosmos bounded by Time's rope, wound round the primum mobile. As Fludd proceeds to the "Supernatural, Praeternatural and Contranatural History of the Microcosm," the geocentric cosmos gains three further circles. They represent the spheres of the empyrean world with its angelic hierarchies who are not subject to time. Neither, in some respects, is man. Beside his physical body, which corresponds to the worlds of the elements and the planets, he has three higher vehicles corresponding to the angelic realms: Reason (*ratio*), Intellect (*intellectus*), and Mind (*mens*). The latter is the highest type of mental activity, which is illuminated by the rays of the divine, pictured here as a blazing triangle outside all the circles. *UCH* II, 1, 1, title page.

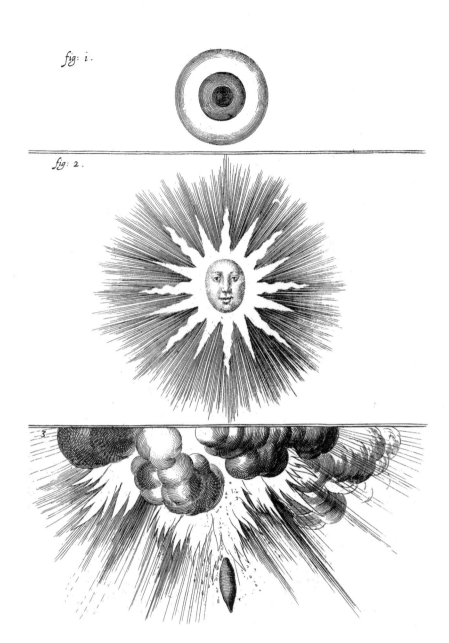

4.2. The Trinity and the Generation of the Elements

Unity is the starting point, and Duality is the firstborn of Unity, the mean between Unity and Trinity. From the Dyad proceeds the Third, the Holy Spirit, which is one in essence with the Father and the Son, and in turn binds them together (pp. 25–26). Thus Fludd unites theology with arithmology. In the associated plate, fig. 1 represents the Trinity in the form of an eye. The Father is the white, the Son the iris, the Spirit the pupil. Fig. 2 draws an analogy with the sun: the Father is the orb, the Son the light, the Spirit the heat. In fig. 3 the analogy continues on the elemental level. The Father here is a consuming fire, the Son, being the divine Word, is likened to the sound of thunder, and the Spirit to the lightning flash. The final outcome is a "thunderstone": in fact, the common fossil of a belemnoid (a squid-like creature of the Mesozoic era), that was believed to be a special stone produced by thunder. *UCH* II, 1, 1, p. 27.

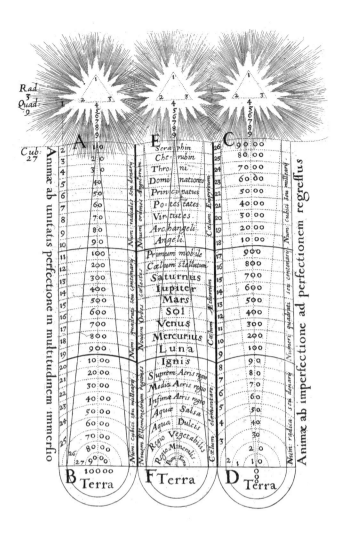

4.3. Descent and Ascent of the Soul

The vertical inscriptions read (*left*) "The soul's plunge from the perfection of unity into multiplicity" and (*right*) "The soul's return from imperfection to perfection." The downward and upward journeys, familiar from the Hermetic writings, are represented in numerical terms. The left-hand column represents the pyramid of matter, which vanishes at the top of the empyrean world; the right-hand column, the pyramid of form, which ends at the center of the earth. Each pyramid is numbered in accord with its increasing or decreasing influence, in a system that goes from units to tens, hundreds, and thousands. Accordingly, each world has nine subdivisions, named in the middle column where both pyramids are drawn. In order to bring the divisions of the lower worlds up to nine each, Fludd adds the primum mobile and the starry heaven to the seven planets, and in the elemental world divides the air into three regions, water into two (salt and fresh), and adds vegetable and mineral regions. The diagram belongs to a family of symbols representing the positive and negative forces in the cosmos, such as the pillars of Mercy and Severity in Kabbalah, the pillars Jachin and Boaz in Freemasonry, the yin-yang diagram of Taoism, and the good and bad thieves crucified on either side of Jesus. *UCH* II, 1, 1, p. 45.

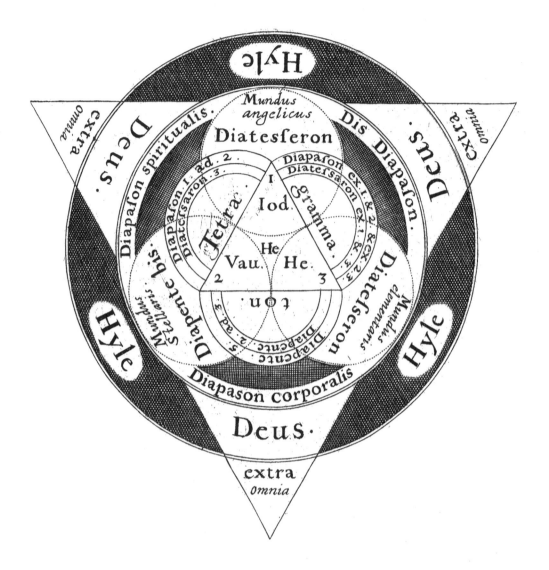

4.4. Threefold Manifestation

The light triangle of the Trinity represents God, who remains "beyond all things," seen against the black hole of chaos (compare ill. 2.4). As a result, three worlds arise: empyrean, ethereal, and elemental. In the center is the Tetragrammaton IHVH, with the "pre-cosmic" numbers 1–3 (see ill. 4.3). These are joined by arcs showing their harmonic relations. *UCH* II, 1, 1, p. 62.

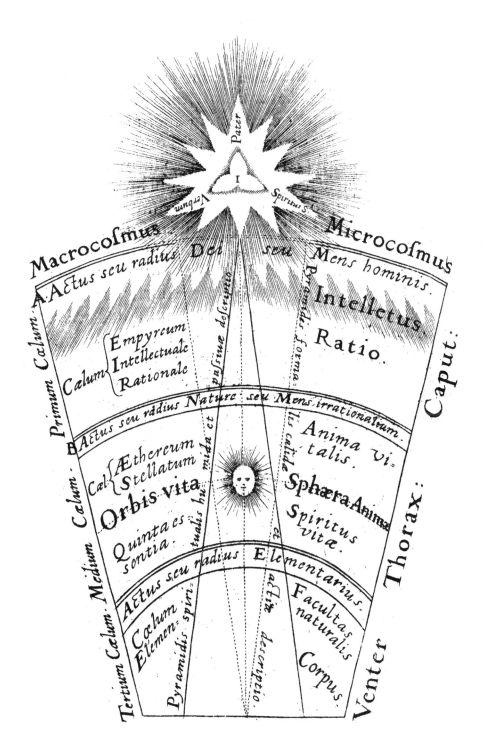

4.5. Pyramids Uniting Man and Cosmos

This applies the symbol of intersecting pyramids to the correspondence of microcosm with macrocosm. On the left are the three heavens: the empyrean, in which God acts; the ethereal, in which nature acts; and the elemental, where the active agent is not mentioned, but is presumably also nature. These heavens correlate, on the right, with man's higher vehicles (see ill. 4.1, pp. 130–31), his soul and vital spirits, his natural faculties and body. *UCH* II, 1, 1, p. 82.

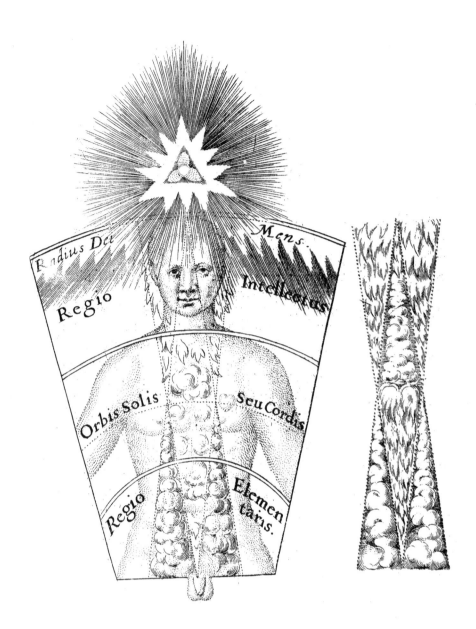

4.6. Spiritual and Sensual Pyramids

In more picturesque form, Fludd shows the fundamental duality of man. His loftiest faculty, the *mens* or higher mind, receives the direct rays from God. From his genitals rise the intoxicating vapors of sensuality. The two contrary forces meet in equality at the heart. *UCH* II, 1, 1, p. 83.

4.7. The Harmony of the Human Soul

The right-hand arc reads: "The essential harmony by which the human soul draws into its own constitution any portion of the regions of the three worlds." This means that man can operate on any of the levels of being, from seraphic to earthly. He does this through his complex organism, whose members Fludd defines in the key:

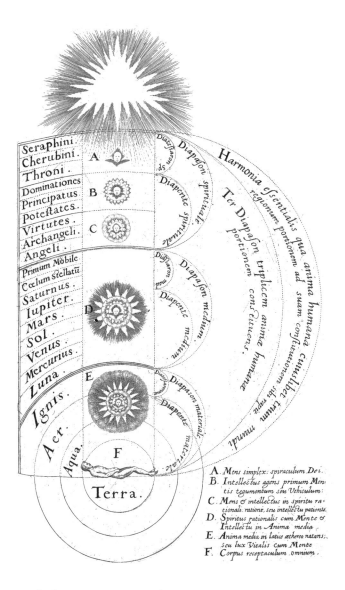

Seraphini.
Cherubini.
Throni.
Dominationes
Principatus
Potestates.
Virtutes.
Archangeli.
Angeli.
Primum Mobile
Cœlum Stellatū
Saturnus.
Iupiter.
Mars.
Sol.
Venus.
Mercurius.
Luna.
Ignis.
Aer.
Aqua.
Terra.

A. *Mens simplex: spiraculum Dei.*
B. *Intellectus agens primum Mentis tegumentum seu Vehiculum.*
C. *Mens & intellectus in spiritu rationali. ratione, seu intellectu patiente.*
D. *Spiritus rationalis cum Mente & Intellectu in Anima media.*
E. *Anima media in latice æthereo natans;. seu lux Vitalis cum Mente.*
F. *Corpus receptaculum omnium.*

A. Simple Mind: the opening to God

B. The Active Intellect, the first sheath or vehicle of Mind

C. Mind and Intellect in the Rational Spirit, open to Reason or Intellect

D. The Rational Spirit with Mind and Intellect in the Middle Soul

E. The Middle Soul swimming in ethereal fluid, or the Vital Light with the Mind

F. The Body, receptacle of all things

This is a fascinating image to those familiar with the Hindu system of Yoga, which situates seven chakras or energy centers in the human body and represents them as lotuses with various numbers of petals. The highest chakra is called the "thousand-petaled lotus" and corresponds to the many-rayed triangle at the top of the diagram. The second chakra descending actually has two petals; compare the two wings of the angel marked *A*. The next chakras have sixteen and twelve petals, respectively; compare the nineteen and thirteen rays of *B* and *C*. Levels *D* and *E* do not correlate so well, but the lowest chakra is situated at the base of the spine, and so is the very center of the earthly sphere, as marked by the recumbent figure. *UCH* II, 1, 1, p. 93.

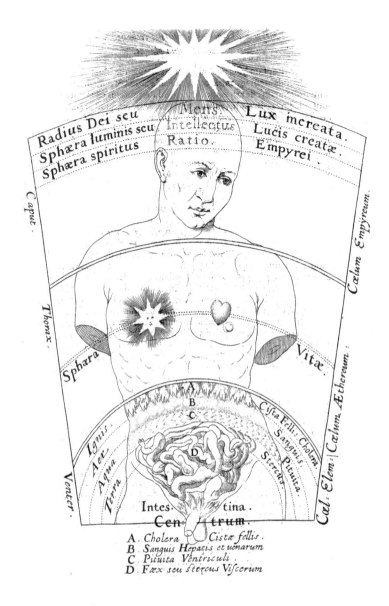

Radius Dei seu
Sphæra luminis seu
Sphæra spiritus

Mens
Intellectus
Ratio.

Lux increata.
Lucis creatæ
Empyrei.

Caput.

Cælum Empyreum.

Thorax.

Sphæra

Vitæ.

Ignis.
Aer.
Aqua.
Terra.

Cista Fellis, Cholera
Sanguis
Pituita
Stercus

Cæl. Elem. Cælum Æthereum.

Venter.

A
B
C
D

Intes — tina.
Cen — trum.

A. Cholera   Cistæ fellis.
B. Sanguis Hepatis et uenarum
C. Pituita Ventriculi
D. Fæx seu stercus Viscerum

4.8. Threefold Man

This sad-looking man, with his arms cut off and belly sliced open, illustrates how the three regions of the body correspond to the three worlds. His three higher faculties correspond as follows: Mind to the ray of God or uncreated light; Intellect to the sphere of light or created light; Reason to the sphere of *spiritus* and the empyrean. The ethereal world corresponds to the thorax, the sphere of life, at whose center is the sun's equivalent in the heart. The elemental spheres of fire, air, water, and earth are marked both on the diagram and underneath with correspondences partly taken from the Galenic theory of the humors:

> A. Choler (gallbladder)
> B. Blood (liver and veins)
> C. Phlegm (belly)
> D. Feces or dung (viscera)

How Man
Is Made

UCH II, 1, 1, p. 105.

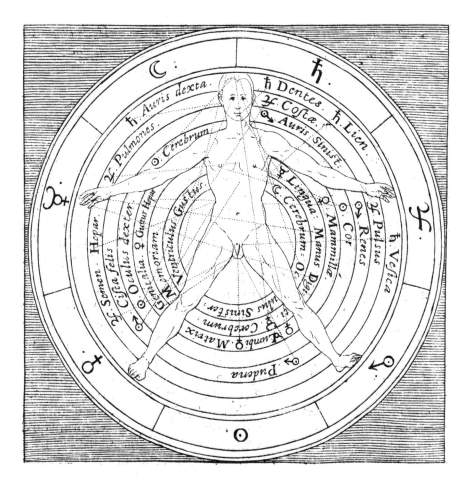

4.9. Planetary Man

The macrocosm-microcosm doctrine found its popular representation in astrology, where each part of the body is ruled by a planet and a sign of the zodiac. This and the next plate show the correspondences that vary somewhat from one astrologer to another, as Fludd presumably applied them in his medical practice. In the rings we learn:

> Saturn rules the right ear, teeth, spleen, bladder
> Jupiter: lungs, ribs, pulse, semen, liver
> Mars: left ear, kidneys, pudenda, gallbladder
> Sun: brain, heart, right eye
> Venus: breasts, loins, womb, genitals, throat, liver
> Mercury: tongue, hands, fingers, brain, memory
> Moon: brain, left eye, belly, taste

On the geometrical correspondence of the human body with the cosmos, Fludd writes: Just as the earth is the center of the greater world . . . thus the center of the lesser world is the point of the genitals or pudenda, and the root of the penis, from which if we measure to the bone of the mucronate cartilage, and from there to the base of the throat level with the collarbones, lastly from there to the top of the head, we will find the geometrical proportions of the Microcosm corresponding in three equal distances to those of the macrocosmic regions or heavens (p. 102). *UCH* II, 1, 1, p. 112.

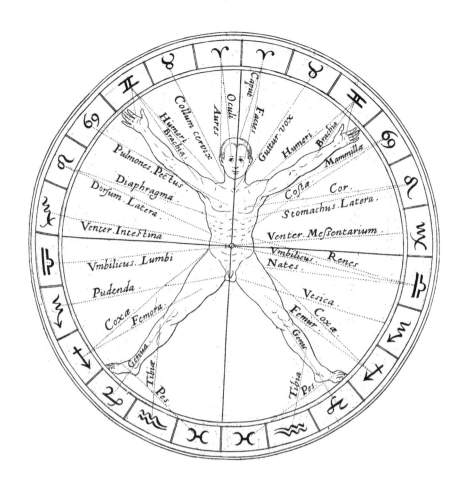

4.10. Zodiacal Man

The rulerships of the signs of the zodiac are more logical than those of the planets, for they go in order from head to toe, as follows:

Aries: ears, eyes, head, face
Taurus: neck, nape of the neck, throat, voice
Gemini: shoulder, arms
Cancer: lungs, chest, ribs, breasts
Leo: diaphragm, back, sides, stomach, heart
Virgo: belly, intestines, mesentery
Libra: navel, loins, buttocks, kidneys
Scorpio: pudenda, bladder
Sagittarius: hips, thighs
Capricorn: knees
Aquarius: shins
Pisces: feet

Whereas in the previous (planetary) circle the man touches the circumference at five points and has his genitals at the center, in the zodiacal circle he divides it into four and has the center at his navel. Fludd comments on this: **There are some who make the navel the center of the microcosmic periphery, with which I do not agree**

for reasons given above. Nevertheless, we will depict such a description of the human circumference here, so as to show the relation between the signs of the celestial zodiac or firmament of the fixed stars and the parts of the human body, and demonstrate the harmony between them (p. 112). Other microcosmic figures (not included here) fill a square, either with legs together and arms outstretched, like Christ crucified, or touching the corners and describing, as Fludd says, a Saint Andrew's cross. The immediate source for them all was probably Cornelius Agrippa's *Three Books of Occult Philosophy*, where all these arrangements appear. *UCH* II, 1, 1, p. 113.

4.11. Flying a Kite

This charming example of Matthaeus Merian's style accompanies Fludd's explanation of how the higher elements have a naturally upward tendency. Fludd has given the example of a lighted candle placed upright in a bowl of water with a glass retort lowered over it. As the candle burns, the water in the retort rises, as Fludd believes, "by the occult faculty of fire." Likewise the kite demonstrates the natural upward motion of air toward the fiery sphere. A third case of the upward tendency of the "vivific spirit" is seen in the fact that live creatures weigh less than dead ones, as Fludd assures us is the case. This is more so with humans than with animals, showing that man contains a greater proportion of vital light than they. Take a man who weighs 200 pounds when alive: his corpse may weigh 140 pounds. The difference of minus 60 pounds weight of vital spirit would be enough to lift his [vital?] body to the sphere of the Sun (pp. 138–41). *UCH* II, 1, 1, p. 139.

4.12. The Three Visions of the Soul ↝

This often-reproduced engraving summarizes Fludd's theory of the three sources of perception and consciousness, and the relation of the soul to the brain.

1. The circles on the left are those of the sensible world, with its elements and the five senses corresponding to them: earth = touch, water = taste, dense air = smell, thin air = hearing, light or fire = sight. Their information lodges in the sensitive soul, whose residence in the brain is behind the forehead. There too comes the input from the imaginable world (second circular system) that contains shadows of the elements and is apprehended by the imaginative soul. Neither of these sources is to be trusted, for the senses can deceive, and imaginations have no substance.

2. True visions come to the central part of the brain. Their source is the intellectual world (*Mundus Intellectualis*) comprising the threefold God and the nine orders of angels, encircled here by rays of light. Fludd writes: **These secrets, such as the ineffable mystery of the three essences, have never been grasped by the senses. Nor can the imagination comprehend them, while reason itself, and the height of human intelligence, can scarcely ever obtain such grace, and only with a mighty illumination of mind. Thus it is that reason at first ascends by divine speculation to the intellect, and then leaps up from the intellect into the sphere of mind, so that in its light it sees spiritual things from afar, and by such a vision is transported with intense joy** (p. 218).

3. The back of the head contains the memorative and motive parts of the soul. The former records, stores, and retrieves things seen in the sensible, imaginative, and intellectual worlds. The motive soul sends its motions down the spinal medulla and thence to all the members of the body. The whole concept was not original with Fludd, but can be seen in cruder illustrations to the works of Albertus Magnus, Gregor Reisch, and Andrea Bacci.* *UCH* II, 1, 1, p. 217.

---

*Hall, *Man, the Grand Symbol,* pp. 135–41; Bacci, *Ordo Universi.*

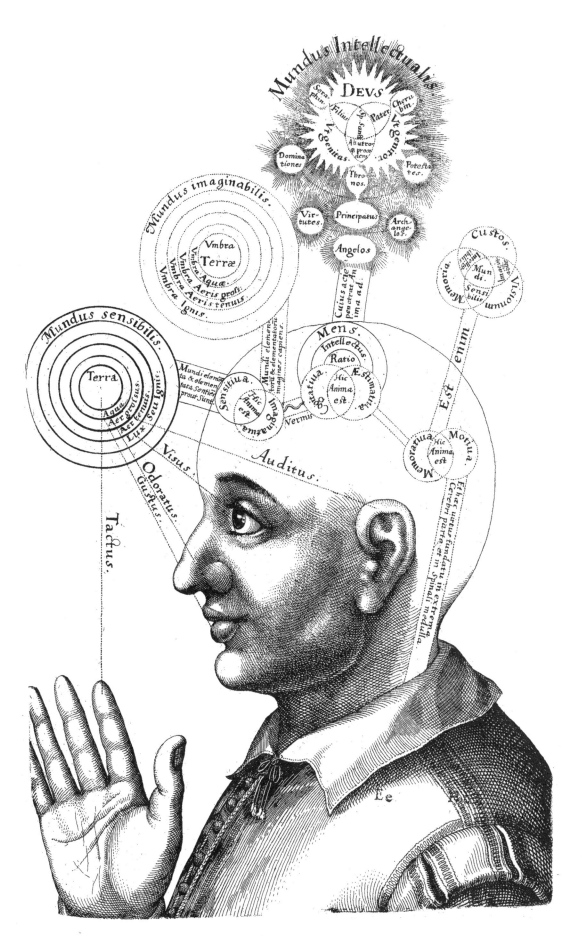

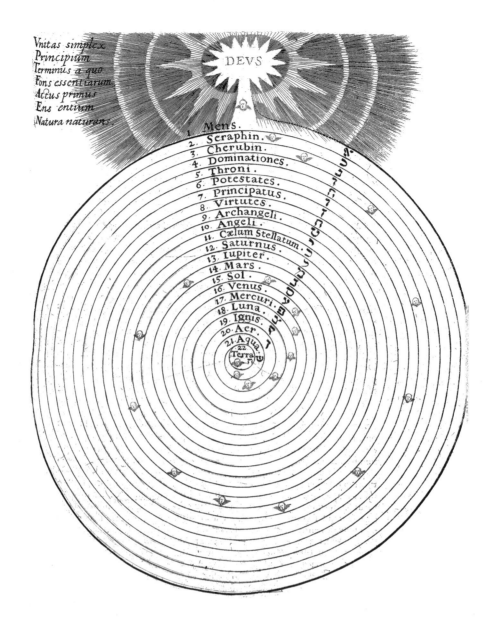

4.13. The Spiral of Creation and Ascent

The Absolute creates by limiting its own infinity, in an act described by the caption: "The simplex unity; the beginning; the starting point; source of essences; the first action, the Being of beings; Nature producing nature." First comes cosmic or World Mind (*Mens*), open on the one hand to God, and on the other entering the constricting vortex of creation. The first of the Hebrew letters, *Aleph,* marks this beginning of beginnings, from which the other twenty-one hypostases emanate. They proceed through the now familiar three worlds: empyrean (angels), ethereal (stars and planets), and elemental. "What God created in the first week does not exceed 22," which is the number of Hebrew letters. While the spiral describes the process of creation, it also represents the path taken by the soul on its mystical ascent. Fludd writes eloquently, even ecstatically, of this process, and of how, after returning to earth, one is endowed with absolute certitude and is henceforth a companion of God. *UCH* II, 1, 1, p. 219.

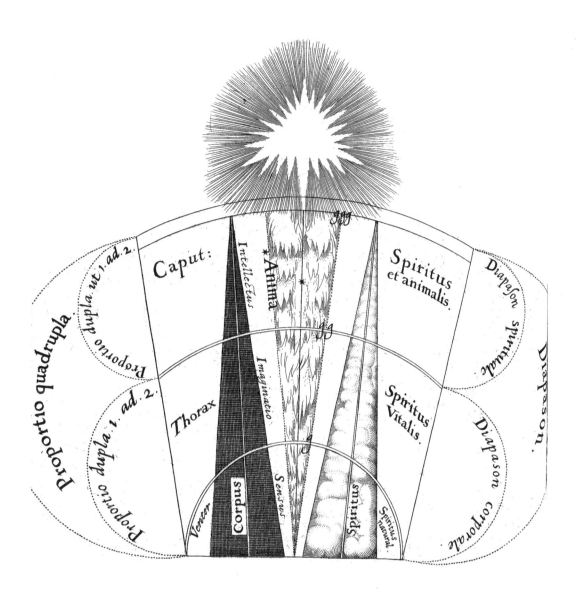

4.14. Pyramids of Body, Soul, and Spiritus

The *spiritus* of Renaissance medicine and natural philosophy was a corporeal vapor, formed in the blood, which vivifies the brain and provides the link between the body and the soul. To avoid confusion with the immortal spirit, we retain the Latin term. Fludd's system divides *spiritus* into three types of increasing density: animal or animating, vital, and natural. The text explaining this plate is concerned with finding the harmonic intervals between the different densities, between the faculties of intellect, imagination, and sense, and between the head, thorax, and belly. It represents Fludd's compulsion to integrate his metaphysical concept (the pyramids of form and matter) with physiology, both material (parts of the body) and subtle (*spiritus*), and with harmonic proportions, which ultimately rest on number. *UCH* II, 1, 1, p. 248.

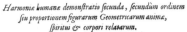

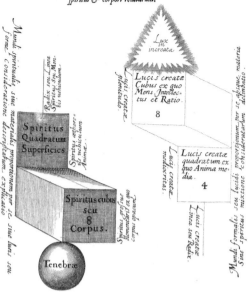

4.15. Line, Surface, and Solid

Fludd's analysis of the pyramids of form and matter involved all the arts of the quadrivium: Arithmetic, as seen in the "Descent and Ascent of the Soul" (ill. 4.3), Music, as in plate 4.4. with its harmonic proportions, Astronomy, with the continuous reference to the planetary and stellar spheres, and now Geometry in this plate. The diagram draws a parallel between the three degrees of *spiritus* and of light with the geometrical progression of line, surface, and solid. The legend written upward (*on the right*) reads: "Delineation of the proportions of the formal or lucid world, to be considered in itself and without the mixture of matter or *spiritus.*"

The texts beneath the triangular burst (*upper right*) of "uncreated light" read thus:

Fullness of created light: Cube of created light from which [come] mind, intellect, and reason

Mean of created light: Square of created light from which [comes] the middle soul

Line or root of created light

The legend written downward (*on the left*) reads:

Explication of the proportions [reading *proportionum*] of the spiritual or material world in itself, to be described without [reading *sine*] consideration of light or form

The texts above the sphere of darkness read thus (*from bottom to top*)

Gross elementary *spiritus* from which [comes] the opaque body; Cube of *spiritus* or body

Ethereal *spiritus,* vehicle of the soul; Square of *spiritus*, surface

Root or line of *spiritus* or vehicle of mind

UCH II, 1, 1, p. 251.

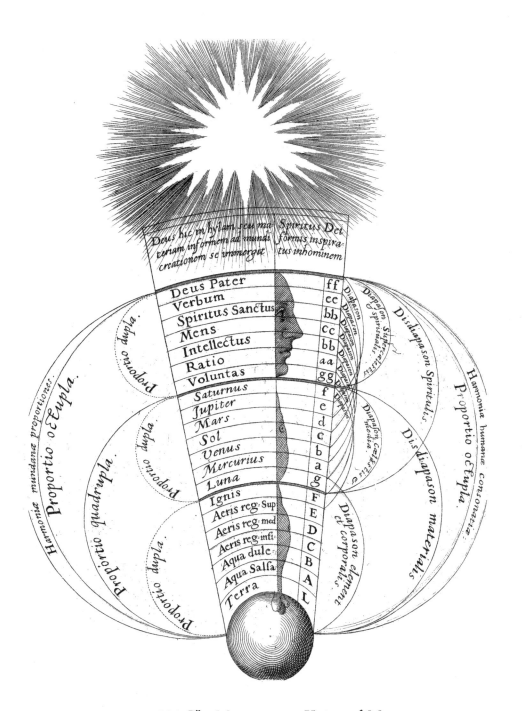

The labels within the illustration read:

Deus hic in hylam, seu materiam informem ad mundi creationem se immergit — *Spiritus Dei formis inspiratus in hominem*

Left column (top to bottom): Deus Pater, Verbum, Spiritus Sanctus, Mens, Intellectus, Ratio, Voluntas, Saturnus, Jupiter, Mars, Sol, Venus, Mercurius, Luna, Ignis, Aeris reg: Sup, Aeris reg: med, Aeris reg: infi, Aqua dulc, Aqua Salsa, Terra

Right column: ff, ee, bb, cc, bb, aa, gg, f, e, d, c, b, a, g, F, E, D, C, B, A, Γ

Outer arcs (left): *Harmonia mundana proportiones.* *Proportio octupla.* *Proportio quadrupla.* *Proportio dupla.* *Proportio dupla.* *Proportio dupla.*

Inner arcs (right): *Diapason Supercaelestis & spiritualis.* *Diapason caelestis media.* *Diapason elementi et corporalis.* *Disdiapason Spiritualis.* *Disdiapason materialis.* *Harmonia humana consonatia.* *Proportio octupla.*

4.16. The Macrocosm as Universal Man

This plate, though different in appearance from ill. 4.14, is an elaboration of it. The legend at the top reads "God thus immerses himself in *hyle* or unformed material for the creation of the world. God's forming spirit is drawn into man." The human profile shows the three bodily regions of head, thorax, and belly. The column *to the right* of it names the musical notes of the three corresponding octaves. The column *to the left* introduces the divisions of the macrocosm, dividing each of its worlds into seven to match the musical scale. They are the supercelestial and spiritual world (here using "spirit" in its superior sense) in which the Holy Trinity acts, and which man accesses through his mind, intellect, reason, and will; the celestial and middle world with the familiar seven planets; and the elemental and corporeal world. *UCH* II, 1, 1, p. 254.

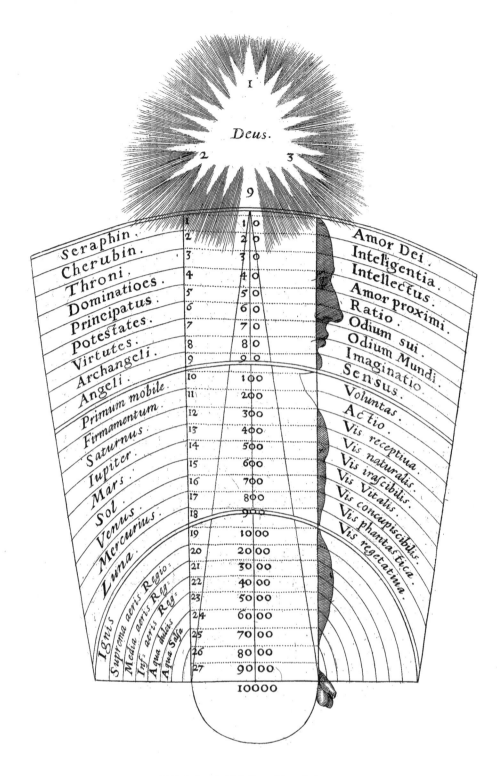

4.17. Man's Higher Faculties

Whereas the preceding illustration had a musical basis, this one has an arithmetical basis derived from the "Descent and Ascent of the Soul" (ill. 4.3). Consequently, each of the three worlds and their reflection in man is here divided not into seven circles but into nine, and extra spheres have to be added to make up the difference. Instead of the harmonic arcs we see the series of twenty-seven numbers (the limiting number of the world's creation as recounted in Plato's *Timaeus*) and the progression of tens, hundreds, and thousands that Fludd equated to squares and cubes. *UCH* II, 1, 1, p. 259.

4.18. The Ladder of Ascent

How amazing it is that things so disparate as the vile body and the immortal spirit
should be joined together in man! No less miraculous it is, that God himself should have
contracted into corporeality; and that man should be so made that he can participate in
eternal beatitude. What joy there is in this world comes alone from the presence of the
spirit in the corruptible body. How much greater, then, must be the bliss of heaven,
where the rational spirit enjoys God's proximate presence! To attain this, it is necessary
to turn away from exterior things and turn inward, indeed, to penetrate through one's
very center (p. 273). The ladder of perfection shows the steps that must be taken
to mount from earth to heaven: from the world of Sense to the inner world of
Imagination; thence through Reason, or disciplined thought, to Intellect, the inner
organ of knowledge; to Intelligence, or the object of direct inner knowledge; and
finally to the Word itself, which opens the supercelestial realm. *UCH* II, 1, 1, p. 272.

4.19. Microcosmic Day and Night ⤳

The body is formed of food, hence of the four elements. This inert matter is vivified by the soul, which is of another order of existence altogether. The wonderful harmony of these two extremes is brought about by the Spiritus Mundi, the limpid spirit, represented here by a string. It extends from God to the earth, and participates in both extremes. On it are marked the stages of the soul's descent into the body, and its reascent after death (pp. 274–75). The three worlds are shown as concentric circles, marked, on the left, "Empyrean Heaven of the Microcosm," "Ethereal Heaven of the Microcosm," and "Elemental Heaven." They correspond to man's head, thorax, and belly, or on the mental plane to intellect, imagination, and sense. But what of his legs? Here at last they are given their due, supporting and stabilizing man's whole universe "as though on the shoulders of Atlantes" (p. 276). In the macrocosm they correspond to the inert mass of the earth, which as Fludd insists is totally devoid of light and form. Thus the legend at the bottom of the plate reads: "A mass of microcosmic earth: two columns by which his universe is supported at right angles."

This final plate of the volume also introduces the theme of "macrocosmic day and night." The sun's orbit around the earth ("Via Solis") makes it visible for half the time, illuminating the upper semicircle that contains all of man's conscious life. For the other half it is invisible and apparently underneath or inside the earth. Thus Fludd applies his pervasive theme of a cosmos compounded of form and matter, light and darkness, to the cycles of time. *UCH* II, 1, 1, p. 275.

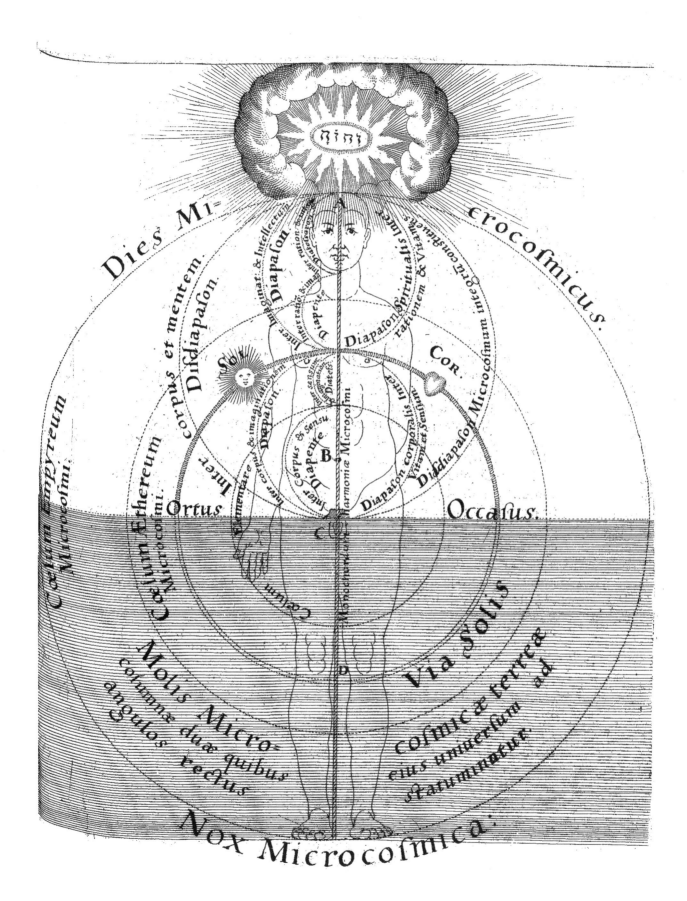

Five

Psychology and Divination

5.1. Inner Arts and Sciences

Whereas Fludd's *History of the Macrocosm* treated the arts and sciences as applied in the outside world by "nature's ape," the *History of the Microcosm* deals with those that apply to man himself. Whether or not by design, the man pictured on the title page contrasts with the confident youths of Fludd's previous title pages (see ill. 2.1, pp. 30–31, and ill. 4.1, pp. 130–31). Instead of spanning the universe, he stands with a moronic expression, scratching his backside. Yet the ape is confined beneath his feet, and around him are the magnificent prospects of prophecy, the prediction of the future through geomancy, the art of memory, and the reading of character and destiny through horoscopes, physiognomy, and palmistry. *UCH* II, 1, 2, title page.

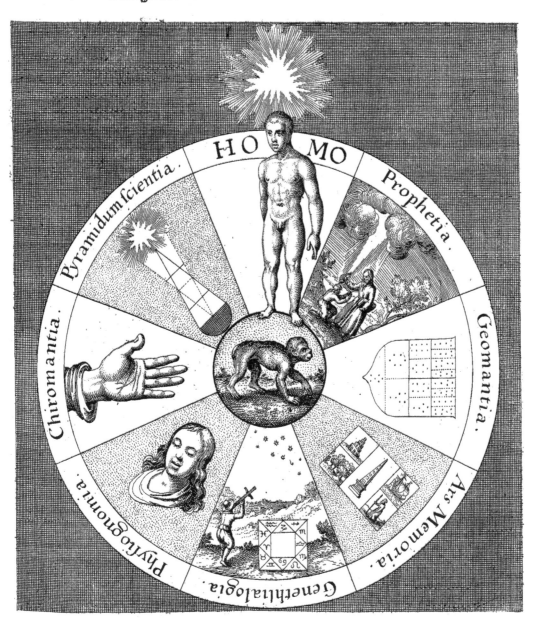

TOMI SECVNDI
TRACTATUS PRIMI,
SECTIO SECUNDA,
De technica Microcosmi historia,

in

Portiones VII. divisa.

AUTHORE

ROBERTO FLUD aliàs de FLUCTIBUS

Armigero & in Medicina Doctore Oxoniensi.

5.2. Prophecy

Craven interprets this scene as Elijah anointing Elisha with a horn of oil, thus endowing him with the prophetic gift (1 Kings 19:16).* The engraver Merian sets the scene in one of his characteristic landscapes, into which the Holy Spirit bursts from the clouds. The gift of prophecy, says Fludd, can come directly from God, or else indirectly through the help of demons. He cites the examples of many biblical characters, and also credits the gift to pagans such as Hermes Trismegistus, Plato, Orpheus, the Sibylline and Chaldean Oracles, Apollonius of Tyana, Cassandra, and Merlin. In our own day, he adds, we have Nostradamus.

Just as the sun shines perpetually on all men, so God incessantly offers his pearls of wisdom, and those who receive them become prophets. But the evil demons can also give knowledge, inasmuch as they had it before the fall (pp. 8–11). In his *Medicina Catholica* Fludd gives examples of how contemporary people have received true prophecies (see appendix 6, "Three Stories of Prophecy"). *UCH* II, 1, 2, p. 3.

---

*Craven, *Doctor Robert Fludd,* p. 103.

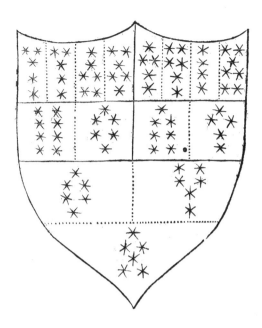

5.3. Geomancy

The standard matrix for European geomancy is this shield-shaped container of fifteen regions, which are filled with a series of possible patterns made by the random casting of pebbles or soil (hence the name "divination from earth") or by making marks on paper. In his *History of the Macrocosm* Fludd had already related his geomantic experiences in France and supplied many charts and tables for interpretation. Here he gives the art a strong and reasoned defense, both against theological objections and against the ridicule in which many people held it. First, he explains why we cannot know the deep causes behind the phenomenon: **Thus while the divine mind produces marvelous effects in man and acts marvelously, the obstacle of the flesh and of darkness prohibits correct knowledge of the reason for these actions. For the mind acts in the intellect, which patiently accepts the act of its lord, and thus the principal cause lies hidden in the center of the mind, namely in the divine word** (p. 38). Second, he emphasizes the need for due preparation: **When we are sound and healthy in body, undisturbed in mind, not laden with food or drink, not laboring in poverty or wealth, unassailed by the vices of lust or anger, then we may enter this prophetic sanctuary** (p. 41). And that is the least of it, for the state of mind to which the geomancer aspires is similar to ecstasy or the prophetic rapture. At the end of this section Fludd lists some other forms of divination: *hydromantia* (from water), *lecanomantia* (from pills in a dish of water), *aeromantia* (from signs in the air), *pyromantia* (from fire), *capnomantia* (from smoke), *axinomantia* (from axes), *cleromantia* (from drawing lots), *botanomantia* (from ingesting herbs), *clidomantia* (from a key), *coscinomantia* (from a sieve), *umbilicomantia* (from the navel), *physiognomia* (from the face), *chiromantia* (from the hand), *necromantia* (from the dead), and *augurium* (from birds). *UCH* II, 1, 2, p. 37.

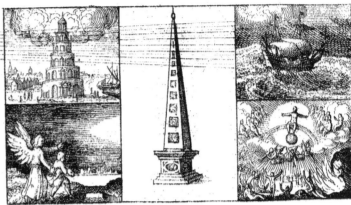

Oculus Imaginationis.

5.4. The Art of Memory

The art of memory teaches how to transmute concepts into visual images, and arrange them spatially, so that they can be stored in the brain and retrieved at will. The man is imagining a fivefold image that groups (*left*) the Tower of Babel, Tobias and the angel, (*right*) a storm at sea, and the Last Judgment around an obelisk. The subjects are probably not significant in themselves, because in practice it is not the images themselves that matter, but the associations that one makes with them. Fludd describes the mechanics of the process as follows:

Physicians say that retention of the species of natural memory is done through the contraction of a sort of worm or vermiform organ in the middle of the brain, and that their loss comes from the expansion or extension of the same. But the retention of artificial memory is done by a constant act of imagination, imprinting the species of truth in memory's unguent jar with vain and fictive ideas and pictures. Given the nearness and vicinity of its action to the cell of memory, and since it is recent and continuous, it seems to strike the memory repeatedly and as though with a live action (though made from invented and inanimate species); whereupon by striking, it presents the species of memory to be retained, just as a dumb man learns to indicate and state something by a sign in place of words (p. 49). *UCH* II, 1, 2, p. 47.

5.5. Theatre of the Globe

One prepares for the art of memory by forming an ordered collection of "memory places" in the mind's eye. Fludd recommends a theatre as a suitable locale, containing as it does many available places such as doors, windows, columns, and the spaces between them. These then serve as locations for the things to be remembered, which one imagines placed in them. As with a theatre, the places can be cleared of images and reused again and again. This plate achieved fame when Richard Bernheimer and Frances Yates suggested that with its title *Theatrum Orbi,* it might be an actual drawing of Shakespeare's Globe Theatre.* *UCH* II, 1, 2, p. 55.

---

*See Yates, *Theatre of the World,* pp. 156–61.

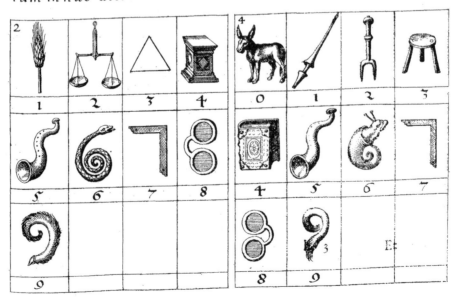

↰ 5.6. Memory Symbols

Fludd suggests several ways of remembering letters and numbers. For the Latin alphabet of twenty letters he supplies six lists of names: masculine and feminine, both current and classical, names of birds, and those of animals. The latter list (not pictured) reads: *Asinus, Bos, Camelus, Dama, Elephas, Felis, Gryphus, Hydra, Jumentum, Leo, Mulus, Nereus serpens magnus, Ovis, Panthera, Questor, Rhinoceros, Simia, Tigris, Ursa* (none supplied for *X* or *Z*). In addition, every letter of the alphabet and the numerals from 0 to 9 can be visualized in some picturesque form, as suggested in this plate. If you want to express the number 432, make an image of a man holding a book in his left hand; on the left side you will imagine a baker or a farmer holding a fork, and in the middle a woman seated on a tripod, giving these persons suitable actions (p. 62). *UCH* II, 1, 2, p. 61.

5.7. Astrologer at Work

In this beautiful engraving we see an astrological consultation with the tools of the astrologer's trade: a globe, dividers, spectacles, books of tables, and—here differing from his modern counterpart—direct observation of the skies. But there the realism ceases, for the sun, moon, and stars are all shining simultaneously. Since Fludd had already published a long exposition of practical astrology, he devotes this one mainly to the question of the "natal genius," whether angel or demon. Drawing principally on the Neoplatonists Porphyry and Iamblichus, he explains the various theories of beings who govern and enter the human soul at its birth. His own theory, preferring Christian doctrine, concludes that each person carries the influences of not one but several angels, mediated through the planetary genii, and that they can be identified through the natal horoscope. *UCH* II, 1, 2, p. 71.

5.8. Physiognomy

The science of physiognomy studies the "middle soul" of man as revealed in the body. This includes the skin color, gait, posture, deformities, hair, and every feature of the head, hands, nails, and legs. Fludd states dogmatically the psychological and moral conditions to be deduced from each variation. He then reverses the process by listing the features under the headings of the four humors and the planetary influences. Here are some typical observations: *large and fleshy feet* indicate foolishness in love, adultery, and love of injustice; *very hairy arms* indicate insanity, or rusticity; *a nose that nearly reaches the mouth* denotes a worthy and magnanimous man; *baldness* is a sign of subtlety and astuteness. The couple on the title page display *round faces* indicating deliberation, forethought, gentleness, and hiding their anger, *prominent upper lips* indicating prudence, and *large ears* promising good memory and long life, though with a tendency to guile and arrogance. *UCH* II, 1, 2, p. 116.

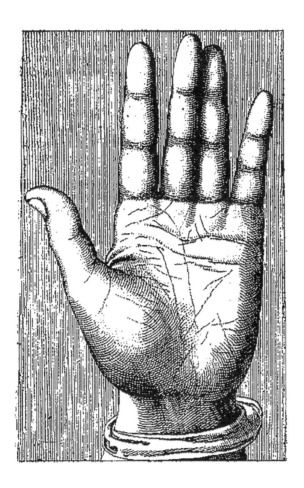

5.9. Chiromancy

Chiromancy and physiognomy, like their parent art of astrology, assume that a person's character is given at birth, and that the spiritual influences that formed his or her soul are visible in the body. However, this does not exclude a certain freedom, as Fludd explains. For the wise man, as is often said, dominates the stars, and much more so with the signs in physiognomy and chiromancy that warn of evil, in which the sidereal influences are immediately visible. For instance, if one sees a sign in a hand that the person should end their days at sea and suffer death in the waves, he will be able, if wise, to use two remedies against this danger. First, he should learn from the characters of his hand of the real danger to his life. Then with that in mind, he should restrain and control the voluptuous desires of his flesh and avoid sea voyages. In this way he will be less exposed to that danger that the fates have imposed on him according to the natural constitution of his birth. Thus he will escape from the malignity of the stars, and be ruled by his mind and protected by its guardian angel (p. 141). *UCH* II, 1, 2, p. 140.

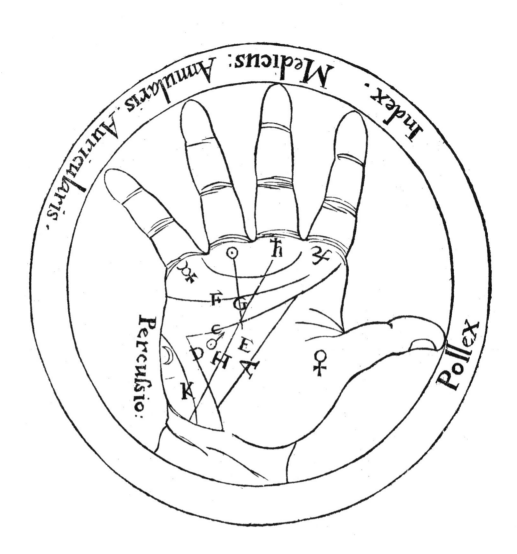

5.10. Parts of the Right Hand

This woodcut of a hand, copied from Cornelius Agrippa, shows the close relation to astrology in the areas or "mounds" named after the seven planets. This and the naming of lines after the head, the heart, and the liver suggest that the hand corresponds to the whole body: it is a microcosm of the microcosm, as it were. Marin Mersenne, in his attack on Fludd, was particularly averse to this science, and invited his opponent to interpret the markings of a palm that he illustrated. Fludd is not known to have responded to the challenge, though he believed that palmistry could reveal not only character but "women's secrets," including virginity or otherwise, and the sex of an unborn child. *UCH* II, 1, 2, p. 143.

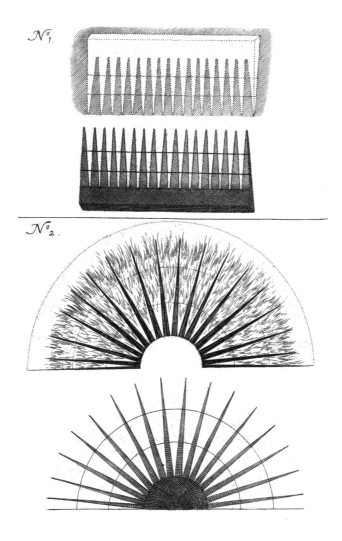

5.11. Dark and Light Combs

The inclusion of a "science of the pyramids" among the traditional psychological and divinatory arts is a surprise. Fludd had treated it exhaustively in his *History of the Macrocosm,* yet he always had more to say about it. He regarded it as one of his chief discoveries, and as giving the essential clue to understanding man: the two-sexed creature in whom form and matter, light and darkness, the divine and the chaotic meet. Thus he returns to it as the culmination of these studies, and offers two novel visualizations: We can also represent these dark and light pyramids as two combs: a light one representing the downward-pointing spiritual forces, and a dark one for the material world (see No. 1). As an adaptation of these combs, we present the two hemispheres of No. 2, the upper one corresponding to the male, generative nature, and the other to the female, receptive to the seed of light. This material hemisphere is like wax that can be formed by the seal of spirit (p. 188). The faint lines crossing the combs' hemispheres denote the three worlds, or the three parts of the human being, in which this process takes place. *UCH* II, 1, 2, p. 188.

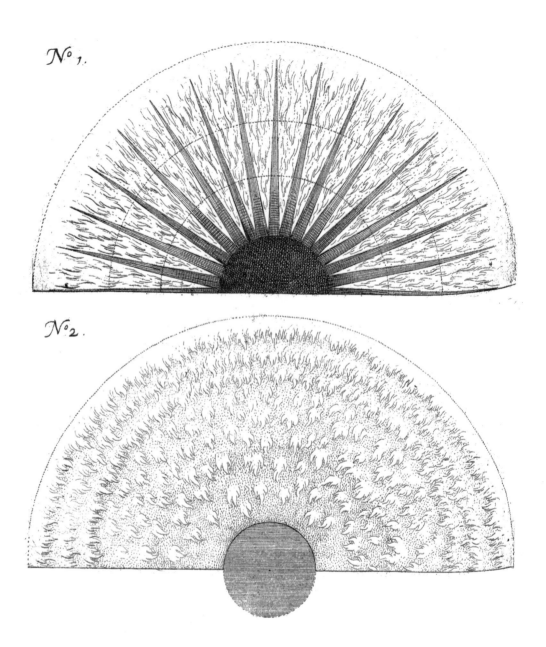

5.12. The Hemispheres United

We must now imagine the dark and light hemispheres united, so that no empty space remains between their interstices (No. 1). The actual result of this mixture is to be seen in No. 2, where the spiritual fire diminishes gradually as it approaches the earth. With this engraving Fludd concludes the current work, assuring the reader that knowledge of the material and formal pyramids is the principal key to our doctrine, or the portal by which one enters the enclosure of this Philosophy and indeed of every true natural science. But since few will be able to attain the mysteries of the heavens' constitution, for lack or difficulty in the true knowledge of these pyramids, I have set it out succinctly in this book, whereby lovers of this science may more quickly and easily reach the happy goal and end of their desire and honest aspiration (p. 191). *UCH* II, 1, 2, p. 190.

Six

Kabbalah

6.1. Jehovah's Wings

The devotee kneels before the Most High, saying "Under the shadow of thy wings will I rejoice" (Psalm 63:7). The Rosicrucian manifesto of 1614, *Fama Fraternitatis,* concluded with the same quotation. The clouds have parted so as to allow him direct vision of the Tetragrammaton, the unpronounceable four-lettered name of God usually written IHVH. It is commonly found in Christian iconography, especially Protestant. Christian Kabbalists such as Fludd could accommodate the three different letters to their doctrine of the Trinity. The fact that the letter *He* occurs twice was explained by the Holy Spirit as both joining the Father (*Iod*) to the Son (*Vau*) and proceeding from them. *UCH* II, 2, 1, folio A3'.

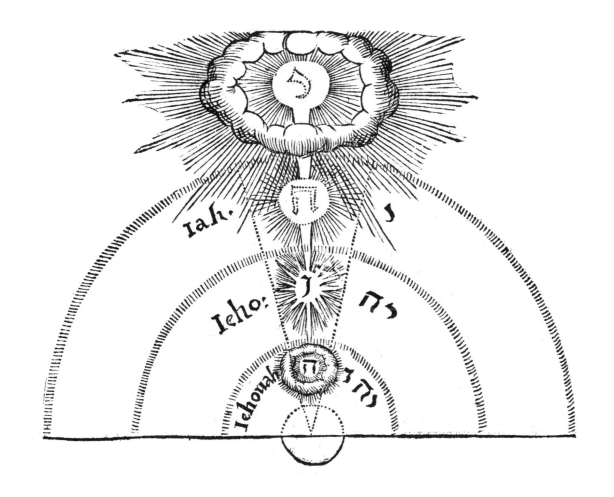

6.2. The Tetragrammaton in the Macrocosm

Hermes says that the world is an image of God, and Moses that man, too, is made after God's example. Hence all Kabbalists refer these lower realms to the archetypal one. This plate shows how the ineffable Name is imprinted on the universe. Above and beyond all is *Iod* י, the letter from which all proceeds and which conceals in itself the whole Name. From it emanates the empyrean world, symbolized by *He* ה. The psalmist says that God has placed his tabernacle in the Sun, and this we may interpret as follows: God forms around the Sun the ethereal world (*Vau* ו), dividing the empyrean from the lower *He* ה, the elemental world (pp. 5–6). The plate also shows how God's full name unfolds stage by stage: I, IH, IHV, IHVH, and encloses the letters within Fludd's symbolic pyramids, this being the descending pyramid of light or form. *UCH* II, 2, p. 6.

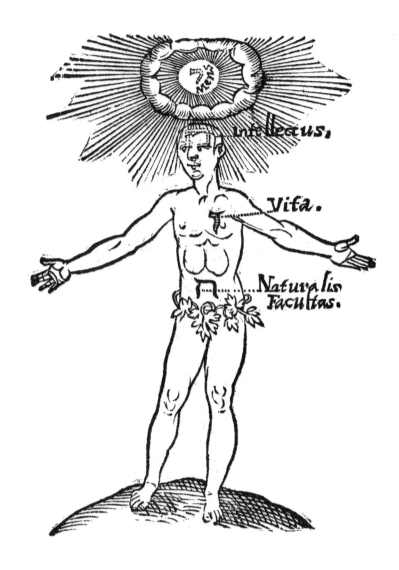

6.3. The Tetragrammaton in the Microcosm

As Fludd has frequently explained, man's faculties correspond to the regions of the universe. Thus they, too, can be seen as manifesting the divine Name. *Iod* is the higher mind, not contained by the physical body (compare ill. 4.1). Hence it is above the man's head, just as in the previous plate *Iod* is above the three worlds. *He, Vau,* and the lower *He* are, respectively, intellect, life, and the natural faculty. *UCH* II, 2, p. 8.

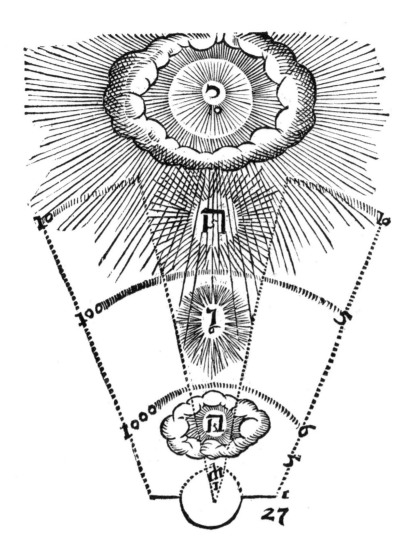

6.4. *The Tetragrammaton Numbered*

Here Fludd integrates the Tetragrammaton with two other numerical schemes of great importance to him: the series of simple, squared, and cubed numbers whose limits are 10, 100, and 1,000, and the number 27, which is the cube of 3 and the limiting number of the creation scheme of Plato's *Timaeus*. His procedure is ingenious, if somewhat forced. Since in Hebrew gematria (letter-number equivalents) the letters *Iod* (10), *He* (5), *Vau* (6), *He* (5) total only 26, Fludd adds *Aleph* (1) to bring the total to 27. He observes that there are only three different letters in the Tetragrammaton, and the third power of 3 is also 27. Moreover $3 \times 3 = 9$, and by taking three nines he arrives at 999, **denoting the nine roots of the world, namely the nine orders of angels, the nine orbs of the firmament, and the nine spheres of the elements.** By adding *Aleph,* he arrives at the limiting number of 1,000. *UCH* II, 2, p. 9.

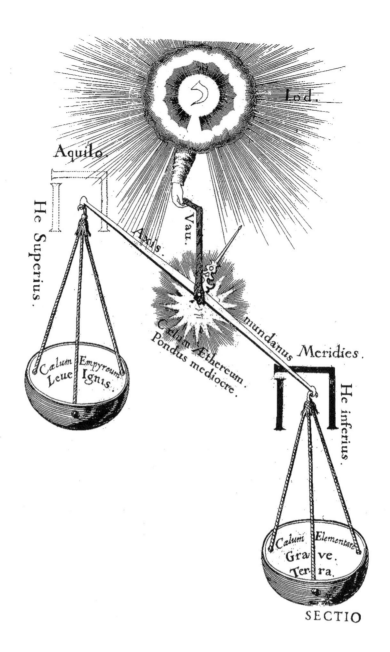

6.5. Weighing the Worlds

Another arrangement of the Tetragrammaton shows *Iod* as the supreme Deity holding a pair of scales. The point of balance is the Sun, whose pivotal position in the middle of the ethereal world Fludd emphasizes time and again. In a clever conceit, the two letters *He* are assigned to the two sides of the balance, one above the Sun, the other below. The left-hand balance rises because it represents the empyrean heaven, made of "light fire"; the right-hand one falls, being the "heavy earth" of the elemental heaven. The ethereal heaven is of "medium weight." The balance bar is the "axis of the world," joining north (Aquilo) and south (Meridies). Because Fludd's cosmos is geocentric, this is not merely the axis of the earth but that of the entire system centered around it. *UCH* II, 2, p. 11.

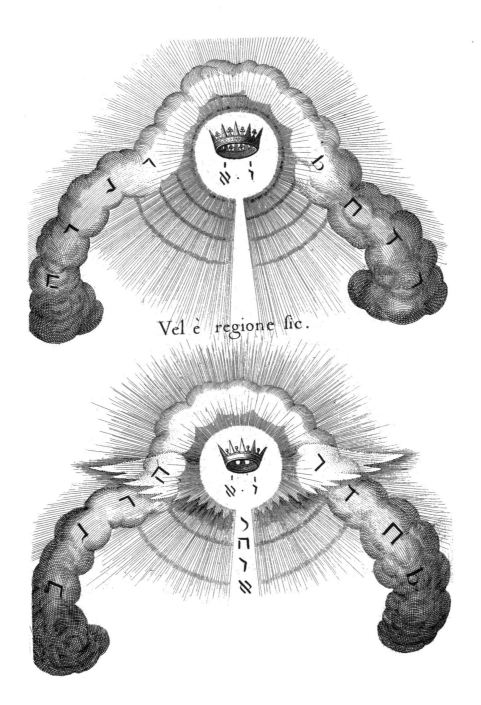

Vel è regione sic.

6.6. The Mystery of the Number 5

The engraver's lack of clarity in Hebrew lettering is aggravated here by one of Fludd's more confusing verbal explanations. The context is his assertion that while God and nature are not identical (as pantheists believe), God in some of his aspects is to be found in nature. Consequently we must use nature in our approach to God, like the rungs of Jacob's ladder, because otherwise the difference between our nature and God's is too great to be bridged (p. 41).

Fludd's text is largely inspired by the *Sepher Yetzirah,* the only non-biblical source he cites here. It encompasses the three worlds, the names of God, creation as a process involving higher elements, the simple numbers of 1 to 9 divided into odd and even, with 5 in central position, and the return of the soul to God. The plate borrows its

(ill. 6.6 continued from page 173)

basic form from ill. 6.1. God is represented here by a crown, the name of Kether, the highest of the *sephiroth.* Fludd signifies it both by the first letter of the Hebrew alphabet, *Aleph,* whose number is 1, and by the primal letter *Iod,* whose number is 10. In the clouds of the upper figure (*left*) the letters continue the alphabetical and numerical progression from *Aleph* to *Beth* (2), *Gimel* (3), *Daleth* (4) and *He* (5). These align, says Fludd, with the first five members of a ninefold cosmic hierarchy: three divisions of angels, the stars and upper planets, and the sun. Whereas in the previous plate, the sun was assigned the letter *Vau,* here it has the letter *He* and the privileged number 5, because it is at the midpoint of the three worlds with their nine divisions. The sun is God's particular tabernacle in the center of the universe, hence the most visible evidence of his presence in nature. All of this is supported with quotations from the Psalms and other biblical sources.

On the right, the series of Hebrew letters goes from *Iod* to *Mem, Cheth, Daleth,* and *Resh.* Fludd's reasons for choosing these letters, which do not make an arithmetical series, are obscure. He explains that whereas the *Aleph* here is the "Dark Aleph," symbol of the ultimate void before creation, *Iod* is the "Light Aleph," symbol of God the creator. *Mem* and *Cheth* are "the remainder of the darkness, from which creation is made," gate-shaped *Daleth* is "the gate through which wisdom enters the world," and *Resh* is "the life produced in the world by that wisdom" (p. 44).

The text mentions the return of all things to God "through what we wrongly call death." This gives a clue to the lower figure as complementary to the upper one, for it adds the protecting wings of God as seen from the human standpoint, and reverses the order of the Hebrew letters. The central column reads *Iod, He, Vau, Aleph,* glossed by Fludd as "the two formal letters embracing the two material letters" and spelling the name conventionally written "Jehovah." *UCH* II, 2, p. 42.

6.7. God's Omnipresence

Fludd's diagrams often show the earth as a dense sphere in the center, excluded from his celestial schemes. This plate takes up the theme of God's presence throughout nature, including the material earth. As in ill. 6.2, it assigns the four letters of the Tetragrammaton to God and the three worlds. But the copious quotations that Fludd gives concerning the bottom sphere (the material earth) support the current theme: "The Spirit of the Lord filleth the world" (Wisdom 1:7), "God is everywhere in heaven, in hell, in the uttermost parts of the sea, in night, in darkness" (paraphrase from Psalm 139), "Know therefore this day, and consider it in thine heart, that the Lord he is God in heaven above, and in the earth beneath there is none else" (Deuteronomy 4:39). *UCH* II, 2, p. 74.

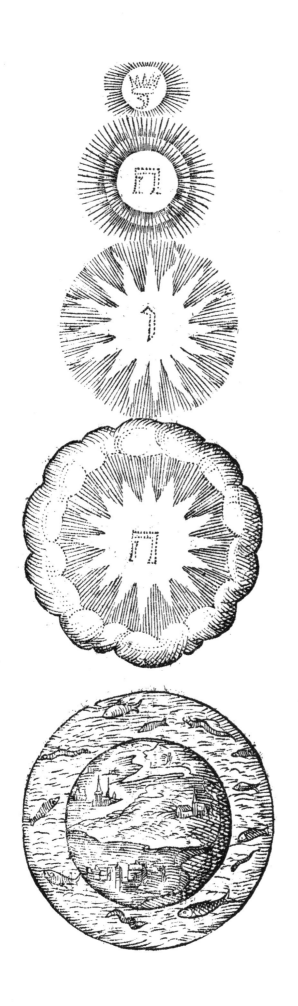

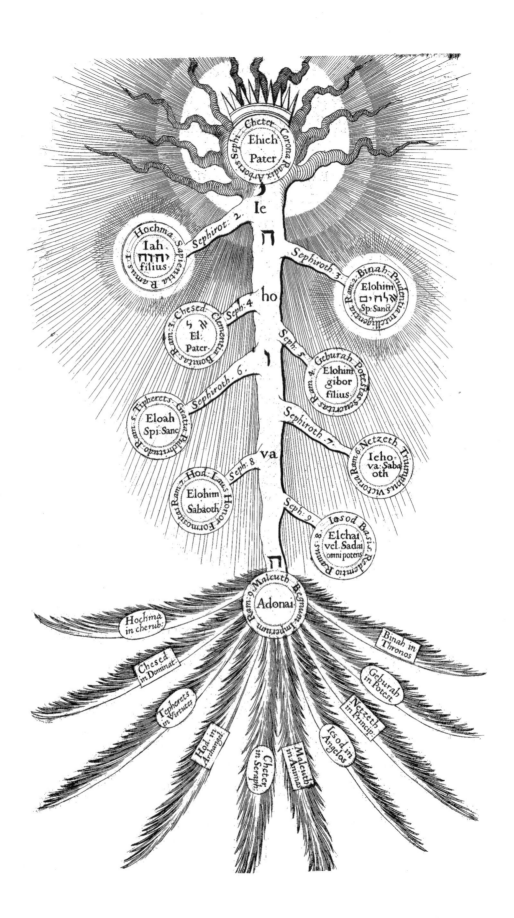

6.8. Sephirothic Tree

Fludd's idiosyncratic interpretation of the traditional Sephirothic Tree has its roots in Kether, the highest *sephira,* and the next eight emanations as branches on either side of a central trunk. Each globe contains, in the center, one of the names of God in Latin and sometimes Hebrew letters, and in the case of the first six *sephiroth,* identification with the Father, Son, or Holy Spirit. Around the circumference is its Hebrew name, a Latin translation, and its number (*ramus* = "branch" 1, 2, 3, etc.). Most interesting to Fludd is the bottom globe, Malkuth, from which sprout ten palm fronds, each again bearing the name of a *sephira* and one of the nine orders of angels (Seraphim, Cherubim, Thrones, Dominions, Virtues, Powers, Principalities, Archangels, Angels) plus *animae,* souls.

Thanks to his Kabbalistic studies, Fludd's system now achieves its complete form, with four worlds instead of his previous three. Kabbalah teaches that there are four levels of being: Atziluth, the "pure world" independent of manifestation, thus still contained by God; Briah, the world of creation, which is Fludd's empyrean world, inhabited by the angels; Yetzirah, the world of formation, which is Fludd's ethereal world of stars and planets; and Assiah, the material world, which is Fludd's elemental world. The bottom *sephira* (Malkuth) of each world becomes the source of the next lower world, which reflects it with its own version of the *sephiroth.* The present plate illustrates the process as it occurs in the two highest worlds. *UCH* II, 2, p. 157.

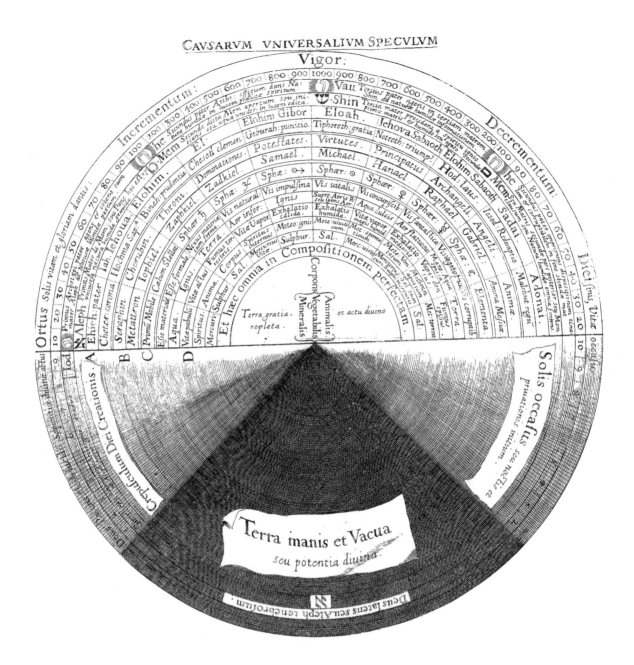

6.9, 6.10. Mirror of Universal Causation

Fludd offers this plate at the conclusion of his book on Kabbalah as a "treasure beyond price." It is one of his most complex and ingenious designs, combining three of his fundamental doctrines: emanation, correspondence, and cyclicity. Illustration 6.10 provides the helpful translation published by Manly Palmer Hall.* (The expression "Divine Power" in the bottom sector would be better phrased "Divine Potency," for it refers to God's quality of nonaction.)

The theory of emanation explains that higher principles do not create lower beings out of nothing, but emanate them as manifestations of themselves on inferior planes of existence. We read down one "chain," as an example, starting from the

*Hall, *Secret Teachings,* p. cxxii.

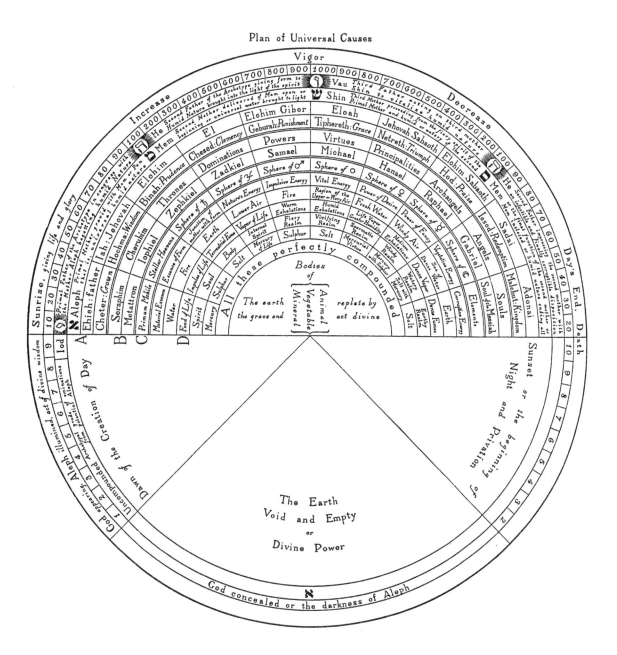

Hebrew letter *Vau* at the top of the chart. *Vau*, the archetypal Son or Word of God, emanates *Shin*, the Spirit that manifests as *Eloah*, the personal God. He emanates the *sephira* Tifereth, the grace or beauty of the universe that is built by the order of angels called Virtues. In the ethereal world this manifests through the archangel Michael, who resides in the Sphere of the Sun. The sun gives vital force, rules the upper region of the air, and causes humid exhalations and the "enlivening meteor." Of the three alchemical principles, it relates to salt.

The doctrine of correspondence teaches that each level of the hierarchy of being reflects the ones above it. So Michael's position among the archangels is like that of the sun among the planets, the heart in the body, gold among metals. The whole of magic rests on this doctrine, for it assumes that actions taken on one level will have repercussions in the corresponding ones. In making ritual objects of gold, for example, one is drawing down the solar forces into them and thus into the user.

KABBALAH

(ill. 6.9, 6.10 continued from page 179)

The third principle—that of cyclicity—is that time is not a straight line from infinity to infinity but a system of cycles, wheels within wheels, each unrolling in imitation of its superiors, from atomic particles up to galaxies and beyond. Humans experience these cycles as day and night, the seasons of the year, the individual's course from birth to death, the ages of world history, and so on. Fludd's diagram shows it on the outside ring as the sun's daily course. The cause of all these cycles, as hinted by the inscriptions on the dark part of the chart, is God's dual quality of action and nonaction (compare ill. 9.1, pp. 218–19).

Fludd offers this image not just for contemplation but, like all his circular charts, for practical use. He gives examples of how one can consult it to ascertain the causes behind phenomena, and especially the planetary and meteorological influences affecting humans. For instance, how would one discover the nature of the angel that ruled a person's birth, and that of the Olympian or elementary demon subject to it? What is the strongest power of his vital soul? What will be any man's more fortunate and unfortunate days? For this question, one should consider the sephiroth of the ruler of his horoscope and the ruler of the day in question. Which of two men fighting or litigating with each other will prevail in a certain contention, on a certain day? There you must consider the sephira of each one's nativity, with the strength or weakness of the lord of the heaven on the given day (p. 197). *UCH* II, 2, p. 181.

6.11. Mirror of the Macrocosm

This and the next plate (ill. 6.12) conclude Fludd's treatise on Kabbalah. They derive from the cyclical idea expressed in the previous plate, but make use of the whole circle rather than one-half of it. The principle is that everything begins in the darkness of potentiality, emerges into light, and returns to the darkness. The starting point is at the bottom, and progress is clockwise.

This plate expresses the origin and destiny of the macrocosm. The outer ring contains the four letters of the Tetragrammaton. *Iod,* says Fludd, is the Absolute Father, shrouded in incomprehensible darkness, who manifests through the Son and the Holy Spirit. The second ring contains the three "mother letters," which have a privileged place in Kabbalah: *Aleph, Mem* (in both normal and final forms), and *Shin. Aleph* can be both light and dark, expressing God's positive and negative aspects, so this circle begins with one and ends with the other. The third ring begins with potentiality, called the "upper waters" in the Genesis creation myth, and the

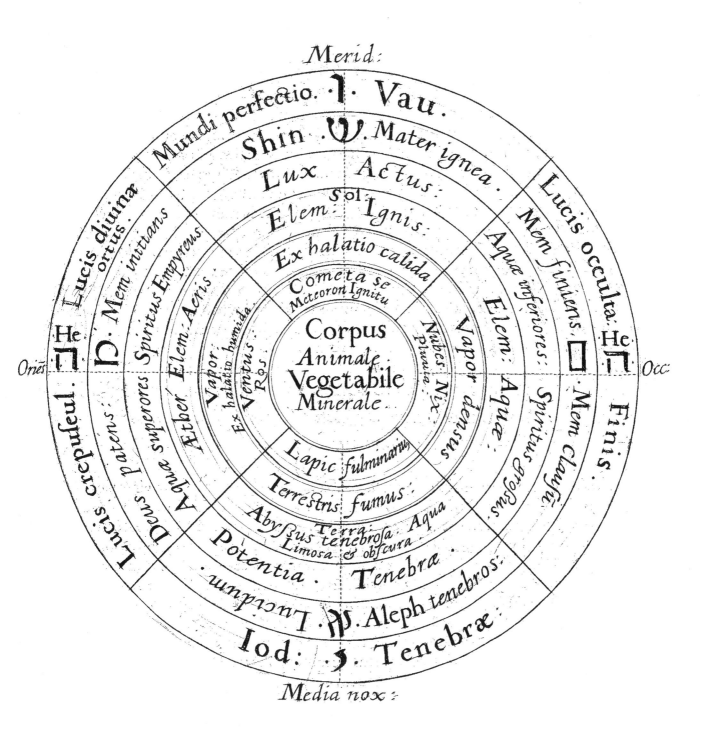

empyrean spirit. These culminate in perfect light and action. Proceeding round the ring we come to the lower waters and the gross spirit, allied to the darkness. The fourth ring contains the four elements. The fifth ring is the higher realm of "meteors," consisting of finer and denser vapors. The sixth ring shows meteors of the lower realm: dew, fiery comets, clouds, snow, rain, and the thunderstone. In the center is body, which can be animal, vegetable, or mineral. *UCH* II, 2, p. 198.

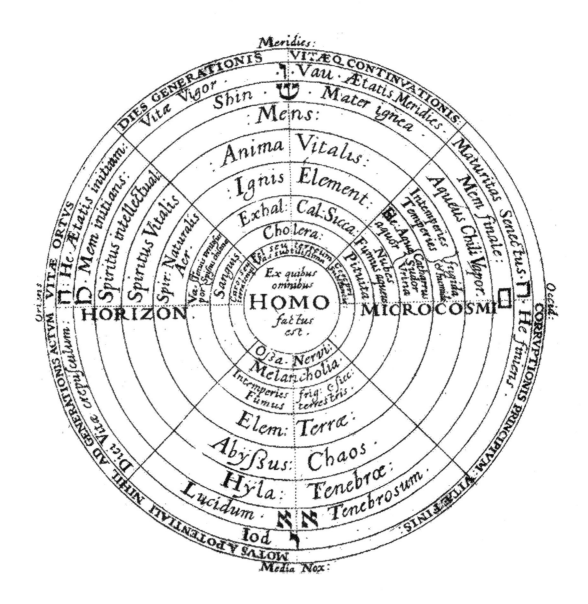

6.12. Mirror of the Microcosm

This plate complements the previous one by applying the same principle to the microcosm. The outermost ring summarizes the course of human life. It reads: "Motion from the nothingness of potentiality to the act of generation, the origin of life; the daytime of generation and the continuation of life; the beginning of corruption; the end of life." The second and third rings contain the two sets of Hebrew letters. The inner circles reflect the cosmic processes as they manifest in the microcosm, through psychic elements, subtle and material substances, weather conditions, humors, and organs, "from all of which man is made," as it says in the center. *UCH* II, 2, p. 199.

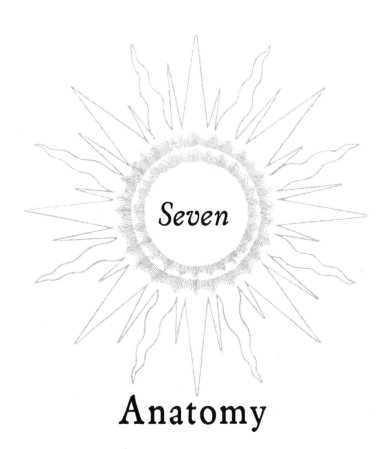

Seven

Anatomy

7.1. Soul, Body, and Bread ↷

The title page of Fludd's *Theatre of Anatomy* announces the three themes of the book: his experiment with wheat, the anatomy of the human body, and mystic anatomy. The figure embracing the large circle is "Man, or the Microcosm: the admirable receptacle of all these subjects." Within are three lesser circles:

1 (*above*): "The external image of man's mystic anatomy." The sacred monogram IHS (Jesus) is at the center, around which are two rings marked *A* and *B*. The small circle to the left explains them: Jesus is the "light or center of men," and the first of man's three internal members, the others being *spiritus* or air (*A*) and the soul (*B*). This diagram also shows and names the four winds, issuing from angelic heads at the four corners. They are ruled by the archangels Gabriel (north), Michael (east), Uriel (south), and Raphael (west), and have the respective properties of congesting, generating, dissolving, and conserving. Much of the treatise is concerned with the influences of these winds on the human body and the ailments and cures associated with them.

2 (*left*): "The bright mirror of the anatomy of wheat or bread." Wheat, the "preeminent food of man," was the subject of an alchemical experiment of enormous significance to Fludd. He describes it in the first part of this book, telling of how he separated wheat into its four elements and its quintessence, along with the many macrocosmic conclusions he drew from this process (see ills. 7.2–7.17, pp. 186–87). The tall bottle resembles that in which Fludd had separated the five elements of wine (see ill. 2.16, p. 49). The small circle (*bottom*) reads: "Three things are necessary to make anatomy accessible." They are the subject—here bread (*A*) and wheat (*B*), the dissected members or elements (*C, D, E, F, G*) and the instruments—alembic and retort (*I, K*).

3 (*right*): "The living effigy of common anatomy." A scene of dissection is treated in a similar threefold way. The small circle reads: "Three watch over common anatomy": the subject of dissection (*A*), the dissector (*B*), and his instruments (*C*).

The three large circle are joined by a triangle along whose side are written the words "Heaven or *spiritus*," "Earth or body," and "The food of man." C. H. Josten has pointed out that the three apexes join the monogram IHS with the level in the bottle equivalent to air, and the surgeon's ear. He suggests that they "probably meant to convey the idea that the Word of God (as nourishing to man as wheat or bread) is manifested to him by sound propagating itself through the medium of air".[*]
AA, title page.

---

[*]Josten, "Robert Fludd's 'Philosophical Key,'" p. 23.

ANATOMIÆ AMPHITHEA
TRVM EFFIGIE TRIPLICI, MORE
ET CONDITIONE VARIA, DESIGNATVM

Authore
Roberto Fludd, *alias de Fluctibus, Armigero & in Medicina D: Ox:*

Francofurti Súmptibús Iohannis Theodori de Brÿ 1623.

THE EXPERIMENT ON WHEAT

As prelude to his treatise on anatomy, Fludd undertakes to expound "the exact anatomy of bread or wheat," which is also "the lesser philosophic key." The illustrations are not engraved, but are small and rather crude woodcuts. The book opens with images of a sheaf of wheat (7.2, *AA*, p. 3) and of stalks growing on a mound (7.3, *AA*, p. 4). Fludd begins with a series of biblical quotations about wheat and bread, from which he distinguishes between heavenly and earthly bread (7.4, *AA*, p. 5). They correspond to the soul and body of man, and also to the hidden and literal meaning of the Scriptures. In both cases, by investigating the outer form, one learns about the inner and mystical content (p. 9). As man is to the animal world, so is wheat in the vegetable world: its most excellent member, and God's tabernacle. For this reason Jesus chose bread to represent his own body. Containing all four elements plus the quintessence, it serves as man's perfect food and the maintainer of health.

Fludd chose for his experiment the time of planting, when wheat seeds are put to putrefy in the soil. He seems to have put the seeds with water in a large glass vessel, then embedded it in straw containing rotting horse dung. This provided a gentle heat that reduced the matter to a putrid mass (7.5, *AA*, p. 25). A stronger heat came from placing the vessel over an underground fire, whereupon a column of smoke "nearly ten cubits high" arose from it (7.6, *AA*, p. 27). Then, just as in the Alps a dense fog resolves itself as rain, the cloud was converted to drops of water (7.7, *AA*, p. 28).

The next procedure was to separate the unwanted part of this water, just as the human body discards part of its fluid intake as urine. Fludd illustrates three different heating devices (7.8, *AA*, p. 29). By varying the heat, he distilled a liquid that was different from ordinary water: it was the same fluid as attracts *spiritus* into the blood and into human and animal seed. He describes seven experiments performed with it. The first resulted in a crystalline substance somewhat like snow or fine hail, which upon heating resolved into a liquid resembling potable gold (7.9, *AA*, p. 30).

The second experiment referred not to the present process but to a memory from Fludd's travels in Provence. When he was in Nîmes and practicing swimming, he dived down to the bed of a river and picked up two stones. Clashing them together made a terrible sound "because of the air included in the water" (p. 30). This confirmed that all water contains air or *spiritus* within it. The third experiment returns to his laboratory, where his assistant, a Frenchman, suddenly called him to see an extraordinary phenomenon. On a thin sheet of iron, which had covered the pot of putrefied wheat for about five weeks, ten thousand spikes were sprouting like yellow wheat shoots (7.10, *AA*, p. 30). This proved that the *spiritus* from the material could penetrate iron.

The fourth experiment placed the white crystalline *spiritus* in the sunlight. After a few hours its color had turned ruby red. Fludd deduced that an analogous

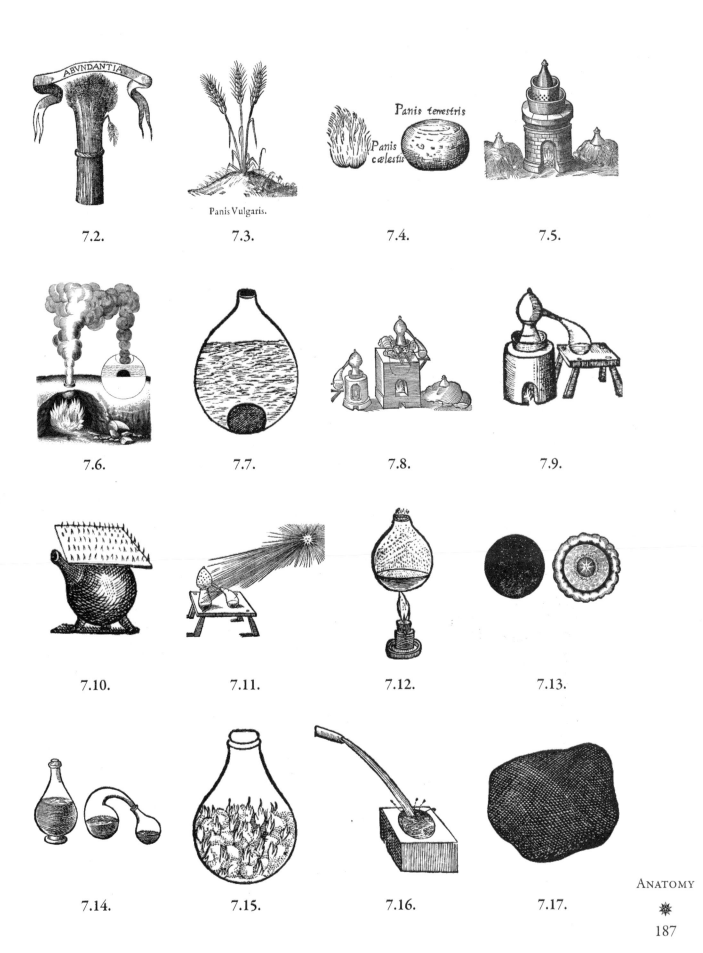

ABVNDANTIA

7.2.

Panis Vulgaris.

7.3.

Panis terrestris

Panis cælestis

7.4.

7.5.

7.6.

7.7.

7.8.

7.9.

7.10.

7.11.

7.12.

7.13.

7.14.

7.15.

7.16.

7.17.

process causes the growth of vegetables, uniting the active, masculine sunlight with the passive, feminine material (7.11, *AA*, p. 31). In the fifth experiment Fludd observed "with diligent speculation" that the *spiritus* diffused throughout the world is the denser and more material part of the quintessence. The sixth experiment showed that the slightest application of heat caused the crystalline *spiritus* to fragment into myriad atoms (7.12, *AA*, p. 32). It reminded Fludd of Epicurus's doctrine that all things are made from atoms. In the seventh and last experiment of this series, he discovered that a single grain of wheat, immersed for a few days in this *spiritus,* became diaphanous and glass-like.

This experiment, which Fludd describes with much more theorizing than practical details, demonstrated what he already knew from his cosmological studies: that the four elements, plus the quintessence, derive ultimately from the primordial chaos. He had depicted it memorably in his *History of the Macrocosm* (see ill. 2.7, p. 40). Now he shows a smaller version, setting it side by side with a diagram of the elements (7.13, *AA*, p. 33). Another set of experiments follows. The first explains "How the element of fire produces melancholy and dark or diabolic illnesses." Devils have bodies of air (which is why we do not see them), but their inner nature is the subtler element of fire. Whereas God's fire gives life, that of the devils works in the contrary way, causing corruption and diseases such as delirium, insomnia, desperation, lycanthropy, and insanity. The parallel with this simple distilling device seems extremely forced (7.14, *AA*, p. 35).

Fludd's ultimate vision presents "that which alchemists call the quintessence, the philosophers aether, and poets the Elysian Fields." The culmination of the experiment with wheat was the extraction of this from a dark, spongy substance in the alembic (7.15, *AA*, p. 36). It was a most laborious task, he says, requiring a new sort of heat. **Then truly I saw with open eyes how wonderfully this balsam was constituted, for with minimal heat it became liquid, blood-red in color, filling the whole vase with atoms; and with the cooling of the air it immediately rained down in a diaphanous and lucid substance like a precious stone, partly crystal-clear, partly of the golden tincture of the hyacinth, like a crystal glass, everywhere glittering with sparks like tiny bright stars.** After this awe-inspiring vision Fludd modestly warns the reader that he has not achieved the pure quintessence of the Philosophers, but only made it visibly distinguishable from the other four elements.

Fludd now washed out his vessel, discarding the burnt matter that seemed useless to him. He poured it into a hollowed stone used for collecting rainwater. After five days he found the water full of thin, white worms (7.16, *AA*, p. 38). Since no such creatures had ever appeared there before, he realized that they had come from the quintessence, and that it functions the same way in animals as in vegetables: hence the life-giving quality of bread. Fludd's next experiment was to cure a chronic pain in his hand by anointing it with the "golden balsam." He also noted the delicious perfume that distinguished the substance from those made from other elements (p. 39).

Finally Fludd was left with the *caput mortuum,* the alchemical equivalent of the utter darkness at the center of the earth. He tried burning it by pouring on oil and lighting it like a lamp wick, to no effect, then threw it into the fire, where it glowed like a coal. After it had cooled, it had more of a metallic quality, and Fludd abandoned it on a heap of wood. However, after five hours it began to burn again, and if it had not been noticed and extinguished, it would have set the house afire (7.17, *AA,* p. 41). Thus, with a narrow escape from disaster, his alchemical experiment concluded.

FLUDD'S ANATOMICAL ILUSTRATIONS

Fludd opens his treatment of physical anatomy with a Latin oration that he gave in 1620 before the College of Physicians. It displays his usual florid style and pious sentiments, exalting the human body as the microcosmic mirror of God's creation, its perfection in design and function, yet its capacity for temptation and sin. Presumably it was followed by the demonstration of dissection, made by a barber-surgeon with Fludd's commentary. After this Fludd makes a surprising disclaimer, saying that the anatomical illustrations that follow were included against his wishes but at the insistence of the publisher, Johann Theodor de Bry (pp. 62–63). The latter had argued that this would save Fludd from trouble and expense, and that it would make the work cheaper and more accessible to students. Thus Fludd was forced to accept the insertion of nearly fifty engravings that de Bry had made for a publication of 1605: Gaspard (Caspar) Bauhin's *Theatrum Anatomicum,* dedicated to Landgrave Moritz of Hesse. What Fludd does not mention is that virtually all of these engravings were careful copies from Andreas Vesalius's *De Humani Corporis Fabrica Libri Septem* (Basel, 1543). That work founded the modern science of anatomy, and its superbly detailed woodcuts set the standard for anatomical illustration. Eighty years later they were still being borrowed, copied, and plagiarized, while the science itself had made negligible advance, owing to the extreme difficulty of obtaining human corpses for dissection. As far as anatomical accuracy was concerned, Fludd could not have done better.

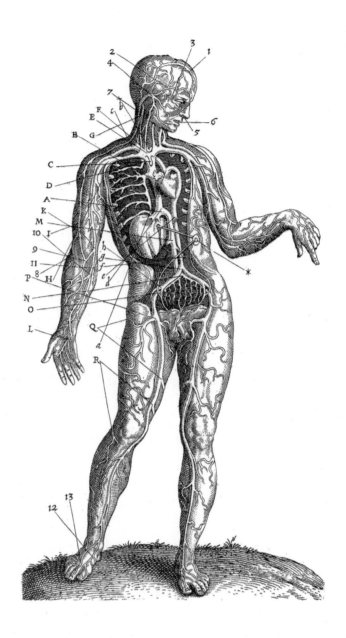

7.18. The Venous System

This, with 7.21, is one of the few illustrations not taken from Bauhin. It is ultimately derived from Vesalius, and shows the latter's detailed mapping of the venous system, each vein being identified by a letter or number. However, it does not take account of William Harvey's discovery of the circulation of the blood, which Fludd readily accepted for symbolic as much as for anatomical reasons (see comment to ill. 9.19, pp. 236–37). *AA*, p. 84.

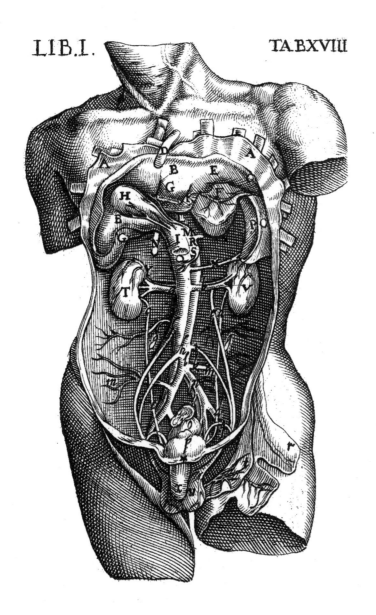

7.19. The Torso Dissected

This dissection, taken from Vesalius (book V, fig. 20), shows the connections of the liver, spleen, and gallbladder with the male genito-urinary system. According to the modern editors of Vesalius, it shows his occasional reliance on animal rather than human dissections, for the position of the kidneys is as in the ape, and the kidneys are those of a dog.* *AA,* p. 113.

———————
*Vesalius, *Illustrations from the Works,* p. 166.

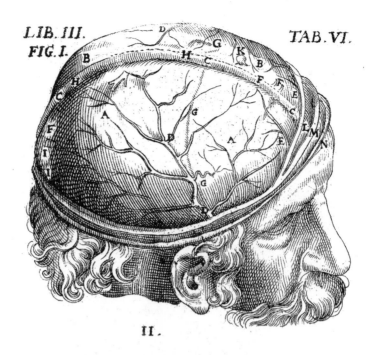

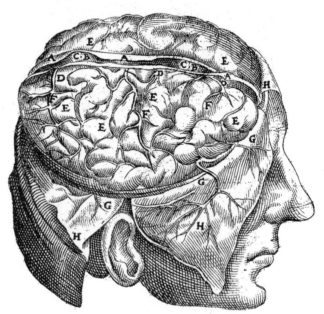

7.20. The Brain

The engraving reproduces the first stage of Vesalius's dissection of the brain.* Its origin is from sperm, whence it is white. Its substance is soft, liquid, and similar to marrow, the better for it to receive impressions and sensible properties from the operations of the soul. Its size is greater in man than in animals of the same weight and dimensions, for nature has fashioned it to include more capacities and consequently more functions (p. 157). *AA*, p. 156.

*Vesalius, *Illustrations from the Works,* p. 189.

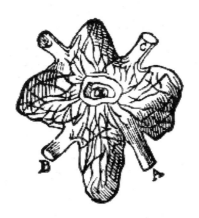

7.21. The "Wonderful Net"

This small woodcut is included for the insight it gives into Fludd's anatomical studies. It depicts the *rete mirabile,* a network of blood vessels in the brain, whose function, says Fludd following Galen, is "to contain the vital spirits flowing from the heart into the brain." The image was specially copied from one of the engravings in Bauhin's *Theatrum Anatomicum* that was not included in Fludd's book.[*] It originates from Vesalius,[†] who established that the human brain contains no such organ. Galen had found it in the brains of sheep and cows, and wrongly assumed that it occurs in humans too. Bauhin explains all this clearly.[‡] We have already noted Fludd's annoyance at having Bauhin's plates used to illustrate his own book. This detail, so significant in the theory of *spiritus,* shows that Fludd had not had access to Bauhin's book, and possibly not even to Vesalius's. *AA,* p. 168.

---

[*]Bauhin, *Theatrum Anatomicum,* p. 607. On this, see Sugg, *The Smoke of the Soul,* p. 286.
[†]Vesalius, *Illustrations from the Works,* p. 199.
[‡]Bauhin, *Theatrum Anatomicum,* p. 609.

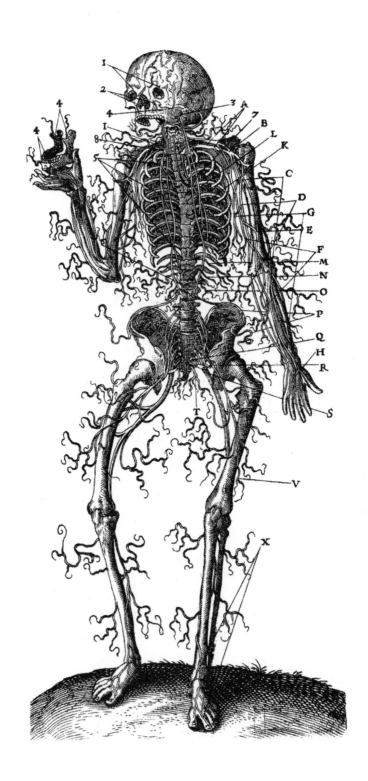

7.22. *The Skeleton and the Nerves*

This haunting illustration, not taken from Vesalius, is titled "Universal mirror of the nerves, both of the brain and the spinal cord, emerging from the appropriate bones." *AA,* p. 184.

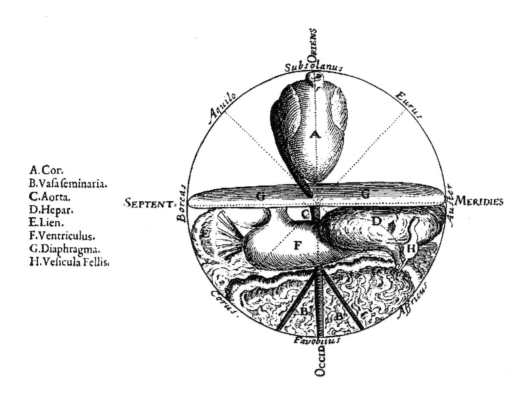

A.Cor.
B.Vafa feminaria.
C.Aorta.
D.Hepar.
E.Lien.
F.Ventriculus.
G.Diaphragma.
H.Veſicula Fellis.

7.23. Mystic Anatomy

With the conclusion of his "vulgar anatomy," Fludd returns to more congenial ground
and to illustrations in symbolic mode. Man the microcosm, he says, is naturally
oriented to the four directions: his face to the east, his right to the south, his left to
the north, and his back to the west. From those directions come the four winds, which
are the bearers of health and disease. Four organs serve as the principal receptors of
their influences. This schematic diagram shows the heart (*top*), which corresponds
to the east; the spleen (*left*), which receives the effects of the north wind; the liver
(*right*), from the south; and the spermatic vessels (*below*), from the west. *AA*, p. 214.

7.24. The Great Monochord (overleaf)

Fludd's treatise on anatomy continues with his answer to Johannes Kepler's criticisms,
titled *Monochordum Mundi*. For this he prepared the most complete representation
of his syncretic cosmology. At the top are four all-embracing statements that combine
Hermetic, Platonic, and Kabbalistic doctrines.

> The monad generates a monad and reflects its ardor in itself.
> The One is all things and all things are the One.
> GOD is all that there is: from him all things proceed and to him all things
>   must return.
> The infinite dimension of the Tetragrammaton: in and between all things.

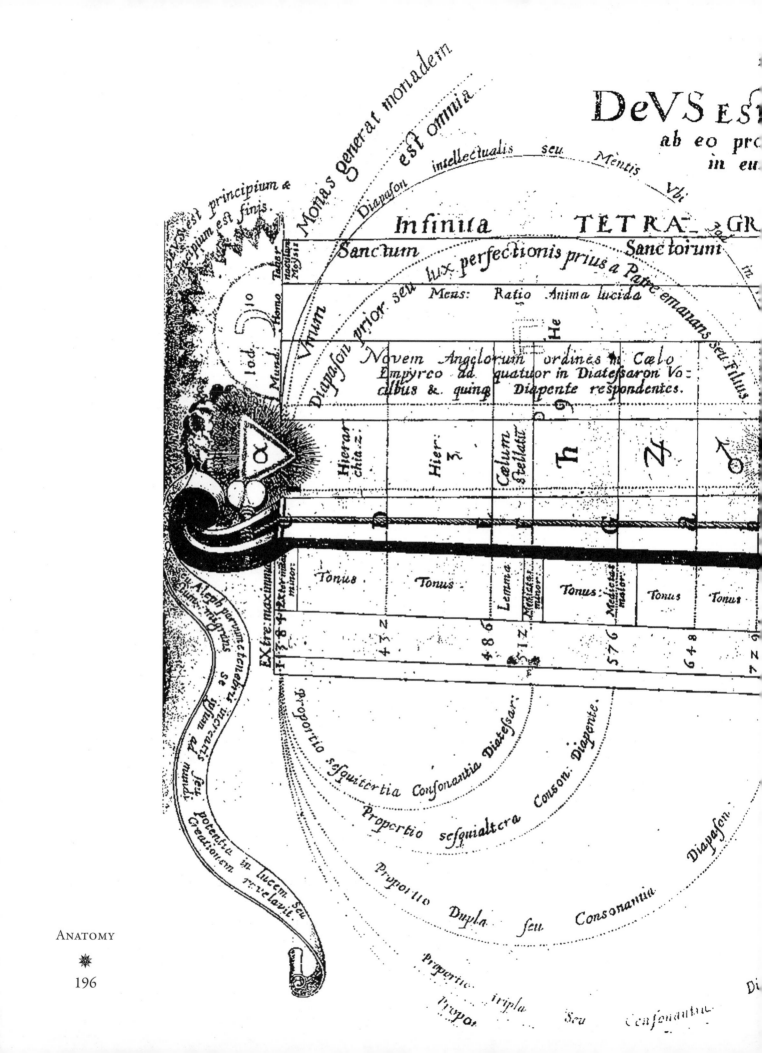

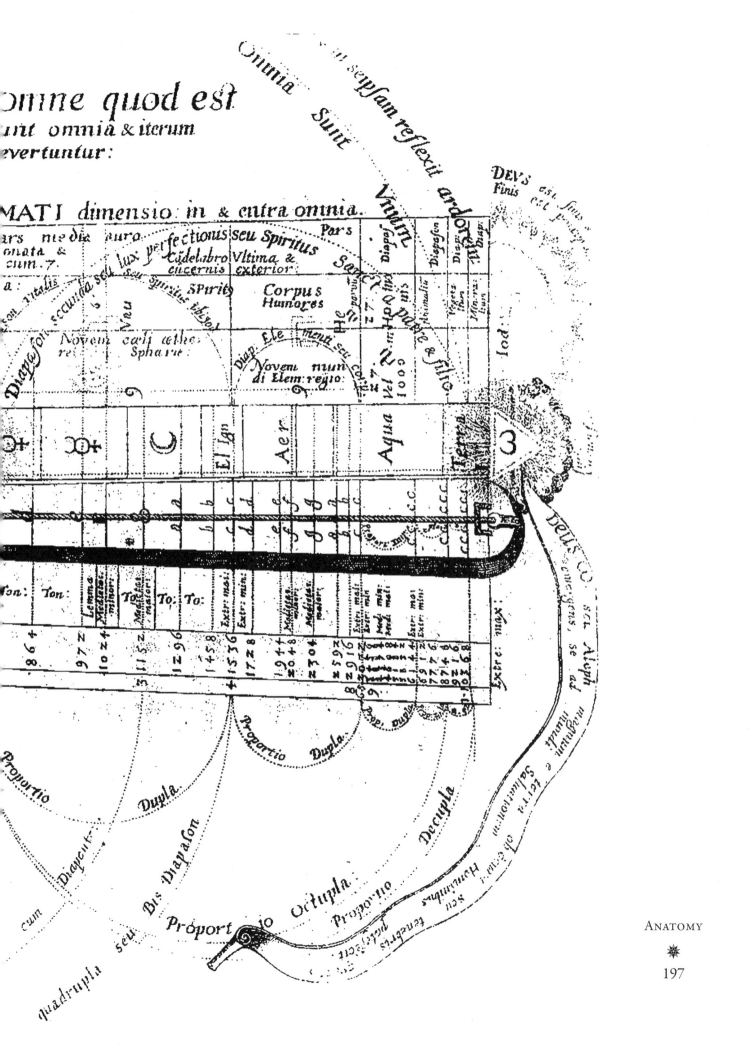

(ill. 7.24 continued from page 195)

Turning the page so that the tuning-peg of the monochord is at the top, we see an *alpha* in a blazing triangle. This is the symbol of God as beginning: "The central principle or Dark Aleph." At the other end of the string is an *omega,* symbol of God as "end and circumference." Toward the upper corners are parallel statements: "God is the beginning, and the beginning is the end"; "God is the end, and the end is the beginning." Another symbol of this reciprocity is the Tetragrammaton, spelled out in palindromic form: *Iod, He, Vau, He, Iod* and drawn in dotted lines from one end to the other.

The scrolls issuing from the *alpha* and *omega* read:

> "God (alpha), or the Lesser Aleph of the uncreated darkness, or potency, reveals itself for the world's creation by changing to light, or act."
> "God (omega), or the Greater Aleph, emerging from dark earth or the created darkness, reveals itself to men for the world's salvation."

The chart combines several of Fludd's favorite systems—Kabbalistic, harmonic, Platonic, cosmological, mystic-anatomical—which do not always align with each other. On the string of the monochord are the notes of the diatonic scale for three octaves from C to c3 (wrongly written *cc*), and thereafter the octaves alone up to c6 (correctly written *ccccc*). This is musically correct, as are the proportions of string length and the intervals marked on the lower arcs. Between c6 and the bridge at the omega end, there is in theory an indefinite series of higher octaves. Similarly, the numerals in the left-hand column, which give the proportions of string length for each scale tone in the lowest possible whole integers, could continue from 10,368 to infinity if space allowed. The intervals between the steps (*tonos, lemma,* etc.) are named in the adjacent column.

To the right of the monochord string are the symbols of the planets, part of the familiar system of three worlds or heavens (compare ill. 2.27) that are defined in the adjacent column:

> Nine orders of Angels in the Empyrean Heaven, corresponding to the four notes of the diatessaron (fourth) and five of the diapente (fifth)
> Nine spheres of the Ethereal Heaven
> Nine regions of the Elemental World

Whereas the musical system began at the top of the monochord and culminated at the *omega* with infinitely small intervals, the divisions of worlds begin with the earth and increase in size (each one, we recall, being a sphere concentric with the earth) until they reach the all-containing infinity of the *alpha*.

The next column to the right names the corresponding parts of man (compare ill. 4.5): Mind, Reason, Lucid Soul; Life, *Spiritus*; Body, Humors. They are glossed on three diminishing semicircles:

> The octave of Intellect or Mind, where *Iod* is in *He*
> The octave of Life or *Spiritus* where *Iod* [*sic*]
> The elemental or corporeal octave

These constitute the "lesser Aleph." Beneath is the "least Aleph" of the animal, vegetable, and mineral creations, each an octave in its own right.

The final row refers to the parts of the Tabernacle of Moses, also divided into three: the Holy of Holies; the middle part decked with gold and with seven candlesticks; the last, the exterior part. The seven candlesticks of the menorah, which symbolizes the six planets grouped around the sun, may be the reason for the second sun engraved here in the middle of the appropriate region. *AA,* pp. 314–15; *SM,* pp. 54–55.

Eight

Meteorology

8.1. Cosmic Meteorology ↝

Fludd applies the term "meteor" to any heavenly phenomenon, from the weather to the planets and even the fixed stars. In this book, titled *The Holy and Truly Christian Philosophy, or Cosmic Meteorology,* he surveys them all, refuting the notions of Aristotle, whose *Meteorologia* still passed as authoritative. Fludd's object is to demonstrate how the divine influences proceed down the chain of being from God to the angels, from these to the planets, thence to the winds, and finally to man. The title page with its vivid scenes shows the results of "macrocosmic meteors," most of which are catastrophic. Various combinations of wind, water, and earth are the immediate causes, producing rains of fire (*upper left*), tempests at sea (*upper right*), earthquakes (*lower left*), and the devastating combination of wind, thunder, lightning, rains, and falls of stones from the sky (*upper center*). Only the scene at *lower right,* where the south wind blows, is pleasant and pacific.

The side panels show some meteors of the upper regions, together with two of the archangels who play a large part in the meteorological economy. On the left is Michael, the solar angel of the east, subduing the dragon, and above him are three suns beneath a rainbow. Similar pictures appeared both before and after Fludd's time to illustrate the rare and awe-inspiring phenomenon of multiple images of the sun known as *parhelion* or "sun dogs." On the right-hand panel, the archangel Gabriel interprets to the prophet Daniel his dream of the four beasts, seen at their feet. Above Daniel are comets of various shapes, which Fludd later catalogues (see ill. 8.3, pp. 205–9).

The bottom panel shows microcosmic man. His internal organs are pictured with their correspondences to the cardinal directions and winds, as Fludd had explained in his previous book (see ill. 7.23, p. 195). *PS,* title page.

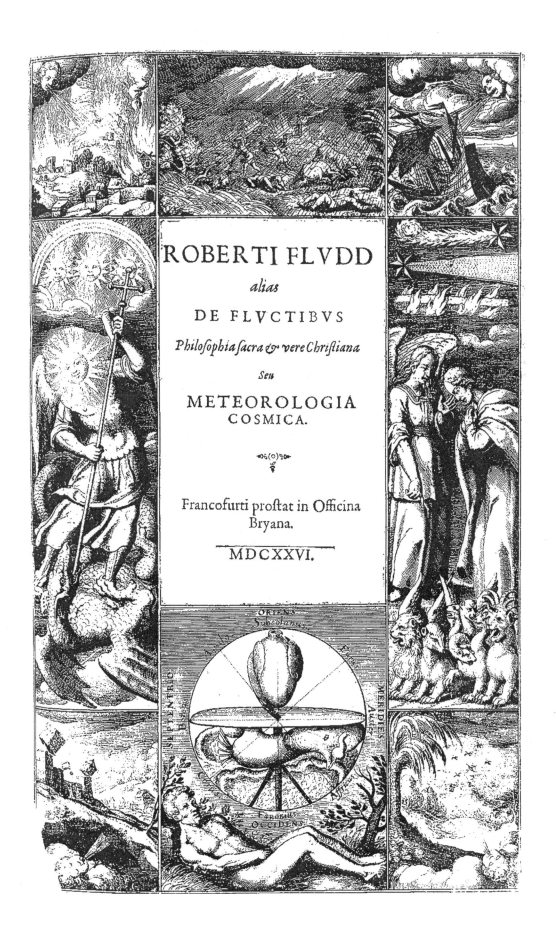

ROBERTI FLVDD
alias
DE FLVCTIBVS
Philosophia sacra & vere Christiana
Seu
METEOROLOGIA
COSMICA.

Francofurti prostat in Officina
Bryana.

MDCXXVI.

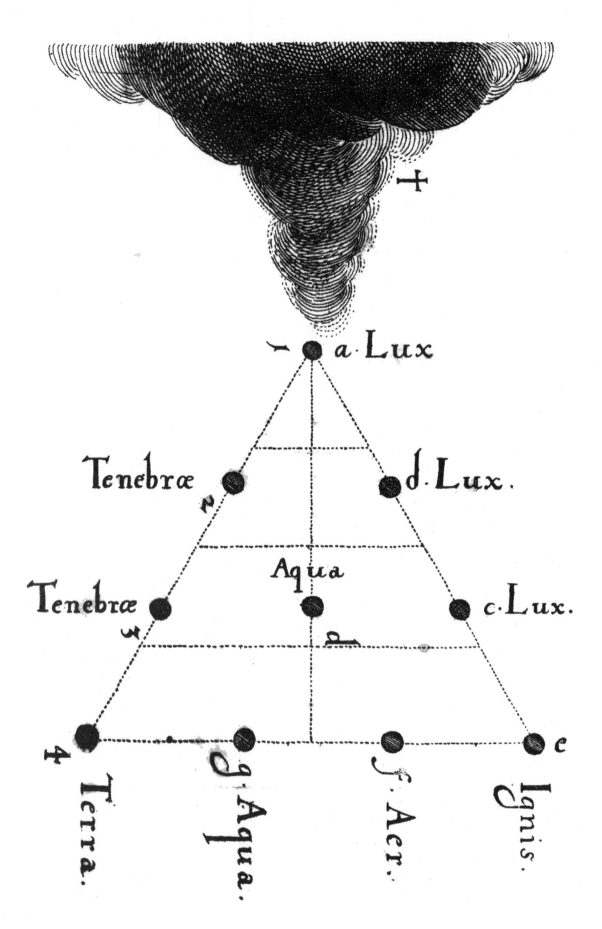

Among the models of creation that Fludd integrated into his system was the *tetraktys*, the symbol of ten dots in triangular form, revered as sacred by the Pythagoreans. Fludd adapts it here to the creation myth of Genesis. We see light (*a*) as God's first creation from the cloud of chaos. This is the Monad. The Dyad is the division of light from darkness (2, on the *left*; *b*, mistakenly written *d*, on the *right*). The Triad (*d*) is the "humid spirit" that emerges between them, and from that comes the Tetrad of elements (4, *g, f, e*), bringing the number of principles up to ten. Fludd borrowed this mathematical philosophy from Francesco Giorgio, whose *De Harmonia Mundi* (1525) also supplied him with his ideas of musical proportion as a universal scheme. *PS*, p. 33.

8.3. The Great Meteorological Chart (overleaf)

Every heavenly phenomenon that can affect or afflict mankind is shown in this remarkable chart. At the top, as always, is God, symbolized by the Tetragrammaton. Since no image can represent, nor any human mind comprehend him in his infinity, the Kabbalists and secret theologians use also the word Ensoph, which signifies infinitude (p. 142). Flanking God are ten compartments that are the emanations from his ten Hebrew names. Each name or aspect of God "gushes forth" through the channel of one of the ten *sephiroth* (see ill. 8.6, p. 212). The names give life and essence to the orders of angels, who in turn direct the circles of the ethereal world. The correspondences are shown in the table on page 209.

God's special relationship with the sun is indicated in the upper center, where the angel Michael descends. One of Fludd's favorite quotations, "He hath placed his tabernacle in the sun" (Psalm 19:4), is written close by.

The large semicircle that dominates the central panel contains an encyclopedic collection of meteorological phenomena. Fludd categorizes them (pp. 145–46) as (1) those which exist and are seen, (2) those which exist but are not seen, and (3) those which are seen but do not exist. The first category includes the various types of comets depicted in the outside crescent (*left to right*):

> Trabs, a blazing beam-shaped comet
> Lances, a long, spear-like comet
> Xiphias, a shorter one, like a pointed sword
> Mercurialis, a small bluish comet with a long thin tail
> Miles, a red comet

METEOROLOGY

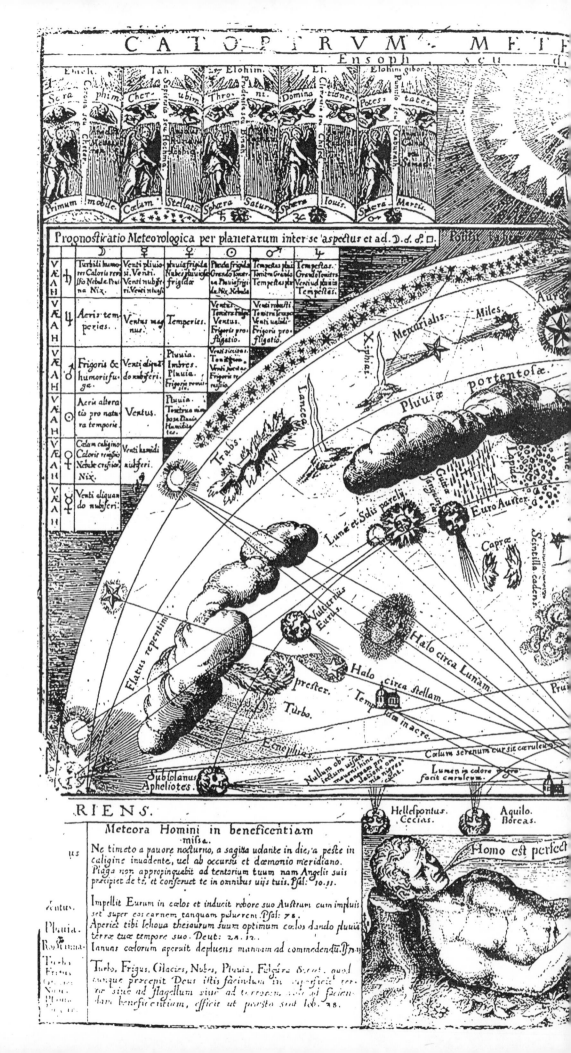

(ill. 8.3 continued from page 205)

Aurora, which looks like a star, but excels all in brightness and splendor

Rosa, a large, round comet with a human face

Tenaculum, which stands on a fiery base

Niger, a dark comet with a short tail

Ceratias, which has the shape of a horn or flame

Chasma and Scintilla volante, brief appearances of flames and flying sparks

Other things both visible and credible are the clouds in the next arc, and the things that fall out of them: "sudden winds," causing invisible hurricanes and whirlwinds as well as fiery exhalations, "monstrous showers" of blood, stones, frogs, thunderstones, hail, ordinary rain and snow. The sun's rays, penetrating the fissures in the clouds, cause "perpendicular lines," and when reflected from clouds in the evening they produce the illusion of a red sky.

Below the clouds, the twelve winds blow. In the lowest region are the real phenomena of "goats" (meteors that throw off jumping sparks), falling and shooting stars, and lightning flashes. Here the vapors form that cause hail and dew. The unreal phenomena are haloes round the sun, moon, or stars, mirages such as temples in the sky, rainbows, colorations of the moon, and magnification of the setting sun by vaporous air. The blueness of the sky is explained (*lower left*) by the combination of light with blackness.

The triangular chart on the left shows the influences of planetary aspects on the weather, according to the four seasons (*V* = spring, *AE* = summer, *A* = autumn, *H* = winter). Conjunctions, oppositions, and squares are treated alike for purposes of prognostication. On the right is another circle of planetary aspects, from which one can predict the "opening of the great gates of heaven" in the upper sphere. This occurs when the moon is passing out of conjunction, square, or opposition with the Sun, Jupiter, or Mars, and directly transiting Saturn, Mercury, or Venus—or vice versa. Then, in the opinion of all astrologers, there will be abundant rains and consequently great floods. The inner circle of the diagram shows the aspects that cause the opening of the lesser doors of heaven, with consequent rainfall. This is a secret that the astrologers seldom divulge, but it will be found very useful (p. 275).

The recumbent man in the lower panel says, "Man is the perfection and end of all creatures in the world." He seems to represent Adam before the Fall. *On the left,* a list of "meteors sent for man's benefit": good angels, wind, rain, dew, manna (thought to be derived from dew), storm, cold, ice, clouds, rain, and lightning. *On the right,* the "meteors sent for man's chastisement and punishment": bad angels, fiery whirlwinds (with and without demons), wind, rain, springs, thunder, lightning, and hail. All these are supported with biblical quotations of which the sources are given.

NAME OF GOD	SEPHIRA	ANGELIC ORDER	CHIEF ANGEL	ETHEREAL CIRCLE
Ehieh	Kether	Seraphim	Metatron	Primum Mobile
Iah	Hokhmah	Cherubim	Ruziel	Fixed Stars
Elohim	Binah	Thrones	Zabkiel	Saturn
El	Chesed	Dominions	Zadkiel	Jupiter
Elohim Gibor	Geburah	Powers	Samael	Mars
Eloah	Tifereth	Virtues	Michael	Sun
Jehovah Sabaoth	Netsah	Principalities	Anael	Venus
Elohim Sabaoth	Hod	Archangels	Raphael	Mercury
Sadai	Yesod	Angels	Gabriel	Moon
Adonai	Malkuth	Souls	Soul of the Messiah	Elements

PS, pp. 140–41.

8.4. Creation of the Primum Mobile

In expounding his meteorological theories, Fludd went back to first principles. On page 157 he reproduces the "FIAT" plate from the *History of the Macrocosm* (ill. 2.10, p. 43) and on the next page the "Creation of the Empyrean Sphere" (ill. 2.11, p. 44) from the same series. He then adds a new type of image, which would have filled the gap in the stages of creation as he had formerly depicted them. **When the darkness had been dismissed to the region of the earth, God made the Primum Mobile which gives movement and life to all the inferior spheres. It is the bearer of his wisdom and will, which are effected here below by the angels. For want of words to describe how God's wisdom acts in the whole world before the creation of the Sun, we depict it thus with the pen** (pp. 159–60). Here is proof, if proof were needed, that Fludd designed his famous cosmological diagrams himself. But it took the engraver's skill to give them elegant and memorable form. This new image, of the divine source of light sending out one of its rays to create a secondary, radiant center, would reappear several times. *PS,* p. 160.

8.5. Divine and Human Will

In this plate, as in the previous one, a greater source of light kindles a lesser source, which blazes in its turn. Here the sun sends its rays to meet light and dark objects. The upper one responds by giving off light; the lower remains dense and clouded. Both objects are heart-shaped, indicating the microcosmic aspect of this macrocosmic principle. For the human heart can either receive God's light and love, in which case it gives them out again, or it can refuse to let them penetrate the clouds of its own darkness. Fludd explains: **God acts out of will: not, as the Peripatetics say, out of necessity. Nothing is done in heaven or earth that does not derive its motion from the divine will. Only the dark mass of matter receives ill the acts of the divine mind, and "the darkness comprehendeth it not"** [John 1:5]. We could compare this to the action of the sun, which shines indifferently upon the whole earth, but whose rays are variously received according to the nature of bodies. The sun can make plants grow, yet it can also shrivel them. Similarly, the intellectual and invisible sun is one in its act but various in its effects (p. 164). *PS*, p. 165.

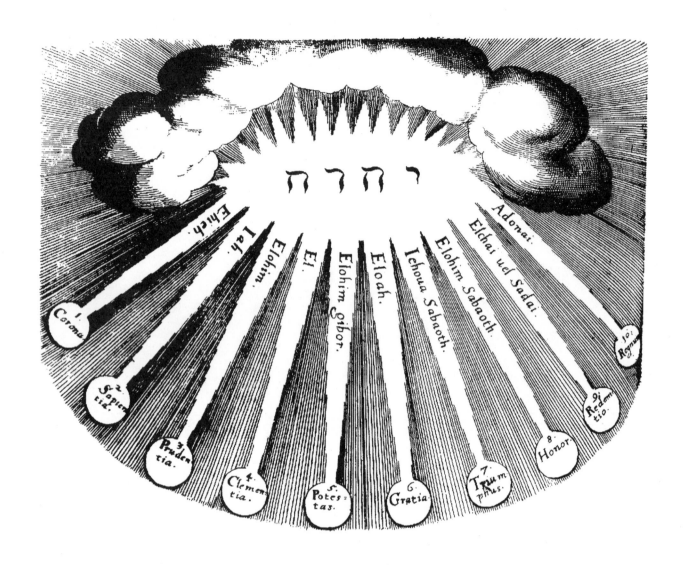

8.6. Emanation of the Sephiroth

The God of the Hebrew Scriptures is called by several different names, some of them derived from prior and polytheistic religions. Monotheism had to accommodate them all, and it did so with the concept of a God of one essence but multiple operations. This diagram represents the primordial self-revelation of the one God as IHVH through the Tetragrammaton, inscribed in the burst of light. Ten of its rays carry his other names, and each emanates one of the *sephiroth* or principles of manifestation. Their Latin names mean (1) Crown, (2) Wisdom, (3) Prudence, (4) Mercy, (5) Power, (6) Grace, (7) Triumph, (8) Honor, (9) Redemption, (10) Kingdom. *PS,* p. 170.

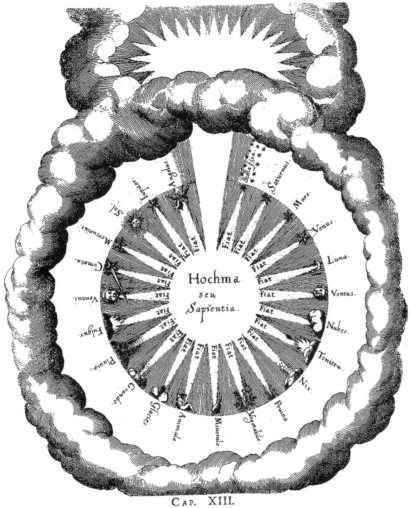

CAP. XIII.

Quod voluntas DEI esset, quod stellæ fixæ in sua sphæra forent creatæ, ipsæque in momento factæ sint.

8.7. Wisdom's Creations

Of all the *sephiroth,* the second, Hochma, holds a special place in the Hebrew Scriptures. Usually translated as "Wisdom," it takes on a character, even a personality (and a female one, at that), especially in the books of Job, Psalms, Proverbs, and Ecclesiastes. Fludd uses for his exegesis the same graphic concept as in ills. 8.4, 8.5, and 8.8, depicting a greater light source creating a second light that radiates in its turn. Here we see one of the ten rays of the previous plate, the one that produces Hochma, and the productions of the latter. *Clockwise from the top,* we read Fixed Stars, Saturn, Mars, Venus, Moon, wind, clouds, thunder, snow, frost, vegetables, minerals, animals, ice, hail, rain, lightning, wind again, comets, Mercury, Sun, Jupiter, and angels. The placement of the winds on the horizon of the diagram reflects their crucial function as mediators of celestial influences, explained in the following plates. *PS,* p. 174.

METEOROLOGY

213

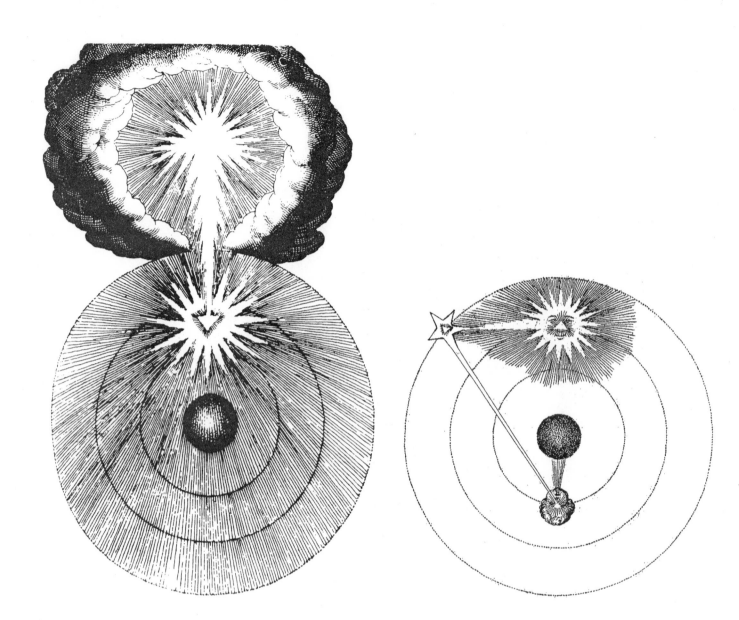

8.8, 8.9. Origin of Winds

Fludd ascribed enormous importance to the winds, believing them to be the proximate agents of God's will on Earth. The first plate again uses the image of a great light emerging from clouds to kindle a lesser light. The latter is the sun, shown in Fludd's usual manner at the midpoint of three concentric worlds surrounding the dark earth. The second image (which precedes the first in Fludd's text) is the significant one. The sun sends out one of its rays to the outermost planetary sphere, that of Saturn, in Fludd's words "inhabiting and animating" that planet and endowing it with power of its own. Saturn's ray, in turn, penetrates to the elemental world where it vivifies the appropriate wind, Boreas. That is the north wind, which finally pours its influences upon the earth, causing the meteorological and medical phenomena to which Fludd devotes much attention, both here and in *Medicina Catholica. PS,* pp. 190, 189.

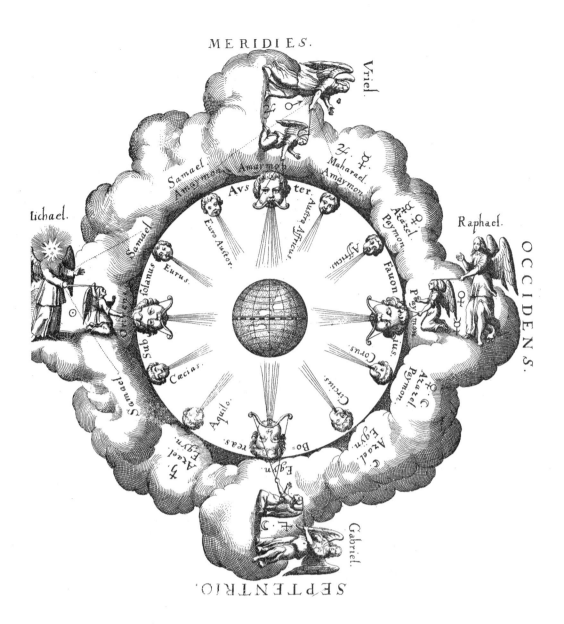

8.10. Archangels and Winds

The four archangels Michael, Gabriel, Raphael, and Uriel, whose stations are traditionally at the four corners of the earth, delegate their powers to the spirits of the winds. These dwell in the sphere of air surrounding the earth. We see them here as winged, kneeling figures with the archangels' scepters on their heads. They control their winds like the rider of a horse, with a bridle connected to a bit in the wind's mouth. Each of the twelve major and minor winds is under the influence of one or more planets, whose symbols accompany their names. Each is associated with a cardinal point and an element: fire in the east, air in the south, water in the west, and earth in the north. From all of these one can deduce their qualities. Austro Affricus, for example, the wind in the southwest, is ruled by the demons Maharael and Amaymon, and affected by Mercury and Jupiter. The exact qualities, effects, and astrological factors are the subject of some hundreds of pages in *Philosophia Sacra* and *Medicina Catholica. PS,* p. 267.

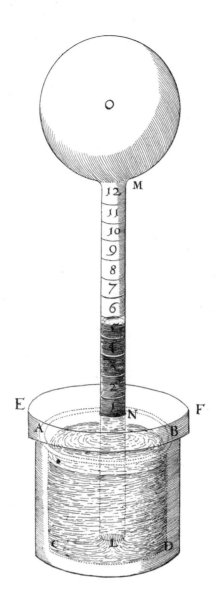

8.11. First Weatherglass

Toward the end of *Philosophia Sacra,* Fludd returns to the "old experiment," which played so important a role in his first treatise (see ill. 2.23, pp. 56–57). He reused the engraved plate twice in his new book, but over ten or more years his interpretation of the experiment had matured. He now says nothing about light purging out the "dense and dark air," but realizes that heat simply makes air expand, while cold contracts it. He also admits that this apparatus is not easy to make, and instead proposes a simple design. It might pass as the first thermometer, had it not already been described by Galileo and pictured in Giuseppe Biancani's *Sphaera Mundi* of 1617. It uses a tub of water with a pierced lid, and a long-necked glass flask. You heat the glass bulb, he says, then immerse the stem in the water. As the air in the bulb cools, the water is sucked up the tube. If you heat it again, it goes down. He suggests coloring the water with copper sulfate ("blue vitriol"), both to resist freezing if used in frigid weather and because it looks beautiful. Fludd now realized that heat = expansion and cold = contraction: a priceless clue for his spiritual cosmology (see ill. 9.8, p. 226). *PS,* p. 287.

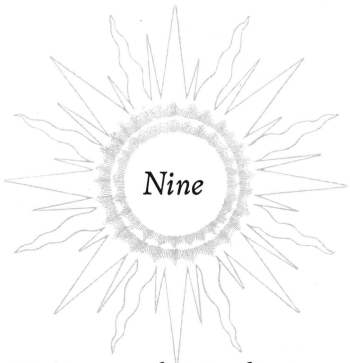

Nine

Universal Medicine

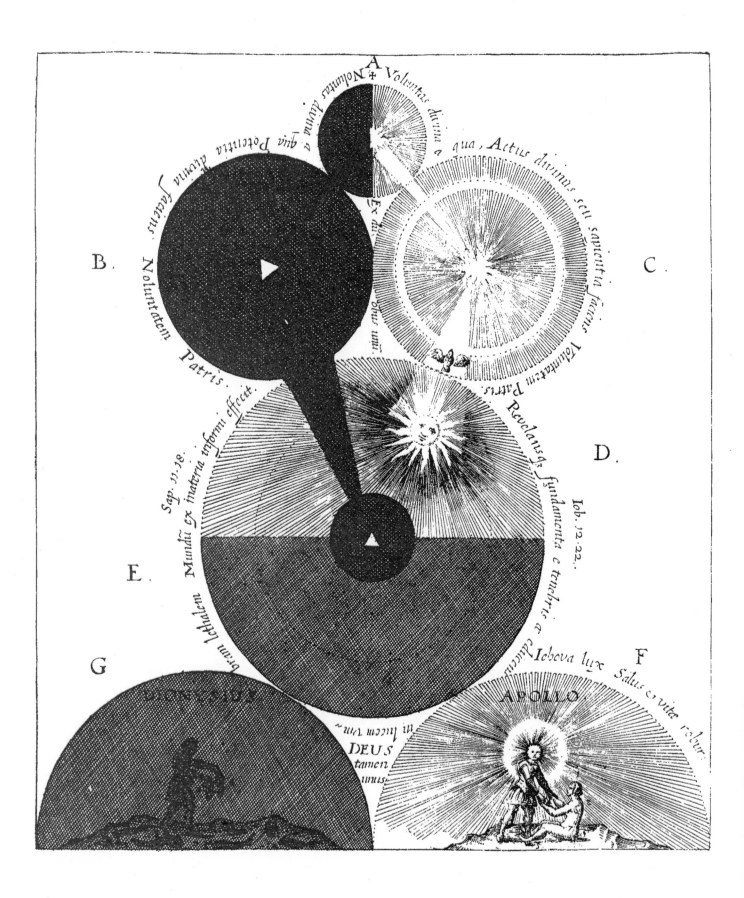

9.1. Primeval Duality (i)

This is one of the most important plates for the understanding of Fludd's metaphysics, as well as the basis of his medical theory. He explains it as follows: There is one God, one Supreme Being, one Essence, one Divine Mind, *vel volens, vel nolens*—either willing or not willing. [This is the upper circle.] These are like a man's dual faculties of affirmation and negation; and just as both can be good, so God is good whether he wills or not, for in God there is no evil. Thus Hermes says, in the Pimander, "the monad generates a monad [God's affirmation] and reflects its ardor in itself [God's negation]."

In the dark circle, all is in the primal state of chaos, before the creation of the world. God is in the middle, in his essence and light, but he does not send it out. Pimander calls this "an infinite shadow in the abyss"; it is the Dark Aleph of the Kabbalah. This divine property manifests as darkness, silence, death, disease, etc., as can be seen by its connection to the central circle, that of the world. And if we could visit the center of the earth, we would doubtless find there the cornerstone of light [*lapis lucidum angularis*]. God's other property gives the world its life, light, form, and harmony. It is the Word of God, the spiritual Christ filling all and the incorruptible Spirit in all things.

According to the Ancients, there is an archetypal Sun through which all is adorned with beauty and harmony. They attribute the mystery of the visible created Sun to this divine Sun, Apollo, who carries life, grace, and health in his right hand but in his left a bow and arrow as a sign of his severity. Similar to him is Bacchus or Dionysus, by whom creatures are torn to pieces. But he is the same being, known by day as Apollo and by night as Dionysus, the Prince of Darkness [see the lower hemispheres]. As Dionysus tears man into his seven pieces by night, so Apollo restores him by day to his sevenfold constitution. They are both none other than the one God, who works all in all (pp. 5–8).

The legends around the circles read as follows:

A–C: "Divine will, from which comes the divine act or wisdom, doing the will of the Father."

A–B: "Divine not-willing, from which comes divine potency, doing the Father's not-willing."

D–F–E: "And revealing the foundations from the darkness and bringing to light the lethal shadow, it creates the world from formless matter," citing Job 12:22 and Wisdom 11:18.

Between *G* and *F:* "God is still one."

F: "Jehova the light, health, and strength of life."

MC I, 1, fol.):(1'; *MC* I, 2, 1, p. 23; *PM*, title page.

9.2. Primeval Duality (ii)

A simpler version of the previous plate removes all superfluous matter and serves as a perfect emblem of Fludd's fundamental theology.

MC I, 1, p. 37.

9.3. The Fortress of Health

In the center *Homo Sanus,* the "healthy man," prays to God, saying "Show thy servant the light of thy countenance, and save me for thy mercy's sake" (Psalm 31:16). God replies: "No plague shall come nigh thy dwelling; for I will give my angels charge over thee, to keep thee in all thy ways" (Psalm 91:10–11).

From north, south, east, and west the angels whom we saw in ill. 8.10 (p. 215) allow their bridled winds to spew forth noxious plagues. Each is led by a demon, mounted on a monster of the earth, water, air, or fire. It has been remarked that the winged insects surrounding each demon may be the first illustration of the idea of

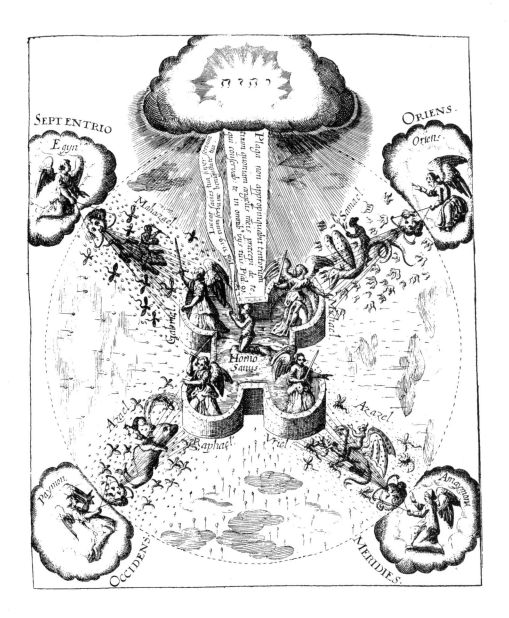

germs as carriers of disease. But Fludd thought of the contagion as purely aerial, and mentions that his friend and printer William Fitzer, fleeing from the plague in Cologne, saw it descending on the city like a reddish cloud (p. 338).

Fludd explains the existence of demons, death, and disease as a consequence of God's dark side, which will become clearer through the following plate (ill. 9.4). Here he writes: **They are not under Divine Justice, but come from Injustice, which is a figment of the Divine Darkness. Health is from God alone, given by his Angels whose ruler is Jesus Christ, the first emanation before creation and the mediator between God and his creatures. God's will is carried out by both good and evil Angels, but we, as creatures of the Light, can only be saved and remain healthy by prayer to God** (folios 1'–5'). Man has as his protectors the archangels Michael, Gabriel, Raphael, and Uriel, who stand in the circular bastions, beating off the assault with their swords. Yet in the earlier image (ill. 8.10) we saw them controlling those same aggressors, so that now they are fighting against their own delegates. This only goes to show how much difficulty Fludd had in explaining the problem of evil. *MC* I, 1, fol.):( ):(2; *MC* I, 2, 1, p. 338.

UNIVERSAL
MEDICINE

221

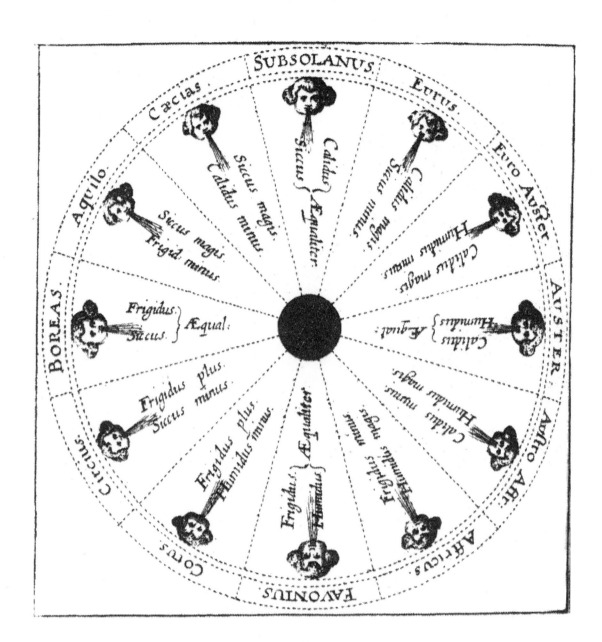

9.4. Qualities of the Winds

The twelve winds are shown with their qualities of hot and cold, wet and dry, which according to Aristotle account for all the differences in the elemental world. For example, Boreas, the north wind, is equally cold and dry; Subsolanus, the east wind, is hot and dry; Aquilo and Caecias represent stages in between. Fludd designed many tables showing the correspondence of winds, elements, and humors, and the effects of their equal and unequal combinations. This, with astrology, is the foundation of *Medicina Catholica*. It rests on the assumption that behind each wind is a malevolent demon intent on sending disease to mankind: something vividly pictured in ill. 9.3. Another lengthy section of the book suggests prayers for warding off these noxious influences. *MC* I, 1, pp. 125, 131.

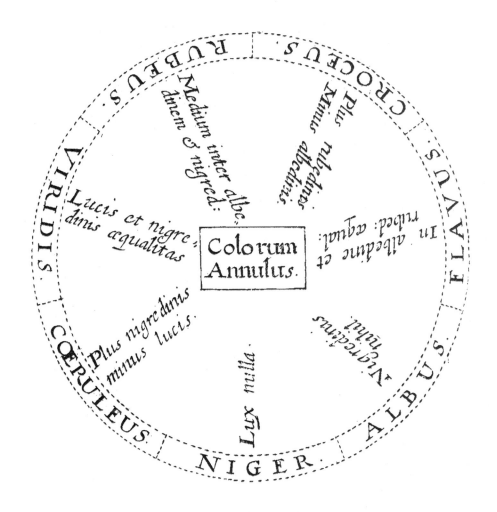

9.5. Color Wheel

Fludd's preoccupation with light and darkness as the primordial qualities, rooted in God himself (see ill. 9.1, pp. 218–19), led him to develop a theory of color in defiance of Aristotelian tradition. Neither cold, nor heat, nor color, nor taste, nor odor are (as the old Philosophers thought) accidents; but essences, placed primordially in creatures by the Creator (p. 147). On this wheel are seven colors, with their compositions of light and darkness: black (*niger*), "No light"; blue (*ceruleus*), "More blackness, less light"; green (*viridis*), "Equality of light and blackness"; red (*rubeus*), "Medium between whiteness and blackness"; orange (*croceus*), "More redness, less whiteness"; yellow (*flavus*), "Equal in redness and whiteness"; white (*albus*), "No blackness." But the ultimate cause of color is the natural and radical sulfur, which is present in all things and causes the rotation of the elements and mutation of forms. The radical sulfur has its root and origin in the Light that first differentiated itself out of the primal mass. Fire is the closest element to it, and most nearly approaches its color (p. 149). As familiar examples, Fludd mentions the colors of fruits, which change as they absorb sulfur from the sun and ripen; also coal, which starts perfectly black, then as it heats and burns turns red, emitting flames of orange and yellow, and even blue and green (p. 153). *MC* I, 1, p. 154.

9.6. The Sickbed

The second installment of *Medicina Catholica,* titled *The Whole Mystery of Diseases,* promises to "describe in a new way, scarcely heard before, the general nature of diseases, or the various reasons for the invasion and attack of the Fortress of Health," with a universal chart of healings and sicknesses, including ways of diagnosing and foretelling the effects of the weather. In the seventeenth century, people were far less insulated from weather and the extremes of heat and cold than we are today. A doctor was expected to take the weather into account and, if possible, predict it. Fludd regarded it as a vital link in the chain of being, joining the human body to the planetary and stellar influences that in turn reflect the will of angels, demons, and ultimately of God. Hence his complex association of medicine with meteorology, astrology, and prayer. *MC* I, 2, 1, title page.

9.7. God's Anger Invades the Fortress of Health ↪

The center of this plate, like the preceding one, shows the sick man in his outward aspect. He lies in bed while the physician takes his pulse and examines his urine. Now Fludd shows the true situation. The demons of the four winds, already familiar from ill. 9.3, are assailing the fortress of health, and Azazel, mounted on a basilisk, has already breached the southern bastion to afflict the patient with the diseases of the south wind. But there is worse. God himself is angry, and no fortress is proof against his wrath. His terrible words resound from the four directions:

North: "Because thou has not hearkened unto my voice, I will afflict thee with cold and will give thee a fearful heart and a sadness of soul until thou perish" (Deuteronomy 28).

South: "Because thou has not kept my commandments, I will afflict thee in summer with corrupt air, and give thee the pestilence to pursue thee until thou perish" (Deuteronomy 28:21); "I shall send fiery serpents among you" (Numbers 21:6).

East: "Because thou hast not observed my precepts, I will afflict thee with a hot, raging, and burning pestilence, and you shall be persecuted by the king's evil, etc." (Deuteronomy 28:22).

West: "I will afflict thee with dropsy" (Luke 14); "I will make thee lunatic, and affected with a heavy spirit" (Matthew 17); "I will dissolve thee with palsy, so that they enterprises are hindered and they mouth stopped, that thou canst not speak" (I Maccabees 9:55). *MC* I, 2, 1, fol. 3–4.

9.8. Fludd's Own Weatherglass

"You see it depicted here just as you would find it in my house," writes Fludd. He has made a classical kiosk, resting on ball feet, with the lower receptacle disguised "to make it more wonderful and entertaining" beneath artificial rocks. He promises that by calibrating the tube (here from −7 to +7) one can quantify the outside temperature: The seventh degree is reached, perhaps, only when the Thames is frozen so that men and animals can safely cross it. The region from 1 to 7 is called the Winter Hemisphere, that from 1 to −7 the Summer one, when the warmed air pushes the water level down. If a sudden drop occurs, say of two or three degrees in four or five hours, it will certainly rain in twelve hours' time. How wrong are the disciples of Aristotle who believe that the rise of the water is due to attraction from the heat of the bulb, analogically to their belief that the Sun pulls the water vapor up! They do not understand the expansion and contraction of air as a factor of heat. Heat and expansion are manifestations of God's own Light; cold and contraction, of his Darkness (pp. 10–13). *MC* I, 2, 1, p. 8.

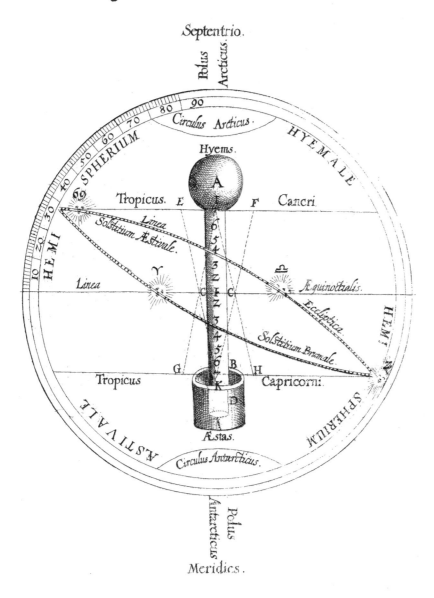

9.9. The Weatherglass as Symbol of the Earth

Here the weatherglass is imagined as the axis of a terrestrial globe. The upper bulb, which the water level approaches in cold weather, is at the wintry North Pole. The reservoir, to which the level falls when the enclosed air expands, is at the South Pole, supposedly the seat of summer. The midpoint is at the equator. The ecliptic circle, shown as an ellipse, adds an imaginary third dimension to the diagram and also introduces the dimension of time. It marks the northern limit of the sun's position at the summer solstice (Tropic of Cancer), the southern limit at the winter solstice (Tropic of Capricorn), and the spring (Aries) and autumn (Libra) equinoxes. The intersecting pyramids of form and matter are drawn in dotted lines in the background. *MC* I, 2, 1, pp. 28, 51.

Vrinarum cum Borealium tum Australium scala.

Septentrio.

Nigra a mortificatione.
Liuida.
Aquea.
Pallida.
Subpallida.
Citrina.
Aurea.
Crocea.
Sub-rubra.
Rubicunda.
Vineta seu color Inopos.
Viridis.
Nigra ab adustione.

Exacta Vrina temporis   Occ | Ori

Meridies.

9.10. The Colors of Urine

This weatherglass is adapted to the science of uroscopy, or diagnosis through the examination of urine. The northern half of the glass marks the degrees of loosening of urine, the southern half those of retention. *On the right* are the colors that may be seen in the urinary flask, reading downward: black from putrefaction, blue-black, aqua, pale gray, light gray, yellow, golden (at the center), orange, reddish, rubicund, vinous, green, black from overheating. All but the central colors indicate diseases, which can then be read from the following plate. *MC* I, 2, 1, p. 60.

9.11. Winds and Diseases

Beginning *from the left,* we read that there are two hemispheres: the cold wintry one and the hot summery one. The north is cold and dry, earthy and melancholic, with three degrees of intensity represented by the north winds Aquilo, Boreas, and Circius. The west is cold and wet, watery and phlegmatic, also with its three winds.

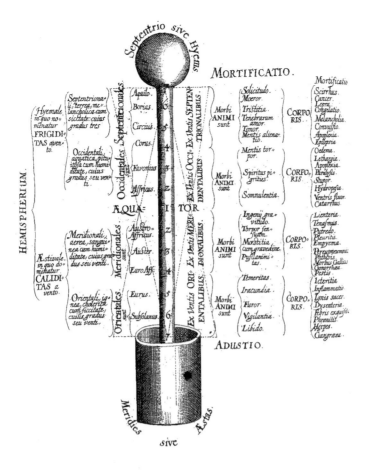

Crossing below the equator is the warm and wet south, whose humor is sanguine, and the warm, dry, choleric east. These neatly match the plus and minus calibrations on the tube, again accompanied by the faint outlines of the pyramids.

The winds coming from the four directions are all potential sources of diseases, which are classified on the right-hand side of the plate. The main tendencies are toward mortification (cold) or inflammation (hot). Here are the ailments, shown in tabular form:

NORTH	EAST	WEST	SOUTH
DISEASES OF THE SOUL	**DISEASES OF THE SOUL**	**DISEASES OF THE SOUL**	**DISEASES OF THE SOUL**
care, grief, sorrow, love of darkness, fear, losing one's mind	mental torpor, sluggishness of *spiritus*, sleepiness	cold, torpor of the senses, depression with catarrh, pusillanimity	rashness, irascibility, fury, insomnia, lust
DISEASES OF THE BODY	**DISEASES OF THE BODY**	**DISEASES OF THE BODY**	**DISEASES OF THE BODY**
mortification, tumor, cancer, leprosy, hardening, melancholy, convulsion, apoplexy, epilepsy	edema, lethargy, apoplexy, paralysis, stupor, dropsy, flux of the stomach, catarrh	lientery, tenesmus, putridity, pleurisy, emphysema, pneumonia, tuberculosis, the French disease (syphilis), gonorrhea, plague	itching, inflammation, erysipelas, dysentery, painful fever, phrenitis, herpes, gangrene

MC I, 2, 1, p. 88.

9.12. Circle of Urinary Colors

This plate is mainly of interest as a medical curiosity and as evidence of Fludd's continuing obsession with uroscopy and urinomancy, which would dominate the last published part of *Medicina Catholica* (see below). With the exception of the physician pictured in the center, it is an exact copy from a fifteenth-century manuscript now in the Bodleian Library, Oxford (MS. Savile 39, fol. 7'). Around the circumference are twenty urine flasks, each connected to one of seven circles. We summarize them as follows, *beginning at the top*:

> Reds, ranging from crocus to intense fire, signify excesses in the digestion.
> Colors resembling liver, white beans, or cabbage stalks indicate overheating.
> Black and leaden colors show bad digestion.
> The colors of spring water, light filtering through horn, milk, or camel hair show indigestion.
> Pallid colors like cooked fat indicate the beginnings of digestion.
> Cider colors show medium digestion.
> Golden colors alone are the sign of a perfect digestion.

MC I, 2, 1, p. 343.

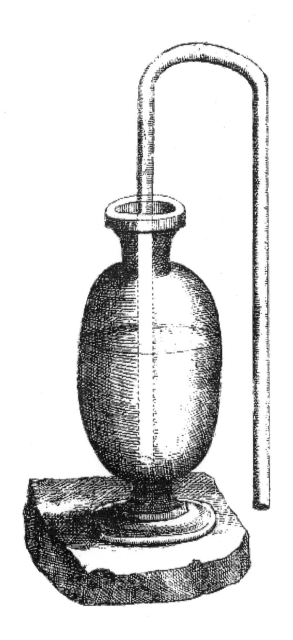

9.13. Siphon

The working of this simple siphon is virtually self-explanatory. When the air is sucked out of the tube, the water rises up it and empties the vase, seemingly defying the law of gravity. In *Philosophia Sacra,* Fludd used this experiment to demonstrate the intimate link between air and water, and nature's abhorrence of a vacuum. He now reuses it in combination with the following plate, to give a medical interpretation. *PS,* p. 91; *MC* I, 2, 1, p. 439.

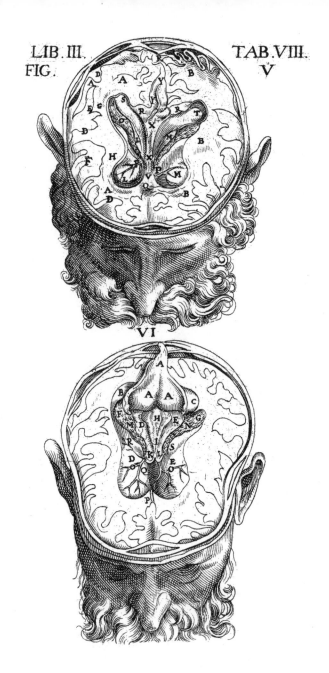

9.14. Catarrh on the Brain

This engraving is taken directly from *Anatomiae Amphitheatrum,* hence indirectly from Vesalius, as explained above (compare ill. 7.20).* In this context it illustrates Fludd's theory of how catarrh is generated in the human body, in an analogous way to the working of the siphon in the previous illustration. He explains that when vapors rise into the head or ventricles of the brain, either the coldness of the brain condenses them into liquid or else they have already risen in liquid form. They then percolate, like milk in a breast, through a sort of sieve in the depths of the front ventricles of the brain, and exit downward through the nose as a mixture of air and catarrhal matter. *AA,* p. 163; *MC* I, 2, 1, p. 440.

---

*See Vesalius, *Illustrations from the Works,* p. 191.

9.15. The Cause of Tuberculosis

Here Fludd returns to the devices described by Hero of Alexandria, which had so interested him in his earlier books. When a fire is lit upon the altar, its heat causes the air inside the reservoir to expand. This in turn forces the water out by its only available routes: up the tubes concealed in the figures, and out of their vases, thus quenching the fire. This fountain demonstrates what happens in tuberculosis: the air contained in the thorax becomes overheated and expands. Some of it escapes through the hidden channels of the veins and arteries, emerging in the viscera as phlegm. At night this rises to the head and, condensing there, falls back into the lungs, making the patient cough. This could lead to many other conclusions: I merely commend it to the consideration of doctors as an entirely new theory (p. 466). *MC* I, 2, 1, p. 465.

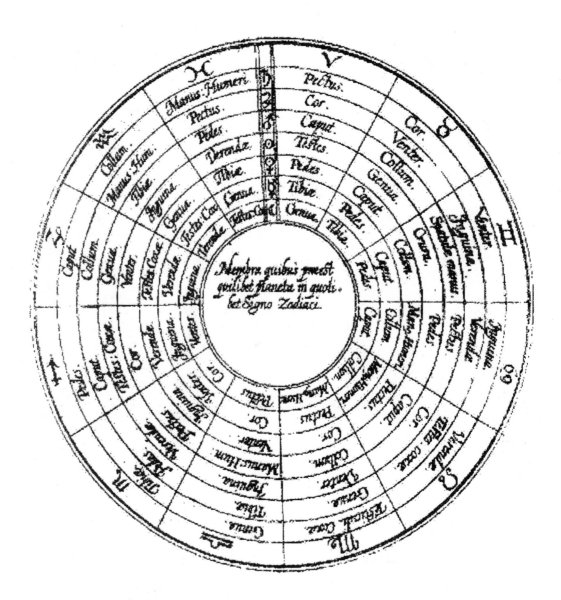

9.16. The Parts of the Body and Their Rulerships

The third part of *Medicina Catholica* contains many tables but fewer engravings. Here is a circular chart that combines the medical influences of the planets (see ill. 4.9, p. 139) and those of the zodiac (see ill. 4.10, pp. 140–41). From it one can find the part of the body that is likely to be affected by any of the eighty-four possible combinations of planets with signs. For instance, when Saturn is in Aries, the chest is affected; when Venus is in Pisces, the shins, and so on. The chart is part of Fludd's grand scheme of astrological diagnosis, which purports to give not only the diseases to be expected from every planetary aspect but also a system for detecting the critical days when the course of a disease may be reversed. *MC* I, 2, 2, p. 183.

9.17. Urinomancy

A doctor of medicine, in Fludd's day, was not expected to perform operations: those were done by barber-surgeons. Instead, he applied his learning to diagnosis and the prescription of cures. On this title page to Fludd's treatise on urinomancy, a well-dressed boy, his hat under his arm, has been to see the patient and has brought, in a basket, a flask of urine. Old-style doctors might examine it carefully, even taste it, but for Fludd a glance at its color suffices. He notes the time of day, the patient's name and age, and then asks the bearer what relationship he has to the patient, and whether he has brought the specimen with the patient's consent or knowledge. On the basis of this information he draws up an astrological chart for the moment and the situation, from which he learns the likely nature and progress of the illness and can predict its course, including whether the patient will live or die. *MC* I, 2, 2, p. 255.

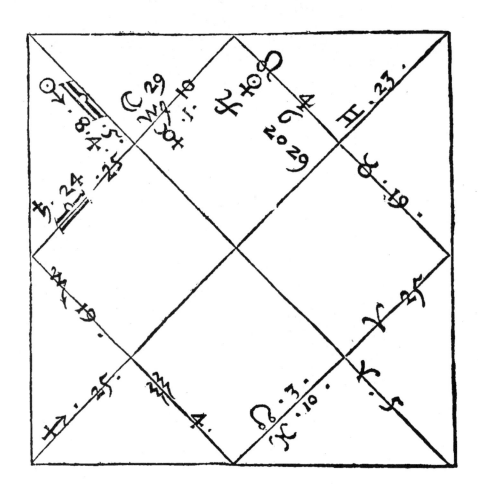

9.18. Urinomantic Horoscope

Fludd offers this chart as one of many examples of his diagnostic method. It is for 11:00 in the morning of August 2, 1600, when a man brought a specimen of his wife's urine for diagnosis, without her consent or knowledge. Fludd states that the planetary positions indicated her imminent death, which occurred at 8:00 the following morning. *MC* I, 2, 2, p. 245.

9.19. The Pulse ⟳

The last installment of *Medicina Catholica* was finished before the previous one (see dates in the bibliography), but published at the end of it. The title reads: "The Pulse, or the new and secret history of the pulses, drawn from sacred sources yet compared with the sayings and authority of the ethnic physicians." The emblem on the title page shows God's hand emerging from the clouds and holding a man's wrist. The adjacent words quote a complaint of Job: "My bones are pierced in me in the night season, and my pulses take no rest" (Job 30:17). The circular device refers to Ezekiel's vision of the valley full of dry bones. Prompted by God, Ezekiel commands the bones to reassemble themselves, and God himself restores them to life with the words "Come from the four winds, O breath, and

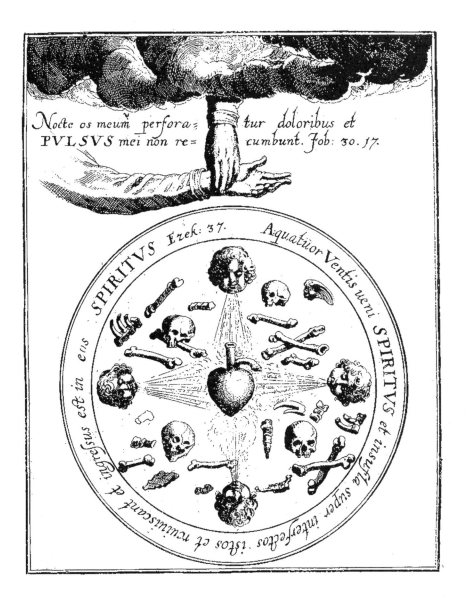

breathe upon the slain, that they may live" (Ezekiel 37:9). The four winds, which play such an important role in Fludd's medical theories, are shown here blowing from the cardinal points into the human heart. As we have seen in previous plates, the winds are the agents of energies that derive from the sun, and ultimately from God himself.

The book in question was finished in 1629, the year when William Harvey published his *Exercitatio Anatomica de Motu Cordis et Sanguinis in Animalibus,* which established the fact of the circulation of the blood. Fludd calls Harvey "an outstanding Doctor of Medicine, brilliant in anatomy and also versed in the deep mysteries of Philosophy, my dearest compatriot and faithful colleague," and praises his discovery (p. 11). But the anatomical details do not greatly concern Fludd. For him, the systole and diastole are signs of the metaphysical duality (see ill. 9.1, pp. 218–19) that manifests in the elemental world as hot and cold, expansion and contraction. The heart receives this dual impulse and responds by expanding and contracting, sending the blood to and fro. *MC* I, 2, 3, title page.

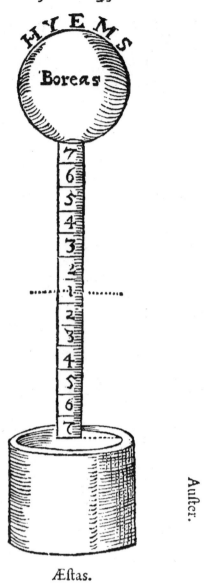

De Pulſuum myſterio.

9.20. The Weatherglass as Symbol

Fludd develops his theory of the pulse by referring the reader to the weatherglass described at the end of his book on meteorology (see ill. 8.11, p. 216), and reminding us of how it demonstrates God's dual effects of expansion and contraction. Thus experience teaches us that darkness is made from contraction, such that clear, rarefied air turns through contraction into dark cloud; tenuous spiritus into dense substance; something tenuous, light, and therefore mobile into a body made slow or even motionless by its grossness and weight; just as we see air transformed into slowly moving water, or into snow, hail, or unmoving ice (p. 6). The weatherglass is redrawn here with the bulb marked "winter, north" and the tub marked "summer, south." The tube is calibrated in plus and minus degrees going from the center. Fludd is no longer thinking practically, but assimilating the device to his other cosmological diagrams. *MC* I, 2, 3, p. 7.

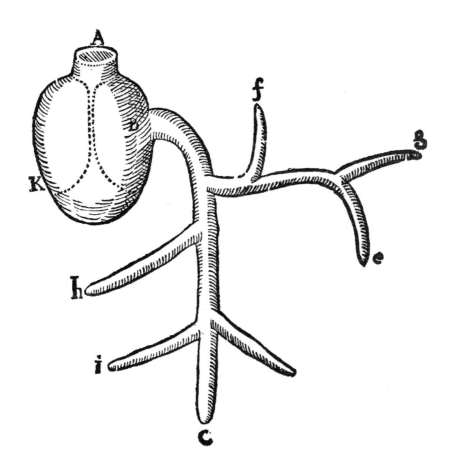

9.21. Experiment with a Heart

Fludd insists, against ancient authorities, that it is the heart alone, not the arteries, that causes the pulse. This experiment is made with a heart, presumably from an animal, with some arteries attached but tied off. Fludd instructs you to put your mouth to the hole at the top of the heart and blow into it. The cavity of the heart and the arteries all expand. When you suck the air out again, they collapse. That proves that it is the heart's expansion and contraction that make the arteries pulsate. But whence comes the original impulse? Likewise the divine spirit, operating in the heart with both of its properties, now contracts the spirit into itself and now dilates it, namely within the heart cavity, at whose motion the arteries are then moved in diastole and systole. *MC* I, 2, 3, p. 29.

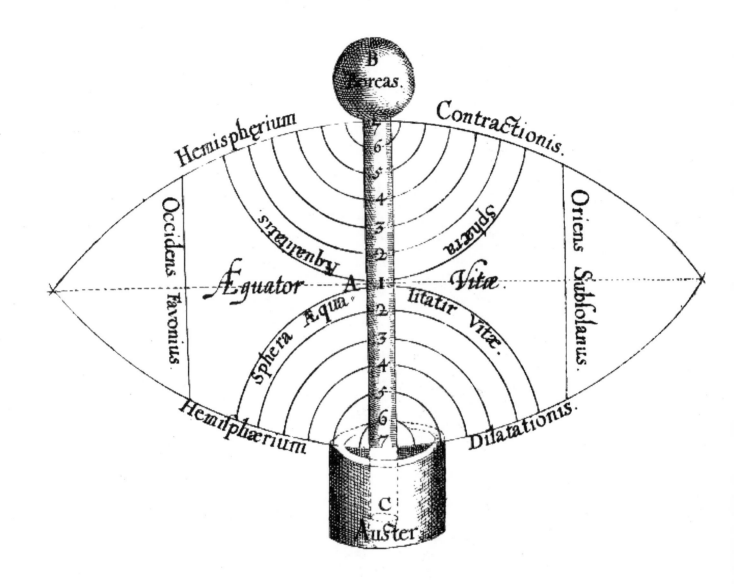

9.22. The Equator of Life

Here the weatherglass is integrated into a typically Fluddean system of contrary qualities mapped along a vertical axis, with each end imagined as a sphere. At the top is the cold pole, where the north wind and the season of winter manifest God's quality of contraction. At the bottom is the warm pole, with the south wind and summer manifesting God's expansive quality. The midpoint is the "equator of life" where the qualities are equal. One of Fludd's guiding principles is that God has "ordered all things by measure and number and weight" (Wisdom of Solomon, 11:20). This must include the winds, he says, and it is they that provide the different degrees of expansion and contraction. *MC* I, 2, 3, p. 46.

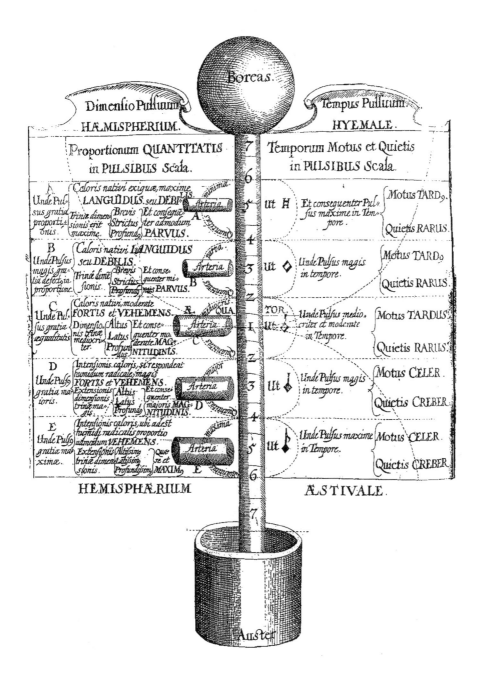

9.23. System of the Universal Pulse

After many developments of the above ideas, including an analysis of the length, breadth, and height of arteries, and a translation of pulsebeats into musical rhythms, here is the most complete development of what started as a simple weatherglass. *To the left* of the tube are arteries of different thicknesses, the thicker ones being at the expansive southern end and favoring a stronger blood flow. The columns *on the right* give pulse speeds in musical notation, and describe their frequent or infrequent rests. *MC* I, 2, 3, p. 78.

UNIVERSAL
MEDICINE

Appendices

1. ASTROLOGY
SOLVES A CRIME

This colorful account of life at Oxford shows Fludd already expert in astrology, but as John Dee had found when he was a student at Cambridge, being too clever could raise suspicion of demonic influence.

While I was working on my music treatise, I scarcely left my room for a week on end. One Tuesday a young man from Magdalen came to see me, and dined in my room. The following Saturday I was invited to dine with a friend from the town, and while dressing for the occasion I could not find my valuable sword-belt and scabbard, worth ten French gold pieces. I asked everyone in college if they knew anything about it, but with no success. I therefore drew up a horary chart for the moment at which I had noticed the loss, and deduced from the position of Mercury and other features that the thief was a talkative youth situated in the East, while the stolen goods must now be in the South.

On thinking this over I remembered my guest of Tuesday, whose college lay directly to the east of St. John's. I sent my servant to approach him politely, but he swore that he had touched nothing of mine. Next I sent my servant to speak to the boy who had accompanied my visitor on that day, and with harsh words and threats he made him confess that he had stolen the goods, and taken them to a place I knew near Christ Church where people listened to music and consorted with women. This confirmed my conjecture that the place was to the south of St. John's, and since Mercury had been in the house of Venus that accorded with the association with music and women. After this the boy was taken into the presence of his companion and flung to the ground. He swore that he had indeed committed the crime, and begged my servant to say no more: he promised to retrieve the belt and scabbard on the following day. This was done,

and I received my stolen property wrapped in two beautiful parchments. It emerged that the music house near Christ Church was the lair of a receiver of stolen goods who had robbed many degenerate scholars, wasting them with gluttony and womanizing. My friend implored me to desist from the study of astrology, saying that I could not have solved this crime without demonic aid. I thanked him for his advice. (*UCH* I, 2, pp. 701–3)

2. THE WISDOM OF
THE ANCIENTS

Here Fludd shows his allegiance to the notion of the *prisca theologia,* the primordial theology or divine wisdom given not only to the Jews but to pagan peoples.

The wisdom of the ancients bears witness that there is in this world a sure and indubitable seat of human beatitude, which some have been fortunate to investigate through long travels and dutiful enquiry. We are taught that Moses, the high priest of divine Philosophy, touched the edge of beatitude, indeed that he spoke with God and mastered the key of knowledge, both supernatural and natural, with the help and illumination of the Holy Spirit. Bezaleel, Joshua, David, Solomon, and all the Prophets possessed this virtue, and some of the ancient Philosophers imitated their wisdom. Mercurius Trismegistus deservedly holds first place among these, for his marvelous knowledge of higher and lower things is vividly shown by his Sacred Sermons, and its science in the Emerald Tablet. Nor should the praise of Apollonius the Pythagorean, celebrated by Philostratus, be consigned to oblivion or passed over in silence. On the latter's authority, Apollonius understood all arcane matters, recalled the dead to life, cured sickness by touch alone, was esteemed for his peculiar sanctity, and overflowed with every blessing of this world.

We also learn there that a brotherhood of the Wise flourished at that time in India, who could predict men's future events and read and divine their conditions, parents, fortunes, and names as though inscribed on their faces in nature's secret characters. The wisdom of the Egyptians and the Ethiopians should be commemorated in eternal monuments, for it was thence, it seems, that Plato derived the Idea of his divine knowledge. Surely all these (if free from diabolic superstition) attained the regal summit of felicity and mundane wisdom. (*TA*, pp. 5–6)

3. FLUDD ON HIS OWN TIMES

Fludd refers here to the system of Johannes Trithemius (1462–1516), which ascribes the rulership of the world to each of the seven planetary angels in turn. Fludd's dating of the creation to 4052 BC (5,314 years before AD 1262) was not shared with many contemporaries.[1] However, knowing that according to Trithemius the period of rulership is actually 354 years and 4 months, and that the sequence of planets follows that of the days of the week in reverse, we can calculate that rulership would pass to the angel of

Jupiter in 1617, the very year that Fludd's book was published, perhaps giving hope for the "universal reformation of the world" called for by the Rosicrucians.

If by careful calculation we seek which planetary spirit rules our present age, we find ourselves living within the 354 years during which the spirit of Venus governs the world. For the Angel of Venus rules over the universe from the year of creation 5314, i.e., 1262 from Christ's birth, until the year 5669. Certainly if we cast our eyes over these times, we find that they accord very well with the nature of the Venereal spirit. For men of this age, in which the spirit Anael rules, are the most cultivated of any age. They incessantly build houses and adorn their cities with regal buildings such as we see in Paris and London, the splendor of which puts to shame the structures of the ancients. They excel in the manual crafts, they invent new arts, their weaving skills are extraordinary; they indulge the pleasures of the flesh beyond all imagination, they are drunk with whoring, they choose the most beautiful wives, they invent games and songs and are everywhere singing to the lute. Most of them either ignore God or serve him for the sake of policy. Thus our age is like the time shortly before the Deluge. (*TA*, p. 136)

1. See Patrides, "Renaissance Estimates of the Year of Creation," p. 318.

4. SYMBOLIC ORNAMENTS

A4.1. The Fall of Icarus

Renaissance initials often show some mythological or biblical figure whose name begins with the appropriate letter. Here Icarus, having flown too near the sun on the wings made by his father Daedalus, plunges to earth, where Pan sits charming serpents with his pipe. But there is another level of meaning here. Since the subject of the book that opens with this initial is the Fall and Redemption of man, we might interpret the winged figure as Lucifer thrust down from heaven.

According to the ancients, Fludd explains in chapter 2 of *Tractatus Theologo-Philosophicus,* the first essence was Demogorgon, the uncreated. The second was Eternity (equivalent to Nature), and the third Chaos, who gave birth to Litigium or Strife. Seeing the damage done by them, Demogorgon flung down Chaos and Strife to earth. Nature then gave birth to another son, Pan, who dwells between the light powers and the dark and regulates the harmony of the spheres with the sevenfold pipes of his syrinx. In the Orphic cosmology, from which this tale is confusedly derived, Pan is far more than the woodland deity of common legend. He is the same as Phanes Protogonus, the father of Saturn and hence the ancestor of all classical gods. Fludd did not delve deeply into this complex theology. It sufficed him to imagine that the ancients had anticipated the role of Christ, sent down by his Father to combat Satan in the hearts of men. It is ironic that the goat-footed, horned Pan was to become the very model and image of the Devil. *TTP,* p. 3; *UCH* II, 1, 2, p. 4.

A4.2. "Shakespearean" Tailpiece

This strapwork decoration, found four times in *Anatomiae Amphitheatrum,* is almost identical to that used repeatedly in the first folio edition of William Shakespeare's works, published in London the same year, 1623. It also appears in the alchemical collection *Aureum Vellus* (Rorschach, 1598), and probably in other books published, as Fludd's was, in the German-speaking lands. Harold Bayley, the first to remark on this, attributed it to an international fraternity of printers with heretical leanings.[*] Manly P. Hall notes that similar or identical decorations appear in the King James Bible (1611) and in publications by Francis Bacon, Walter Raleigh, Edmund Spenser, and others, again suggestive of underground spiritual or political movements.[†] *AA,* pp. 51, 218, 250, 285.

---

[*]See Bayley, *New Light on the Renaissance,* pp. 158–60.
[†]Hall, *Secret Teachings,* p. clxvii.

A4.3, A4.4. Grotesque Tailpieces

Near the beginning of Fludd's book on Kabbalah, two mannerist decorations face each other. One of them pictures a wild man or vegetation god flanked by two hounds; the other, a grinning female with a heavy necklace and beads strung between her nipples, while a nude couple help themselves to fruits from the basket on her head. The first tailpiece appears six times in the book; the second, twice. To the printer, they may have been nothing more than a convenient way to fill out a page, but they are conspicuously pagan in feeling, and in a book illustrated with Kabbalistic diagrams, they stand out as incongruous, even mocking. What did Fludd think when his book arrived from the printer in Frankfurt, too late for him to complain? *UCH* II, 2, fol. A5', pp. 33, 57, 83, 106, 128. *UCH* II, 2, fols. A6, B1.

A4.5. Noah's Ark

Fludd's *Philosophia Sacra* has a second title page bearing the words: *Aer Arca Dei Thesauraria, seu Perspicuum Sanitatis et Morborum Speculum:* "Air, the treasure ark of God or the transparent glass of health and disease." The designer has chosen to ornament the opening page of the text with a printer's device showing Noah's Ark, recalling the greatest meteorological event of all time. *PS,* p. 1.

5. FLUDD FINDS "STAR JELLY"

Star jelly is a name for the mucilaginous substances found in fields, also called by the Welsh name *pwdr sêr* ("star rot"), for which there is no single, definitive explanation. In Fludd's century and in folklore it was always associated with falling stars; more recently, with UFOs.

Once, walking in the fields on a clear night, I saw a meteor star fall near me. After a careful search I found its substance, took it up in my hands and kept it until the next day. On the following dawn I examined it closely and found it compacted from a very viscous and slippery substance, having a consistency like frog spawn. It was dull white and semi-opaque, with many tiny dark spots. Without a doubt this substance was made from a vapor that included the terrestrial spirit. Thus it was not burned, as some would maintain, but, like a mirror, received the light of the stellar rays, just as the stars receive the light of the spiritual heaven and of the sun. It represented a true, natural picture of a star and its light, and doubtless those spots included in its cloudy transparency rendered the material more able to absorb the rays of light. Indeed, if I am not mistaken, they take the place of wicks in the transparent humor, supplying light to it just as the wicks of a lamp give a flame to the oil. We may see the same in the moon's substance, for some parts of it appear denser and darker to our eyes, somewhat resembling tree branches. (*UCH* I, 1, 126)

6. THREE STORIES OF PROPHECY

The anecdotes scattered through Fludd's works show another side of his character, that of an accomplished raconteur.

There was a maidservant in London, in the parish of St. Andrew, Holborn, who had suffered a violent and dangerous delirium, in which she often screamed that she was seeing the devil. When it suddenly stopped, she fell into a calm and peaceful state and seemed to go quietly to sleep. Upon awakening, she said that she had had the most delightful dream, and spoke thus to her mistress: "I am deeply sorry, Mistress, to have been such a disturbance and nuisance to yourself and your household, but I know that no more than three days from now, I will trouble you no longer." The mistress answered: "Be of good cheer, for all the danger (as we hope) is over." The maid replied: "Nay, a quiet place is prepared for me, for at the noon hour on Friday I will leave you and this world. Meanwhile I pray you to bear the trouble that the remainder of my disease and life will cause you." When the said day came, at the exact hour of noon (as she predicted), she expired.

There was a nobleman in the College of Law in the same parish, called Gray's Inn, who showed the signs of smallpox on his body. These worked their way inward, and in three or four days the plague struck him. Toward its end he had a similar dream. He saw himself in a very dark wood, where he was obliged to enter a narrow path on which two could not walk abreast. Another walker approached the same path and contested with him for the place, privilege, and preeminence of first entering. With the arrival of two very solemn men, the argument ceased, "and I," he said, "was permitted to enter, while the other man was denied it." Here is the result of the dream. A little after, the dreamer himself died, and as he was born to burial by many friends, a contention arose with the friends of another dead man on account of the recently made grave or sepulchre. Each group strenuously claimed it as having been ordered and dug for their own friend. Meanwhile two solemn men arrived, to whom responsibility for the church had been assigned for that year, and declared that the place was for the grave of the sleeper.

A noble or highborn Englishman, quite learned, called Litherland, said that he had been warned in his sleep that he would remain inanimate and as though dead for forty-eight hours. He waited long on this prediction, until he was led to place such confidence in his dream that he enjoined his favorite brother strictly and earnestly to take great care around such a time, and ordered him above all, in case he should appear inanimate and dead, to guard against his being taken from his bed before forty-eight hours had elapsed. But it happened that the brother lived together with several other brothers under the same roof, and he forgot Litherland's warning, perhaps putting no credence in dreams. So he went out hunting for two days with his other brothers. Then, suddenly remembering the warning and mandate, he hurried home. There he found everyone in mourning, for Litherland had been taken for dead by the neighbors and the women of the household. They had moved him from his bed, as the country's custom was, and placed him on the cold beams of the room to cool him. On learning this, the brother lamented and mourned vehemently for thus having forgotten Litherland's charge and warning, and straightway placed him in a previously warmed bed, rubbing him often with heated cloths. Around the forty-eighth hour since losing consciousness, he gradually began to move slowly, and finally regained his previous health. Afterward he had the great pleasure of speaking to our King James, to whom he revealed a miraculous vision, seen with his mental eye in the course of that long fainting or swoon, on which I will say a few words in my final volume (if God grants me a happy life) where I have proposed to treat the mystery of death and resurrection. It is clear that if God had not warned Litherland by a veridical dream of his future danger, he would surely have been buried alive. (*MC* I, 1, p. 6)

Bibliography

ABBREVIATIONS

AA	*Anatomiae Amphitheatrum*
AC	*Apologia Compendiaria Fraternitatem de Rosae Crucis*
CP	*Clavis Philosophiae et Alchymiae Fluddanae*
DFA	*Doctor Fludd's Answer unto M. Foster*
MC I, 1	*Medicina Catholica, seu Mysticum Artis Medicandi Sacrarium*
MC I, 2, 1	*Integrum Morborum Mysterium*
MC I, 2, 2	*ΚΑΘΟΛΙΚΟΝ Medicorum χατοπτρον*
MC I, 2, 3	*Pulsus, seu Nova et Arcana Pulsuum Historia*
MP	*Mosaicall Philosophy*
PM	*Philosophia Moysaica*
PS	*Philosophia Sacra*
SM	*Sophiae cum Moria Certamen*
TA	*Tractatus Apologeticus*
TTP	*Tractatus Theologo-Philosophicus*
UCH I, 1	*Utriusque Cosmi Maioris Scilicet et Minoris Metaphysica*
UCH I, 2	*Tractatus Secundus: De Naturae Simia, seu Technica Macrocosmi Historia*
UCH II, 1, 1	*Tomus Secundus de Supernaturali, Praeternaturali et Contranaturali Microcosmi Historia*
UCH II, 1, 2	*Tomi Secundi Tractatus Primi Sectio Secunda: De Technica Microcosmi Historia*
UCH II, 2	*Tomi Secundi Tractatus Secundus: De Praeternaturali Utriusque Mundi Historia*
VP	*Veritatis Proscenium*

PLAN OF FLUDD'S
*HISTORY OF THE MACROCOSM AND THE MICROCOSM**

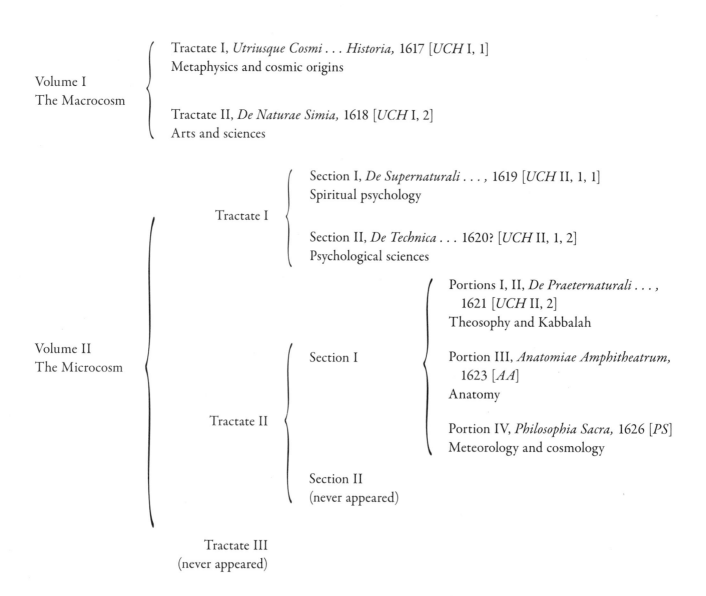

Volume I
The Macrocosm

Tractate I, *Utriusque Cosmi . . . Historia,* 1617 [*UCH* I, 1]
Metaphysics and cosmic origins

Tractate II, *De Naturae Simia,* 1618 [*UCH* I, 2]
Arts and sciences

Volume II
The Microcosm

Tractate I

Section I, *De Supernaturali . . . ,* 1619 [*UCH* II, 1, 1]
Spiritual psychology

Section II, *De Technica . . .* 1620? [*UCH* II, 1, 2]
Psychological sciences

Tractate II

Section I

Portions I, II, *De Praeternaturali . . . ,*
1621 [*UCH* II, 2]
Theosophy and Kabbalah

Portion III, *Anatomiae Amphitheatrum,*
1623 [*AA*]
Anatomy

Portion IV, *Philosophia Sacra,* 1626 [*PS*]
Meteorology and cosmology

Section II
(never appeared)

Tractate III
(never appeared)

*The abbreviations of *Utriusque Cosmi . . . Historia* (*UCH*) and *Medicina Catholica* (*MC*) follow the system used by Johann Rösche. See Rösche, *Der Versuch einer hermetische Alternative,* pp. 584–85.

PLAN OF FLUDD'S
MEDICINA CATHOLICA

Volume I
Causes

Tractate I — *Medicina Catholica,* 1629 [*MC* I, 1]
Winds and demons

Tractate II —
Integrum Morborum Mysterium,
1631 [*MC* I, 2, 1]

Contraction and expansion

Katholikon Medicorum Katoptron,
1631 [*MC* I, 2, 2]

Diagnosis by astrology and uroscopy

Pulsus, 1631? [*MC* I, 2, 3]
The pulse

Volume II
Cures*
(never appeared)

Tractate I —
Observations —
Supercelestial
Celestial
Elementary

External applications

Magnetism and mystic words

Tractate II —
Divine and supercelestial cures
Celestial cures
Elementary cures

*Plan from *MC* I, I, fol. 2.

FLUDD'S WRITINGS

Apologia Compendiaria Fraternitatem de Rosae Crucis Suspicionis et Infamiae Maculis Aspersam, Veritatis Quasi Fluctibus Abluens et Abstergens. Leiden: Gottfried Basson, 1616.

Tractatus Apologeticus Integritatem Societatis de Rosea Cruce defendens. . . . Leiden: Gottfried Basson, 1617.

Tractatus Theologo-Philosophicus in Libros Tres Distributus: Quorum I. De Vita, II. De Morte, III. De Resurrectione. . . . Oppenheim: Johann Theodor de Bry, 1617.

Utriusque Cosmi Maioris Scilicet et Minoris Metaphysica, Physica atque Technica Historia in Duo Volumina Secundum Cosmi Differentiam Divisa. Tomus Primus De Macrocosmi Historia. Oppenheim: Johann Theodor de Bry, 1617.

Tractatus Secundus: De Naturae Simia, seu Technica Macrocosmi Historia in Partes Undecim Divisa. Oppenheim: Johann Theodor de Bry, 1618. 2nd ed. Frankfurt: Johann Theodor de Bry, 1624.

Tomus Secundus de Supernaturali, Praeternaturali et Contranaturali Microcosmi Historia, in Tractatus Tres Distributa. Oppenheim: Johann Theodor de Bry, 1619.

Tomi Secundi Tractatus Primi Sectio Secunda: De Technica Microcosmi Historia, in Portiones VII Divisa. [Oppenheim? 1620?]

Tomi Secundi Tractatus Secundus: De Praeternaturali Utriusque Mundi Historia. In Sectiones Tres Divisa. . . . Frankfurt: Johann Theodor de Bry, 1621.

Veritatis Proscenium: In Quo Aulaeum Erroris Tragicum Dimovetur. Siparium Ignorantiae Scenicum Complicatur, Ipsaque Veritas a Suo Ministro in Publicam Producitur. Seu Demonstratio Quaedam Analytica. . . . Frankfurt: Johann Theodor de Bry, 1621.

Anatomiae Amphitheatrum Effigie Triplici, More et Conditione Varia Designatum. Frankfurt: Johann Theodor de Bry, 1623. Includes *Monochordum Mundi* on pages 287–331, dated December 9, 1621.

Philosophia Sacra et Vere Christiana seu Meteorologia Cosmica. Frankfurt; Officina Bryana, 1626.

Sophiae cum Moria Certamen. In Quo, Lapis Lydius a Falso Structore, Fr. Marino Mersenno, Monacho, Reprobatus, Celeberrima Voluminis Sui Babylonici (in Genesin) Figmenta Accurate Examinat. [Frankfurt], 1629.

Medicina Catholica, seu Mysticum Artis Medicandi Sacrarium, in Tomos Divisum Duos. In Quibus Metaphysica et Physica tam Sanitatis Tuendae, Quam Morborum Propulsandorum Ratio Pertractatur. Frankfurt: William Fitzer, 1629.

Integrum Morborum Mysterium, sive Medicina Catholica Tomi Primi Tractatus Secundus, in Sectiones Distributas Duas. . . . Frankfurt: William Fitzer, 1631.

ΚΑΘΟΛΙΚΟΝ Medicorum κατοπτρον: In Quo, Quasi Speculo Politissimo Morbi Praesentes More Demonstrativo Clarissime Indicantur, et Futuri Ratione Prognostica Aperte Cernuntur, atque Prospicuntur. Sive Tomi Primi, Tractatus Secundi, Sectio Secunda. N.p., n.d. [Frankfurt], 1631. Completed December 17, 1629.

Pulsus, seu Nova et Arcana Pulsuum Historia, e Sacro Fonte Radicaliter Extracta, nec non Medicorum Ethnicorum Dictis et Authoritate Comprobata. Hoc est, Portionis Tertiae Pars Tertia, De Pulsuum Scientia. N.p., n.d. [Frankfurt? 1631?] Completed October 19, 1629. Appended to *MC* I, 2, 2.

Doctor Fludd's Answer unto M. Foster or: The Squeesing of Parson Foster's Sponge, Ordained by Him for the Wiping away of the Weapon Salve. . . . London: Nathaniel Butler, 1631. Latin translation: *Responsum ad Hoplocrisma-Spongum M. Fosteri Presbiteri.* . . . Gouda: Peter Rammazen, 1638.

Clavis Philosophiae et Alchymiae Fluddanae, sive Roberti Fluddi Armigeri, et Medicinae Doctoris, ad Epistolicam Petri Gassendi Theologi Exercitationem Responsum. Frankfurt: William Fitzer, 1633.

Philosophia Moysaica. In qua Sapientia et Scientia

Creationis et Creaturarum Sacra Vereque Christiana (ut Pote Cuius Basis sive Fundamentum Est Unicus Ille Lapis Angularis Iesus Christus) ad Amussim et Enucleate Explicatur. Gouda: Peter Rammazen, 1638.

Mosaicall Philosophy: Grounded upon the Essential Truth, or Eternal Sapience. Written First in Latin, and afterwards thus Rendred into English. London: Humphrey Moseley, 1659.

MANUSCRIPTS

"A Breife Treatise or Hipothesis of One Booke Called Speculum Universi or Universall Mirror." London, Wellcome Medical Library, Ms. 147. Attributed to Fludd in Heisler, "Robert Fludd: A Picture in Need of Expansion" (see general bibliography, below).

"Declaratio Brevis." London: British Library, Ms. Royal 12.c.11.

"De Instrumentis et Machinis." London: British Library, Sloane Ms. 870.

[Eleven pieces for two trebles and bass.] 1. Dr Fluds Dreame. 2. Scale. 3. Pavan I. 4. Pavan II. 5. Changes. 6. Caranto. 7. Almain I or Mottle. 8. Almain II. 9. A Toy. 10. Branle (first treble only). 11. The May Game. New Haven: Yale University Library, Misc. Ms. 170. Filmer Ms. 3.

"On the Divine Numbers and the Divine Harmony." Alnwick Castle: Ms. 600, coll. Duke of Northumberland.

"A Philosophical Key." Cambridge: Trinity College, Western Ms. 1150 [0.2.48].

"Truth's Golden Harrow." Oxford: Bodleian Library, Ms. Ashmole 766.

MODERN EDITIONS AND TRANSLATIONS

"Declaratio Brevis." Edited by William H. Huffman, translated by Robert A. Seelinger, Jr. *Ambix* 25, no. 2 (1978): 69–92.

De Templo Musicae. See English translations under Barton and Hauge, below.

Dr Flud's Dreame and *Caranto.* Transcribed from the Filmer Ms in Barton, "Robert Fludd's *De Templo Musicae*," appendix 3, 202–10.

Mosaical Philosophy: Cabbala. Edited by Adam McLean. Edinburgh: Magnum Opus Hermetic Sourceworks, 1979. Extract from *Mosaicall Philosophy.*

On the Divine Numbers and the Divine Harmony. Edited by Adam McLean, translated by Gen. Charles A. Rainsford (1728–1809). Edinburgh: Magnum Opus Hermetic Sourceworks, 1997. Opening chapters of *UCH* II, a; see Manuscripts, above.

The Origin and Structure of the Cosmos. Edited by Adam McLean, translated by Patricia Tahil. Edinburgh: Magnum Opus Hermetic Sourceworks, 1982. Opening chapters of *UCH* I, 1.

Robert Fludd and His Philosophical Key. Edited by Allen G. Debus. New York: Watson International, 1979.

Robert Fludd: Escritos sobre musica. Edited and translated by Luis Robledo. Madrid: Editora Nacional, 1979.

Robert Fludd: Essential Readings. Edited and translated by William H. Huffman. Western Esoteric Masters Series. Berkeley, CA: North Atlantic Books, 2001. Includes *Apologia Compendiaria,* "Declaratio Brevis," "A Philosophical Key," "Truth's Golden Harrow," *Dr. Fludd's Answer unto M. Foster,* and texts from the Magnum Opus Hermetic Sourceworks series.

Traité d'astrologie générale. Translated by Pierre V. Piobb. Paris: H. Daragon, 1907. Extract from *UCH* I, 2.

Traité de géomancie. Translated by Pierre V. Piobb. Paris: H. Daragon, 1909. Extract from *UCH* I, 2.

"Truth's Golden Harrow." Edited by C. H. Josten. *Ambix* 3 (1949): 91–150.

GENERAL BIBLIOGRAPHY

Allen, Paul M. *A Christian Rosenkreutz Anthology.* New York: Rudolf Steiner Publications, 1968.

Contains an English translation of book IV of Frizius's *Summum Bonum.*

Amman, Peter J. "The Musical Theory and Philosophy of Robert Fludd." *Journal of the Warburg and Courtauld Institutes* 30 (1967): 198–227.

Bacci, Andrea. *Ordo Universi et Humanarum Scientiarum Prima Monumenta.* Rome: Natale Bonifacio, 1581.

Barton, Todd. "Robert Fludd's *De Templo Musicae.*" MA thesis, University of Oregon, 1980.

Bauhin, Caspar. *Theatrum Anatomicum.* Frankfurt: de Bry, 1605.

Bayley, Harold. *A New Light on the Renaissance Displayed in Contemporary Emblems.* London: J. M. Dent, n.d.

Breidbach, Olaf. "World Orders and Corporal Worlds: Robert Fludd's Tableau of Knowing and its Representation." In *Instruments in Art and Science: On the Architectonics of Cultural Boundaries in the Seventeenth Century,* edited by Helmar Schramm et al., 38–61. Berlin: Walter de Gruyter, 2008.

Brianson, Robert de. *L'état et le nobiliaire de Provence.* Paris: Pierre Aubouin, 1693.

Burnett, D. Graham. "The Cosmogonic Experiments of Robert Fludd: A Transcription with Introduction and Commentary." *Ambix* 46, no. 3 (1999): 113–70.

Cafiero, L. "Robert Fludd e la polemica con Gassendi." *Rivista critica di storia filosofia* 19 (1964): 367–410, and 20 (1965): 3–15.

Caus, Salomon de. *Les raisons des forces mouvantes avec diverses machines tant utiles que plaisantes.* Facsimile of Frankfurt 1615 ed. Amsterdam: Frits Knuf, 1972.

Cohen, Simona. *Transformations of Time and Temporality in Medieval and Renaissance Art.* Leiden: Brill, 2014.

Craven, J. B. *Count Michael Maier: Doctor of Philosophy and of Medicine, Alchemist, Rosicrucian, Mystic, 1568–1622, Life and Writings.* Kirkwall: William Peace & Son, 1910.

———. *Doctor Robert Fludd (Robertus de Fluctibus) the English Rosicrucian: Life and Writings.* Kirkwall: William Peace & Son, 1902.

Debus, Allen G. "The Chemical Debates of the Seventeenth Century: The Reaction to Robert Fludd and Jean Baptiste van Helmont." In *Reason, Experiment and Mysticism in the Scientific Revolution,* edited by M. L. Righini Bonelli and W. Shea, 1947. New York: Science History Publications, 1975.

———. *The English Paracelsians.* London: Watts, 1965.

———. "Harvey and Fludd: The Irrational Factor in the Rational Science of the Seventeenth Century." *Journal of the History of Biology* 3 (1970): 81–105.

———. "Renaissance Chemistry and the Work of Robert Fludd." *Ambix* 14, no. 1 (1967): 42–59.

———. "Robert Fludd and the Circulation of the Blood." *Journal of the History of Medicine and Allied Sciences* 16 (1961): 374–93.

———. "Robert Fludd and the Use of Gilbert's *De Magnete* in the Weapon Salve Controversy." *Journal of the History of Medicine and Allied Sciences* 19 (1964): 389–417.

———. "The Sun in the Universe of Robert Fludd." In *Le soleil à la renaissance, sciences et mythes: colloque internationale,* 259–78. Brussels: Université Libre, 1965.

———. "The Synthesis of Robert Fludd." In *The Chemical Philosophy: Paracelsian Science and Medicine in the Sixteenth and Seventeenth Centuries,* 205–93. Vol. I. New York: Science History Publications, 1977.

Emerton, Norma I. "Creation in the Thought of J. B. von Helmont and Robert Fludd. In *Alchemy and Chemistry in the Sixteenth and Seventeenth Centuries,* edited by Piyo Rattansi, 85–102. Dordrecht: Kluwer, 1994.

Fabre, François. "Robert Fludd et l'alchimie I. Le *Tractatus Apologeticus integritatem societatis de Rosea Crucis defendens.*" *Chrysopoeia* 7 (2000–2003): 251–91. Includes a French translation of *Tractatus Apologeticus,* chap. 3, and part of *Apologia Compendiaria.*

Ferté, Patrick. "Robert Fludd et la philosophie hermétique en Provence et à Avignon (1600–1617)." *Provence historique* 44, fasc. 177 (1994): 281–99.

Figala, Karen, and Ulrich Neumann. "'Author cui nomen Hermes Malavici.' New Light on the Bio-bibliography of Michael Maier (1569–1622)." In *Alchemy and Chemistry in the Sixteenth and Seventeenth Centuries,* edited by Piyo Rattansi, 121–47. Dordrecht: Kluwer, 1994.

Foster, William. *Hoplocrisma-Spongus: Or, A Sponge to Wipe Away the Weapon-Salve.* London, 1631.

Frizius, Joachim. *Summum Bonum, Quod Est Verum Magiae, Cabalae, Alchymiae Verae, Fratrum Rosae Crucis Verorum Subjectum . . . Per Joachimum Frizium.* [Frankfurt], 1629. Formerly attributed to Fludd.

Gassendi, Pierre. *Epistolica Exercitatio.* Paris, 1630.

———. *Lettres familières à François Luillier pendant l'hiver 1632–1633.* Edited by Bernard Rochot. Paris, 1944.

Gilly, Carlos. *Cimelia Rhodostaurotica. Die Rosenkreuzer im Spiegel der zwischen 1610 und 1665 entstandenen Handschriften und Drucke.* Amsterdam: In de Pelikaan, 1995.

Godwin, Joscelyn. "Instruments in Robert Fludd's *Utriusque Cosmi . . . Historia.*" *Galpin Society Journal* 26 (1973): 2–14.

———. *Macrocosmos, microcosmos y medicina: Los mundos de Robert Fludd.* Translated by María Tabuyo and Agustín López. Girona: Ediciones Atalanta, 2018.

———. "Robert Fludd on the Lute and Pandora." *Lute Society Journal* 15 (1973): 1–13.

———. *Robert Fludd: Hermetic Philosopher and Surveyor of Two Worlds.* London: Thames & Hudson, 1979.

Godwin, Joscelyn, Christopher McIntosh, and Donate Pahnke McIntosh, trans. *Rosicrucian Trilogy.* Newburyport, MA: Weiser Books, 2016.

Gouk, Penelope. *Music, Science and Natural Magic in Seventeenth-Century England.* New Haven, CT: Yale University Press, 1999.

Guariento, Luca. "From Monochord to Weather-Glass: *Musica Speculativa* and Its Development in Robert Fludd's Philosophy." PhD dissertation, University of Glasgow, 2015.

Hall, Manly P. *Man, the Grand Symbol of the Mysteries.* Los Angeles: Philosophical Research Society, 1932.

———. *The Secret Teachings of All Ages: An Encyclopedic Outline of Masonic, Hermetic, Qabbalistic and Rosicrucian Symbolical Philosophy.* San Francisco: Author, 1928.

Hancock, Joy. *The Byrom Collection: Renaissance Thought, the Royal Society, and the Building of the Globe Theatre.* London: Jonathan Cape, 1992.

Hasler, P. W., ed. *The History of Parliament: The House of Commons, 1588–1603.* London: Boydell & Brewer, 1981.

Hauge, Peter. "Robert Fludd (1574–1637): A Musical Charlatan? A Contextual Study of His 'Temple of Music' (1617–18)." *International Review of the Aesthetics and Sociology of Music* 39, no. 1 (2008): 8–39.

———. *"The Temple of Music" by Robert Fludd.* Farnham, UK: Ashgate, 2010.

Heisler, Ron. "Michael Maier and England." *Hermetic Journal* 43 (1989): 119–125.

———. "Robert Fludd: A Picture in Need of Expansion." *Hermetic Journal* 43 (1989): 139–49.

Heninger, S. K., Jr. *The Cosmographical Glass: Renaissance Diagrams of the Universe.* San Marino, CA: Huntington Library, 1977.

———. *Touches of Sweet Harmony: Pythagorean Cosmology and Renaissance Poetics.* San Marino, CA: Huntington Library, 1974.

Hirst, Désirée. *Hidden Riches: Traditional Symbolism from the Renaissance to Blake.* London: Eyre & Spottiswoode, 1964.

Huffman, William H. *Robert Fludd and the End of the Renaissance.* London: Routledge, 1988.

———, ed. and trans. *Robert Fludd: Essential Readings.* Western Esoteric Masters Series. Berkeley, CA: North Atlantic Books, 2001.

Hutin, Serge. *Robert Fludd (1574–1637), alchimiste et philosophe rosicrucien.* Paris, 1971.

Janacek, Bruce. *Alchemical Belief: Occultism in the Religious Culture of Early Modern England.* University Park: Pennsylvania State University Press, 2011.

Janson, H. W. *Apes and Ape Lore in the Middle Ages and the Renaissance.* London: Warburg Institute, 1952.

Josten, C. H. "Robert Fludd's 'Philosophical Key' and His Alchemical Experiment on Wheat." *Ambix* 11 (1963): 1–23.

———. "Robert Fludd's Theory of Geomancy and His Experiences in Avignon in the Winter of 1601 to 1602." *Journal of the Warburg and Courtauld Institutes* 27 (1964): 327–35.

Kassell, Lauren. "Magic, Alchemy and the Medical Economy in Early Modern England: The Case of Robert Fludd's Alchemical Medicine." In *Medicine and the Market in Early Modern England and Its Colonies, c.1450–1850,* edited by Mark S. R. Jenner and Patrick Wallis, 88–107. Basingstoke: Palgrave Macmillan, 2007.

Kepler, Johannes. *Harmonies Mundi.* Linz, 1619.

Lanovius [François de la Noue]. *Ad Reverendum Patrem Marinum Mersennum Francisci Lanovii Judicium de Roberto Fluddo.* Paris, 1630.

Matton, Sylvain. "Les ténèbres, la matière et le mal chez Robert Fludd et Sade: Du Dieu lacérateur à l'Être suprême en méchanceté." In *Lumière et cosmos: Courants occultes de la philosophie de la nature,* 145–79. Paris: Albin Michel, 1981.

McLean, Adam. "A Source for Robert Fludd's Sevenfold Rose." *Hermetic Journal* 45 (1991): 138–39.

Mersenne, Marin. *Correspondance.* Edited by C. de Waard and R. Pintard. Paris, 1932–70.

———. *Quaestiones celeberrimae in Genesim.* Paris, 1623.

Meyer-Baer, Kathi. *Music of the Spheres and the Dance of Death.* Princeton, NJ: Princeton University Press, 1970.

Nostredame, César de. *L'histoire et chronique de Provence.* Lyon: Simon Rigaud, 1614.

Pagel, Walter. "Religious Motives in the Medical Biology of the Seventeenth Century." *Bulletin of the Institute of the History of Medicine* 3 (1935): 97–128, 213–31, 265–312. Pages 265–86 are on Fludd.

Patrides, C. S. "Renaissance Estimates of the Year of Creation." *Huntington Library Quarterly* 28 (1963): 315–22.

Pauli, Wolfgang. "The Influence of Archetypal Ideas on the Scientific Theories of Kepler." In C. G. Jung and Pauli, *The Interpretation of Nature and the Psyche,* 147–240. New York: Bollingen Foundation, 1955.

Pennick, Nigel. *The Ancient Science of Geomancy: Man in Harmony with the Earth.* London: Thames & Hudson, 1979.

Peuckert, Will-Erich. *Gabalia.* Berlin: Erich Schmidt, 1967.

Rösche, Johannes. *Der Versuch einer hermetischen Alternative zur neuzeitlichen Naturwissenschaft.* Göttingen: V & R Unipress, 2008.

Røstvig, Maren-Sofie. "The Rime of the Ancient Mariner and the Cosmic System of Robert Fludd." *Tennessee Studies in Literature* 12 (1967): 69–82.

Saurat, Denis. *Milton: Man and Thinker.* New York: Dial Press, 1925.

Schmidt-Biggemann, Wilhelm. *Geschichte der christlichen Kabbala, Band 2, 1600–1660.* Stuttgart: Frommann-Holzboog, 2013.

Schuchard, Marsha Keith. *Restoring the Temple of Vision. Cabalistic Freemasonry and Stuart Culture.* Leiden: Brill, 2002.

Scot, Patrick. *The Tillage of Light.* London, 1623.

Sugg, Richard. *Mummies, Cannibals and Vampires: The History of Corpse Medicine from the Renaissance to the Victorians.* London: Routledge, 2011.

———. *The Smoke of the Soul: Medicine, Physiology and Religion in Early Modern England.* Basingstoke: Palgrave Macmillan, 2013.

Szulakowska, Urszula. *The Alchemy of Light: Geometry and Optics in Late Renaissance Alchemical Illustration.* Leiden: Brill, 2000.

———. *The Sacrificial Body and the Day of Doom: Alchemy and Apocalyptic Discourse in the Protestant Reformation.* Leiden: Brill, 2006.

Taylor, F. Sherwood. "The Origin of the Thermometer." *Annals of Science* 5 (1942): 129–56.

Tilton, Hereward. *The Quest for the Phoenix: Spiritual Alchemy and Rosicrucianism in the Work of Count Michael Maier (1569–1622).* Berlin: Walter de Gruyter, 2002.

Van Groesen, Michiel. *The Representation of the Overseas World in the De Bry Collection of Voyages (1590–1634).* Leiden: Brill, 2008.

Vesalius, Andreas. *The Illustrations from the Works of Andreas Vesalius of Brussels.* Edited by J. B. deC. M. Saunders and Charles D. O'Malley. Cleveland: World Publishing Co., 1950.

Waite, A. E. *The Brotherhood of the Rosy Cross.* London: Rider, 1924.

———. *The Real History of the Rosicrucians.* London: Redway, 1887.

———. "Robert Fludd and Freemasonry: A Speculative Excursion." *Transactions of the Manchester Association for Masonic Research* 11 (1922).

Weidhaas, Peter. *A History of the Frankfurt Book Fair.* Edited and translated by C. M. Gossage and W. A. Wright. Toronto: Durndurn Group, 2007.

Weil, E. "William Fitzer, the Publisher of Harvey's *De motu cordis,* 1628." *The Library* 24 (1944): 142–64.

Westbrook, Peter. "The Divine Vina and the World Monochord: Musical Cosmology from Rg Veda to Robert Fludd." PhD dissertation, University of Maryland, 2001.

Wind, Edgar. *Pagan Mysteries in the Renaissance.* London: Faber, 1968.

Wütrich, Lucas Heinrich. *Das druckgraphische Werk von Matthaeus Merian d[er] Ae[lter].* 4 vols. Basel: Bärenreiter, 1966–1996.

Yates, Frances A. *The Art of Memory.* London: Routledge & Kegan Paul, 1966.

———. *Giordano Bruno and the Hermetic Tradition.* London: Routledge & Kegan Paul, 1964.

———. *The Occult Philosophy in the Elizabethan Age.* London: Routledge & Kegan Paul, 1979.

———. *The Rosicrucian Enlightenment.* London: Routledge & Kegan Paul, 1972.

———. *Theatre of the World.* London: Routledge & Kegan Paul, 1969.

Index

Page numbers in *italics* indicate illustrations and captions.

Adam, *206–7,* 208
Agrippa, Henry Cornelius, 17, 141, 164
air
  element of, *48,* 57
  expansion and contraction of, 216, 226
  hot and cold, 75, 123
  treasure ark of God, 248
Albertus Magnus, 142
alchemy
  experiments, 41, *49,* 50, 186–89, *187*
  principles of, *178–79*
Aleph, dark and light, 174, *196–97,* 198, 219,
Allen, Thomas, 4
Altemps, Marco Sittico (Cardinal Sextus Giorgio, "Cardinal Saint George"), 6–7
anatomy, 184, *185,* 189–95, *190–95*
Andreae, Johan Valentin, 8
angel(s). *See also* archangels
  correlated with man's functions, 148
  in Fludd's system, 17, 22, 23, 25–26
  in Great Meteorological Chart, 205, *206–7,* 208–9
  guardian, 163
  hierarchy of, threefold, *62, 64, 65, 73, 74, 91, 92,* 130, *131*
  in Mirror of Universal Causation, *178–79*

as natal genius, 161, 180
nine orders of, 142, *143, 144, 148, 176,* 177, 198
planetary, rule the world, 245
ape, *72, 73,* 82, *83,* 154, *155*
Apollo, *88, 91, 92, 218,* 219
Apollonius of Tyana, 244
archangels
  four, rule the winds, 184, *215,* 220, *221*
  Gabriel interprets dream, 202, *203*
  Michael, 27, 202, *203,* 205
  rulers of world periods, 245
Aristotle, cited or refuted, 16, 202, 222, 226
arithmetical progressions or proportions, 82, *83, 133, 148*
astrology, 18, 82, *83,* 154, *155, 161,* 208. *See also* planets; zodiac
  catches a thief, 244
  diagnosis through, *234,* 235, *236*
  horary, 235, 244
  and palmistry, *164*
automata, *120–27*

Bacci, Andrea, 142
Bauhin, Gaspard, 189, 193
Bayley, Harold, 247
Bearsted Church, 23
Beaulieu, Lord of, 118, 119

Bernheimer, Richard, 159
Biancani, Giuseppe, 216
brain, 142, *143, 158, 192–93, 232*
bread, 184, *185, 187,* 188

Cadenet, Vicomte de, 6
cannon, *115*
car, hand-driven, *118–19*
Casaubon, Isaac, 23
catarrh, cause of, *232*
Catilina, Pompée, 6
Caus, Salomon de, *120, 122, 123, 124*
chakras, *137*
Charles I of England, 23
Charles de Lorraine, Duc de Guise, 4, 6
chiromancy (palmistry), 18, *154,* 163–64
Christ, 22, 27, 219, 246
College of Physicians, 7, 16, 23, 189
color, *223*
combs, dark and light, *166*
comets, 205, *206–7,* 208
Conti (Comti), Carlo, 6
contraction and expansion, 226, 227, 237–40, *240*
Copernicus, Nicolaus, 54
cosmography, 4, *72–73,* 82, *83*
Craven, James Brown, 3n5, 23–24, 156
creation, process of, 36–55, *37–48, 50–53, 55*

Daniel, 202
darkness
    before creation, 36, *37, 43*
    at center of cosmos, *44–48,
        50–52,* 189
    divine potency, *178–79,
        204, 218,* 219, *220*
    microcosmic night, 150
de Bry, Johann Theodor, 8,
    11, 13, 15, 189
    portrait, *10*
    title pages, *14, 31, 83, 131,
        185, 203*
Debus, Allen G., 20, 22n51, 24
Demogorgon, 246
demon(s),
    and angels, 17, 18, 25, 26,
        27, *215, 221, 224, 225*
    can prophesy, 156
    control the winds, 220–22,
        224–25
    of the elements, 220
    Fludd accused of traffic with,
        22, 244
    from God's dark side, 25, 221
    as natal genius, 161, 180
Devil(s), 22, 47, 188, 246,
    249. *See also* demon(s)
Digby, Sir Kenelm, 57
Dionysus, *218,* 219
dissection, 184, 189, *190–94,
    232*
divination, methods of, 154–64
diving, *113*
drawing, *104–7*

Eden, Garden of, *10,* 11, *55*
elemental world (sphere,
    heaven), *40,* 45, *46–48,
    68, 69–70. See also*
    worlds, three
elements, four, 73–74, 138,
    141, *204*
    creation of, *36, 40, 41,
        46–49, 55, 132*
    in Fludd's experiments, *41,
        49,* 184–188
    and humors, 30, *31*

empyrean world (sphere,
    heaven), *38, 44, 51,* 92.
    See also worlds, three
esotericism, Christian, 27
ethereal world (sphere,
    heaven), *38, 45, 53. See
    also* planets; sun; worlds,
    three
experiments
    alchemical, 41, *49,* 50,
        186–89
    with elements, 56, 57, *75–79*
    on a heart, *239*

Ferté, François, 6
Ficino, Marsilio, 26
fire
    element of, *46–48*
    invisible, 46, 74
    of love, 39
    spiritual, 166
    subterranean, *77–79*
Fitzer, William, 16
Fludd, Lewin (nephew), 23
Fludd, Robert, life, 2–24
    death and legacies, 23
    education and degrees, 3–4,
        7
    illustrations, 13
    languages, knowledge of, 3
    medical practice, 7, 16–18
    monument, 23
    parentage, 3
    philosophical system, 24–27
    portrait, *5, 9*
    residences, 3, 16
    steelmaking, 15
    travels, 4, 6–7
Fludd, Robert, works
    Bibliography of, 251–55
    *Anatomiae Amphitheatrum
        (AA),* 4, *14,* 16, 17, 21,
        184–99, 232, 247
    *Apologia Compendiaria
        (AC),* 8
    Clavis Philosophiae (CP), 12
    De Naturae Simia (UCH I,
        2), 13, 15, *82–127*

*De Praeternaturali . . .
    Historia (UCH* II, 2), 131,
    168–82, 248
*De Supernaturali . . . Historia
    (UCH* II, 1, 1), 4, *130–51*
*De Technica Microcosmi
    (UCH* II, 1, 2), *154–66,
    246*
*Doctor Fludd's Answer
    (DFA),* 22–23
*Integrum Morborum
    Mysterium (MC* I, 2, 1),
    57, *224–33*
*Katholikon Medicinae
    Katoptron (MC* I, 2, 2),
    234–36
Medicina Catholica (MC I, 1),
    16–19, *218–23*
Mosaicall Philosophy (MP),
    4, 19, 26
Philosophia Sacra (PS), 5, *43,
    57, 202–216, 231, 248*
Pulsus (MC I, 2, 3), 18,
    236–41
*Sophiae cum Moria
    Certamen (SM),* 21–22,
    196–97
*Tractatus Theologo-
    Philosophicus (TTP),* 8,
    10, 246
*Utriusque Cosmi . . . Historia
    (UCH,* I, 1), 11–16,
    30–79, 249
Veritatis Proscenium (VP), 20
Fludd, Thomas (nephew), 23
Fludd, Sir Thomas (father), 3
Forman, Simon, 18
fortification, *109–10*
Foster, William, 19, 20, 22
Freemasonry, 133
Frizius, Joachim, 12, 22

Galen, Galenic medicine, 7,
    16, 30, 138, 193
Gassendi, Pierre, 20, 22, 23
gematria, 171
Genesis, creation myth of, 27,
    43, 180–81, 205

genethlialogy. *See* astrology

geomancy, 6, 18, 82, *83*, 154, *155, 157*

geometry, *82, 98–100, 146*

Gilbert, William, 19

Giorgio, Cardinal Sextus (Marcus Sitticus Altemps), 117

Giorgio, Francesco, 205

Globe Theatre, *159*

God, 24–27

    anger of, 224–25

    dark side of, 180, *219–221*

    hand of, *64, 73, 172*

    Hebrew name (Tetragrammaton), *72–73, 134, 168–82, 196–97, 212*

    highest mind, *67*

    immersed in matter, *147, 149*

    names of, 178–79, 205–20

    and nature, *72,* 173–74

    Spirit of, *43, 55, 156*

    as Trinity, *32–35, 132, 134, 143*

Goltzius, Hendrik, *14,* 15

Great Instrument, Fludd's, *122*

Great Meteorological Chart, 205–9, *206–7*

Great Monochord, 195–99, *196–97*

Great Spiritual Machine, *121*

Greek fire, *78*

Greuter, Matthaeus, 6

Gruter, inventor, 6–7, *117, 119*

gunpowder, *78*

Hall, Manly Palmer, 24, 40, *178–79,* 247

harmonic proportions, 27, 89

    of cosmos, *60–65, 68–71, 137*

    of man, *134, 145, 147, 151*

Harvey, William, 16, 18, 190, 237

Haslmayr, Adam, 8

health, fortress of, *221, 225*

heart, *136, 138, 211*

    affected by winds, *237*

    experiment with a, *239*

heavens, three. *See* worlds, three

Hebrew letters, *144, 169–82.* *See also* Tetragrammaton

Helt, Justus, 13

Hercules, 121

Hermetic philosophy

    attitude of others, 7, 21

    Fludd's use of, 2, 11, 25, 75, 82, 133, 156, 244

    quoted, 27, 169, 195, 219

Hero of Alexandria, *79, 233*

Holy Spirit, *43, 55,* 156

horoscope, 154, 161, 180, *236*

Huffman, William, vii, 3n2, 24, 27

Icarus, *246*

imagination, *143, 145, 148–51, 158*

inclinometer, *98–100*

intellect (*intellectus*), *131, 137–38, 143, 145–51,* 157

Italian army, 111

James I of England, 13, 15, 22, 250

Jesuits, 6

Jupiter, *53, 139, 196–97, 207–8. See also* planets

    world age ruled by, 245

Kabbalah, Kabbalistic doctrines, 168–82, *195–99, 206–9,* 219

    Fludd's use of, 25–26, 74

    opponents, 7, 22, 23

Kepler, Johannes, 20–21

Kircher, Athanasius, vii, 24, 123

Ladder of Ascent, *149*

Lanovius (François de La Noue), 22, 23

Laud, William, 3

Libavius, Andreas, 7

light

    creation of, *38–39, 43*

    and darkness, *150, 178–82, 218–20. See also* pyramids

    purifying, 57

Logos. *See* Word of God

macrocosm, 30–127 passim

magnetism, 7, 17, 19

Magritte, René, 112

Maier, Michael, 11, 24

Malceau, apothecary in Avignon, 6

Malevich, Kazimir, 36

Mars, *53,* 121. *See also* planets

Marsyas, 92

Maxwell, William, 19

McLean, Adam, 12

medicine, universal, 218–41 passim

memory, art of, 86, *155, 158–61*

menorah, 199

Mercury, 53, 244. *See also* planets

Merian, Matthaeus, *5, 9, 12, 13, 106, 109, 141, 156*

Mersenne, Marin, 20–22, 23, 27, 164

Messiah, 26, 27, *178–79,* 209

Metatron, 26, 27, 74, *178–79,* 209

meteorology, 17, 202–16, *206–7*

meteors, 75, *178–81,* 181, *203, 206–7,* 249

microcosm, 130–216 *passim*

Milgate House, 3

military art, *83, 109–15*

mind (*mens*)

    divine, *144,* 157

    human, *131, 136–38, 143, 146–47, 182*

Mirror of Universal
    Causation, *178–79*
mnemonics, *86*
monochord, *23, 64, 71,* 89–91,
    151
    Great Monochord, 195–99,
        196–97
moon, 18, *53, 55, 74,* 208,
    249. *See also* planets
Moritz von Hesse-Cassel
    ("Moritz the Learned"),
    7, 8, 13, 189
Moses, Tabernacle of, 199
motion, science of, *83*
Muse, *88, 90*
music. *See also* harmonic
    proportions; monochord
    cosmic, 27, *60–71*
    Fludd's treatise on, 4, 6
    human, *88–97*
    and the pulse, 18, *241*
musical instruments
    bells, *112, 127*
    cittern, *95*
    cornett, *88, 96*
    drum, *112*
    harp, *124*
    lute, *88, 89, 93*
    lyre, *88*
    mechanical, *122–27*
    organ, organ pipes, *77,* 89,
        124, 126
    orpharion, *93*
    pandora (bandora), *93*
    pyramidal (triangular), *66,*
        122
    recorder, *67, 77, 96*
    shawm, *96*
    trumpet, *88, 96*
    viola da gamba, *88, 94*
    xylophone, *97*

Nature (personified), 26,
    72–73, 74
Neoplatonism, vii, 92, 161

optics, *101*
Oraison, André, Marquis d', 6

Ovid, 52

painting, *82*
palmistry, *155, 163–64*
Pan, *246*
Paracelsus, 7, 16
Perin, John, 3
perpetual motion, *116*
perspective drawing, 82, *102,*
    104–7
Phanes Protogonus, 246
physiognomy, 18, *155, 162,*
    163
Pico della Mirandola,
    Giovanni, 26
planets, seven
    correlation to angels and
        winds, *206–7, 215*
    genii of, 161
    in Great Meteorological
        Chart, *206–7*
    in Great Monochord,
        196–97
    in macrocosm, *30–31, 55,*
        63–65, 72–74, 131, 144
    in microcosm, *131, 133,*
        137, 139, 147, 148
    in Mirror of Universal
        Causation, *178–79*
    in palmistry, *164*
    relation to sun, *51, 53,* 88
    rulers of body parts, *234*
    Wisdom's creations, *213*
Plato, Platonism, 2, 26, 90,
    148, 195, 245
Plato's Wheel, *86*
primum mobile
    correspondences of, *178–79,*
        209
    creation of, *210*
    limit of ethereal world, *31,*
        130, *133, 137, 148*
prophecy, *155, 156,* 249–50
proportions, arithmetical, *85,*
    133, 148, 196–97. See also
    harmonic proportions
pulse, diagnosis through, *237,*
    241

pyramids of form and matter
    in Fludd's philosophy, 2, 20,
        23, 25
    in Kabbalah, 169, 171
    in macrocosm, *58–71*
    in microcosm, *133, 135–36,*
        145, 148
    science of, *155, 165–66*
    weatherglass and, *227–28*
Pythagoras, Pythagoreanism,
    20, 26, 84, *89–91, 97,*
    204

quadrivium, 146
quintessence, 39, *187,* 188

Rainoldes, John, 3
reason (*ratio*), 131, *137–38,*
    143, 146–51
refraction, *103*
Reinaud of Avignòn, 6
Reisch, Gregor, 142
Renaissance, 27
Renaud, François de, 6
Rösche, Johann, 19–20,
    22n51, 252n
Rosenkreutz, Christian, 8
Rosicrucians, 7–13, *12,* 16,
    168

Saturn, *53, 139, 206–7,*
    208–9, 214, 234. *See also*
    planets
Schmidt-Biggemann,
    Wilhelm, 20, 21n46, 74
Scot, Patrick, 21
Selden, John, 16
Sepher Yetzirah, 173
sephiroth, 74, *173–79,*
    205–9, 212–13
Shakespeare, William, 92, *247*
Siruela, Jacobo, viii
soul (*anima*)
    absent from earth, *52*
    and brain, *192*
    angelic or demonic influence
        at birth, 161, *163,* 180
    controversies over, 20–22

descent and ascent of, *39,
    133, 144, 173*
diseases of, *229*
harmony of, 136, *137*
in man, 27, *135, 137,* 142,
    143–46, 151
of the Messiah, 27, *178–79,
    207,* 209
middle, *162*
relation to wheat, 186
revealed in the hand,
    162–63
of the world, 20, 21, 26, 27,
    72, 74
Spaniards, characteristics of,
    111
spheres, three. *See* worlds,
    three
spiral of creation, *144*
spiritus (vital spirits)
    in controversies, 21, 23,
        182–85
    in Fludd's experiments,
        186–88, *187*
    in the macrocosm, *45*
    in the microcosm, *135, 138,
        145–46, 182, 184*
star jelly, 249
stars. *See also* astrology;
    ethereal world; zodiac
    creation of, *50*
    in ethereal world, 23, 25 `
    influence of, 20, *140, 163,
        42, 45, 57*
    Kabbalistic equivalents, 174,
        177, *213*
    part of meteorology, 202,
        249
sun. *See also* planets
    centrality of, 26, 41, *172–74,*
        214
    creation of, *32, 38, 41,
        51–53,* 219
    effects of, in macrocosm, 55,
        72, 211, 214, 237, 249

experimental effects of, *50,
    57, 76, 123,* 186, *187*
God's tabernacle in, 26, *169,
    174,* 199, 205
as home of Michael, *179*
orbit of, *54, 150*
referred to as Trinity, *33, 132*
separation from earth, *52*
true, 74
sun dogs, 202, *203*
surveying, *83, 98–100*
tank, military, *114*
Taylor, Sherwood, 57
Temple of Music, 89–90,
    91–92
Tetragrammaton, *72, 134,
    168–82, 196–97*
Thoth, 82
thunder and lightning, 78,
    132, 202
thunderstone, *132, 181, 206–7*
timekeeping, *83*
Time (personified), *31, 91,*
    130
Trinity, 32–35, *132, 134, 147*
    in Kabbalah, *168, 176*
Trithemius, Johannes, 245
tuberculosis, cause of, 233

urinomancy and uroscopy, 18,
    228, 230, *235–36*

Venus, *53, 139, 206–7,*
    208–9, 244. *See also*
    planets
    world age ruled by, 245
Vesalius, Andreas, *189–93*

water(s)
    experiments with, *57,
        75–79,* 216, 231, 233
    machines powered by, *117,
        120, 123–27*
    subterranean, *77–78*
    upper and lower, *39, 181*

weapon salve, 7, 19, 22
weather, effect on health, 224
weatherglass, *216,* 226–29,
    238, 240–41
wheat, Fludd's experiment on,
    184, *185, 187,* 188
winds
    bearers of health and disease,
        195, 237
    controlled by demons, *215,
        221–22, 224–25*
    origin of, *213–14*
    planetary influences on, *206*
    ruled by archangels, *184, 215*
    twelve, qualities of, *222*
wine, Fludd's experiment
    with, *49*
Word of God, 26, 74, *147, 149,
    157,* 184
Son of God, *132*
spiritual Christ, 219
worlds, three (*also called*
    realms, spheres, heavens).
    See also elementary
    world; empyrean world;
    ethereal world
    arithmology of, *133, 148,
        171, 196–97*
    correlation with man,
        135–38, 151, 165, 170
    formation of, 38, 45, 55,
        134
    further divisions of, *62,
        72–73, 133, 148, 178–79*
    in Kabbalah, *35, 144, 169,
        172, 176*
    proportions of, *61–65, 137,
        147, 196–97*
    and Trinity, *35, 147*
Wütrich, Lucas, 13

Yates, Frances A., 11, 24, *159*
yoga, *137*

zodiac, *31, 131, 140,* 234